Advances in
LIBRARIANSHIP

Volume 6

Advances in
LIBRARIANSHIP

Edited by

    MELVIN J. VOIGT
    University of California, San Diego
    La Jolla, California

and

    MICHAEL H. HARRIS
    University of Kentucky
    Lexington, Kentucky

    Volume 6

ACADEMIC PRESS   New York San Francisco London   1976
A Subsidiary of Harcourt Brace Jovanovich, Publishers

COPYRIGHT © 1976, BY ACADEMIC PRESS, INC.
ALL RIGHTS RESERVED.
NO PART OF THIS PUBLICATION MAY BE REPRODUCED OR
TRANSMITTED IN ANY FORM OR BY ANY MEANS, ELECTRONIC
OR MECHANICAL, INCLUDING PHOTOCOPY, RECORDING, OR ANY
INFORMATION STORAGE AND RETRIEVAL SYSTEM, WITHOUT
PERMISSION IN WRITING FROM THE PUBLISHER.

ACADEMIC PRESS, INC.
111 Fifth Avenue, New York, New York 10003

United Kingdom Edition published by
ACADEMIC PRESS, INC. (LONDON) LTD.
24/28 Oval Road, London NW1

LIBRARY OF CONGRESS CATALOG CARD NUMBER: 79-88675

ISBN 0-12-785006-6

PRINTED IN THE UNITED STATES OF AMERICA

Contents

Contributors ix
Preface xi
Contents of Previous Volumes xiii

Performance Measures for School Librarians;
Complexities and Potential
EVELYN H. DANIEL
    I. Introduction 2
   II. Why Measure? 5
  III. What is Performance Measurement? 10
  IV. Library Performance Measures—State of the Art 18
   V. Measurement as a Process 36
  VI. A Step-by-Step Plan for the School Library/Media Center
      Practitioner 39
 VII. Summary and Conclusions 45
      References 46

Productivity Measurement in Academic Libraries
THOMAS J. WALDHART AND THOMAS P. MARCUM
    I. Introduction 54
   II. Productivity Measurement 57
  III. Productivity Measurement: A Hypothetical Example ... 66
  IV. Conclusions 74
      References 75

Relevance: A Review of the Literature and
a Framework for Thinking on the Notion in
Information Science
TEFKO SARACEVIC
    I. Preface: Where Lies the Importance of Thinking on Relevance? 81

II.	Introduction: How Relevance Is Involved in Controversy, the History of Science, and Other Fields	82
III.	How Information Science Became Involved with Relevance	85
IV.	How to Construct a Framework for Viewing Relevance from Intuitive Understanding and Then on to More Elaborate Communication Models	90
V.	How the "System's View" of Relevance Developed and How It Has Been Challenged	95
VI.	How the "Destination's View" Emerged, Equating Relevance with Relevance Judgment, and How Experimentation Was Spurred	98
VII.	How Bibliometrics Evolved and How It Is Related to the "Subject Literature View" of Relevance	102
VIII.	How Splitting of the Notion Began and the "Subject Knowledge View" of Relevance Resulted	107
IX.	How the Disenchantment with Relevance Led to Another Splitting and How the "Pragmatic View" of Relevance Evolved	112
X.	How Theories of Relevance Have Covered Different Aspects and Why They Are Important	119
XI.	Back to the Framework	124
	Appendix: Synthesis of the Experiments on Relevance in Information Science	129
	References	135

The Impact of Reading on Human Behavior:
The Implications of Communications Research
ROGER HANEY, MICHAEL H. HARRIS, AND
LEONARD TIPTON

I.	General Introduction	140
II.	The State of the Art in Communications Research: Complexities and Vagaries	141
III.	Pornography and Deviant Sexual Behavior	151
IV.	Violence	165
V.	Reading, Attitude Formation and Change, and Prejudice	176
VI.	Bibliotherapy: Reading in a Therapeutic Context	193
VII.	Implications of Communications Research for Information Professionals	199
	References	202

Trends in Library Education—Europe
DONALD DAVINSON
    I. Introduction and Outline of Problems 218
   II. History and State of the Art in the United Kingdom ... 220
  III. Library Education in Continental Europe 225
  IV. Issues in European Library Education 234
   V. Intervention by Library Associations in Education for
       Librarianship 247
       References 249

The Role of Middle Managers in Libraries
BEVERLY P. LYNCH
    I. The Manager's Work 255
   II. Factors That Influence the Role of the Middle Manager . 259
  III. Leadership in the Context of the Organization 266
  IV. Summary and Discussion 272
       References 274

Author Index 279
Subject Index 287

Contributors

Numbers in parentheses indicate the pages on which the authors' contributions begin.

Evelyn H. Daniel (1), Graduate Library School, University of Rhode Island, Kingston, Rhode Island

Donald Davinson (217), Department of Librarianship, Leeds Polytechnic, Leeds, England

Roger Haney (139), Department of Human Communication, University of Kentucky, Lexington, Kentucky

Michael H. Harris (139), Department of Library Science, University of Kentucky, Lexington, Kentucky

Beverly P. Lynch (253), Association of College and Research Libraries, a Division of the American Library Association, Chicago, Illinois

Thomas P. Marcum (53), Graduate School of Management Library, Vanderbilt University, Nashville, Tennessee

Tefko Saracevic (79), School of Library Science, Case Western Reserve University, Cleveland, Ohio

Leonard Tipton (139), School of Journalism, University of Kentucky, Lexington, Kentucky

Thomas J. Waldhart (53), College of Library Science, University of Kentucky, Lexington, Kentucky

Preface

Of late, librarians have been demonstrating an increased concern with the matter of "accountability," and they have learned, much to their discomfort, that much too little is known about the subject. A major thrust of Volume 6 of *Advances in Librarianship* is thus directed at addressing the questions of "accountability" or "evaluation of productivity," in the hope that they will prove of use to librarians struggling with the problem of meaningfully assessing the value of the library's services to the community.

This volume contains four review papers directly related to this question. The first, by Evelyn Daniel, concerns itself with a detailed examination of the literature relating to the evaluation of library services generally, but with a decided emphasis on school libraries. A second, by Thomas Waldhart and Thomas Marcum, focuses on evaluation in the academic library, and should prove of particular use due to the inclusion of several illustrations of the complicated and frequently misleading process of evaluating productivity.

A third paper, concentrating on a more specific subject—that of relevance in the information context—is contributed by Tefko Saracevic, and represents the thinking of one of America's leading information scientists on a question central to any meaningful measurement of the value of library service. Fourth, Roger Haney, Michael Harris, and Leonard Tipton assess the interdisciplinary literature relating to the question of "what reading does to people." The impact of reading on behavior might well be considered the ultimate question around which the evaluation of the library's effectiveness must be studied, and a review of the literature on the subject should prove of use to all information professionals involved in any critical and substantive analysis of their role and subsequent significance in society.

While the question of "accountability" receives considerable attention in this volume, it remains the intent of the Editors to present a variety of timely topics to the library community in each volume. As a result, librarians will read with interest D. E. Davinson's interpretation of the development of education for librarianship in Europe, and will want to compare it with Lester Asheim's carefully written essay on American library education as published in Volume 5 of these *Advances*.

Finally, Beverly Lynch, the Executive Secretary of the Association of College and Research Libraries, critically examines a topic of growing importance to librarians everywhere. Her analysis of the emergence of "middle managers" in libraries and her assessment of the strengths and weaknesses of this new breed of library administrators, at a time when all librarians are playing a larger role in management, should prove provocative and, perhaps, controversial to all librarians, whether or not they are charged with the guidance of libraries.

Melvin J. Voigt
Michael H. Harris

Contents of Previous Volumes

Volume 1

The Machine and Cataloging
  George Piternick

Mechanization of Acquisitions Processes
  Connie R. Dunlap

Mechanization and Library Filing Rules
  Kelley L. Cartwright

Standards for Technical Service Cost Studies
  Helen Welch Tuttle

The Undergraduate Library Trend at Large Universities
  Robert H. Muller

The Changing School Library: An Instructional Media Center
  Chase Dane

Reference Service to Children—Past, Present, and Future
  Lillian K. Orsini

Progress in Bibliotherapy
  Ruth M. Tews

Effectiveness in Cooperation and Consolidation in Public Libraries
  Ralph Blasingame and Ernest R. DeProspo, Jr.

Library Planning: The Challenge of Change
  Robert E. Kemper

Acceleration of Library Development in Developing Countries
Carl M. White

SUBJECT INDEX

Volume 2

Access to Information
William S. Budington

Control and Dissemination of Information in Medicine
David Bishop

The Computer in Serials Processing and Control
Don L. Bosseau

Micropublication
Allen B. Veaner

The Changing Role of the State Library
Kenneth E. Beasley

Censorship, Intellectual Freedom, and Libraries
Edwin Castagna

Reader Services to the Disadvantaged in Inner Cities
Margaret E. Monroe

Oral History: Problems and Prospects
Louis M. Starr

Armageddon in International Copyright: Review of the Berne Convention, the Universal Convention, and the Present Crisis in International Copyright
Dorothy M. Schrader

AUTHOR INDEX–SUBJECT INDEX

Volume 3

On Beyond 999Z—Patterns of Library Service to Children of the Poor
Binnie L. Tate

Youth as a Special Client Group
James W. Liesener and Margaret E. Chisholm

The Emergence of the Community College Library
Harriett Genung and James O. Wallace

Teaching Library Skills to College Students
Miriam Dudley

Academic Library Buildings in the United Kingdom
H. Faulkner Brown

Academic Library Buildings in the United States
Ralph E. Ellsworth

Federal Grants and Public Libraries
James G. Igoe

Anglo-American Code Implementation
Elizabeth L. Tate

Catalog Use Studies and Their Implications
James Krikelas

Converting Bibliographic Data to Machine Form
Don Sherman

Archive and Manuscript Collections
Robert L. Brubaker

AUTHOR INDEX—SUBJECT INDEX

Volume 4

MARC and Its Application to Library Automation
Roy B. Torkington

Selective Dissemination of Information
Georg R. Mauerhoff

Circulation Automation
Hugh C. Atkinson

Social Responsibility and Libraries
Arthur Curley

Women in Librarianship
Anita R. Schiller

The Use of Resources in the Learning Experience
Johnnie Givens

Reading as Information Processing
John J. Geyer and Paul A. Kolers

SUBJECT INDEX

Volume 5

International Information Systems
Jacques Tocatlian

National Planning for Library and Information Services
Foster E. Mohrhardt and Carlos Victor Penna

Statistics That Describe Libraries and Library Service
Thomas Childers

Coordination of the Technical Services
Helen Welch Tuttle

Trends in Library Education—United States
Lester Asheim

The Technologies of Education and Communication
Gerald R. Brong

Audiovisual Services in Libraries
Irving Lieberman

Sound Recordings
Gordon Stevenson

Joint Academic Libraries
Richard D. Johnson

AUTHOR INDEX–SUBJECT INDEX

Performance Measures for School Librarians; Complexities and Potential

EVELYN H. DANIEL

University of Rhode Island

I.	Introduction	2
II.	Why Measure?	5
	A. External Pressures	6
	B. Internal Pressures	8
III.	What Is Performance Measurement?	10
	A. Definition and Relationship to Evaluation	10
	B. The Search for Goals	11
	C. Norms, Standards, and Library Statistics	13
IV.	Library Performance Measures—State of the Art	18
	A. Inventories and Checklists	19
	B. The Application of Mathematical and Statistical Techniques	25
	C. A Comprehensive Tool for Performance Measurement	33
V.	Measurement as a Process	36
	A. Rubrics of Measurement	36
	B. Building Blocks for Measurement Capability	37
VI.	A Step-by-Step Plan for The School Library Practitioner	39
	A. Stage 1—Exploration and Experimentation	40
	B. Stage 2—Planning	40
	C. Stage 3—Programming	42

	D. Stage 4—Implementation	44
	E. Stage 5—Review and Evaluation	44
VII.	Summary and Conclusions	45
	References	46

I. INTRODUCTION

How do you measure performance? For that matter, how do you measure anything? We are accustomed to measuring distances—how far away, how long, how tall, how wide. We also know how to count numbers of items—how many, how much. In addition, we measure time—how long has it been since . . . the duration of . . . the number of hours or days until . . . . These are simple methods of measurement that we all carry out in our everyday lives. Libraries can be measured in these terms also: how far is the library from . . .; how many feet of shelf space; the number of books, filmstrips, film loops, cassettes, projectors, seats, workers, students, etc.; the time it takes until a book order is received; how long it takes to process an item; the duration of library instruction classes; how much time before that new addition is completed; and so on.

These are simple and effective methods of measurement. They are the basic tools with which more sophisticated methods of measurement can be constructed. For example, simple methods of measurement can be combined. We can measure how many items per measure of distance. This gives us such measures as number of students per square foot of space, average distance traveled by people using the library, number of inches of shelf space per book, per kit, per turntable—or we can combine numbers of items with time measures, such as average number of reference requests per day, number of items added per year. It is easy to bring together other combinations of these simple measures. We often combine two or more different counting measures: number of teaching stations per projector, number of books per student. Often the annual budget for the school library is worked out in these terms—number of dollars per student. When the total school budget is based on number of dollars per average daily attendance, there is a quadruple combination—number of dollars, per year, per number of students, per day.

Not only can we combine simple measurements, we can estimate measures from past measures. If a library circulated 10,000 items the previous year and if conditions for the school and for the library have not changed a great deal, it would seem reasonable to expect that the library might circulate approximately 10,000 items again this year. In addition to estimations based on past performances, we can estimate the total from a small sample. If one-sixth of a raisin cake contains 35 raisins, it is reasonable to assume that the whole cake probably contains about 35 × 6, or 210 raisins. If we measure the library's circulation at selected representative intervals and multiply that result by whatever fraction of the whole is used, we have an estimate of the total circulation—arrived at more easily (and often more accurately) than by laboriously counting each item each day of the school year.

We can combine; we can estimate; we can also make comparisons based on measurements and draw factual conclusions. A library of 10,000 square feet will hold more items, more students, more activities than one of 5,000 square feet. A library with twenty books per student provides more reading opportunities for students than one with five books per student. A jobber who fills orders in thirty days will enable the library to have materials sooner than a jobber who fills book orders in sixty days. A three-year plan of development for a library program provides more opportunities for complex activities than does a one-year plan.

Finally, from all these measurements, combinations of measurements, estimations of measurements, and comparisons of measurements, we can infer quality. On the simplest level, for example, we often infer that "more is better." We can go back to our raisin cake example and say a raisin cake with 210 raisins is "better" than one with 110 raisins. This is not always true. Occasionally, the rule of "more is better" is inverted and we want the exact opposite. After dieting for a year, a person who weighed 250 pounds last year and now weighs 150 pounds would probably say "less is better." A school librarian released from the burden of serving as a study hall supervisor for 1,000 students per day would no doubt also feel that "less is better."

Inferences about quality also take place on other dimensions than greater and lesser quantities. We can produce ranges of comparative figures and say those phenomena that fall within a certain range are "better" than those that deviate from it. A homely example of this might be a cookbook with recipes that can be doubled, tripled, halved, etc., for whatever number of people desired. A raisin cake might call for 1 cup of sugar for a 6-piece cake, 2 cups for 12 pieces, and ½ cup for 3 pieces. A 12-piece raisin cake that had only ½ a cup of sugar or, conversely, had 4 cups of sugar is not going to taste as good as one that has 1¾ cups or one with 2¼ cups of sugar. Neither a library program with scheduled library instruction classes all day long nor one with no library instruction whatsoever is as good as a library program with library instruction interspersed with open library periods for independent use.

Within the library field, this type of measurement is sometimes expressed in tables, but is more often present in considering services in cost-benefit terms. A standard example in this area could be the "balance" of the book collection. Librarians who have put their collection dollars too heavily in one area, such as picture books, may find that other areas are not proportionally as good. (Perhaps the science collection is weak.) School libraries becoming media centers often find that the print collection overshadows the nonprint collection. A "good" library/media center is one in which funds available for collection development have been spent in certain proportions (within certain ranges) in order to relate the dollars spent to the desired end product.

Quality inferences from measurement do not always refer to money. Sometimes inferences about quality, or "goodness" of a library, can be made from measurements of time. If a story-hour program for preschoolers takes more than 25 percent of the elementary school librarian's time, one might infer that service to other groups within the school is receiving too little attention. Many surveys of the activities in the school library begin with a request for a time diary or a comparative estimate of the ways the school librarian spends his/her time.

This preamble is intended to demonstrate a building-block concept of measurement. Quantitative measurement starts with simple counting. Counting several different things and combining them in various ways is a simple step upward but a powerful step in terms of providing more information. From counting individual items to estimating from small samples what the results would be if all the items were counted is another step up in sophistication and power. Comparing the results of these measures with other like measures provides information for making managerial decisions. It is with these tools of measurement that information is produced that can be used to answer questions such as how good a service is and how much good the service does. Measurement data require interpretation. Quantitative data of how much or how many mean nothing alone. Quality must be inferred from quantitative measures. There is no direct link that takes place. Two plus two equals four, we all agree, but whether four is better than three or five is something each of us has to determine on the basis of other criteria.

The most important point to be made about performance measurement is probably that the collection of quantitative data is only a small part of the total process of measurement and evaluation. Before the data are collected, the criteria against which meaning will be extracted from the results must be carefully thought through and specified. The inferences of quality from measures of quantity must be based on prior specification of whether more or less is better or in what combination of quantities does goodness lie. Further, the inferences of quality educed from the collected data must be used as an integral part of the management process of continually changing, shaping, building, and creating a dynamic school media center program. Performance measurement goes hand in hand with performance goals, performance specifications, and the planning process.

II. WHY MEASURE?

"If it's not worth doing, is it worth doing well?"

Probably not one of us questions the value of measurement per se. We all want to know how effective the services offered by the school library media center are. Even if we in the library field accept the value of a library unquestioningly, budget analysts and resource allocators, who talk in terms of "accountability," program budgeting, and behavioral objectives, may not be as satisfied with the acceptance on faith of the library as a "good thing." In addition, we need to be able to demonstrate and articulate, for the principal, the school board, parents, teachers, and students, just who is being served by the school library, in what way, and with what benefit. The librarian needs a means of examining his operation systematically and selecting those activities and services that will be most responsive to the needs of his particular school. He needs a framework that allows him to operate as a manager, a decision-maker, a proactive agent in control of his center and its destiny.

These pressures currently would seem to be having a catalytic effect on school librarians encouraging (perhaps even forcing) us to examine our performance more intensively. The pressures come from both external and internal sources—the former, including all pressures from the outside environment; the latter, those pressures arising from an internal desire to improve and become competent and confident in our mastery of a challenging and complex job. The external pressures may seem the most compelling at the present time, but my own bias is to minimize the importance of the external forces and to emphasize instead the importance of the psychological need for self-knowledge and the psychic reinforcement possible from having accurate and detailed knowledge of our impact on our surroundings. Self-growth will come with information that helps us to determine rigorously the extent to which we are meeting our responsibilities.

A. External Pressures

It is the external pressures, however, that have been the germinating seed begetting a program of analysis, measurement, and evaluation. Certainly the concept of accountability has had, and continues to have, a profound effect on all levels of the educational world. Questions are being asked about the personal responsibility of educators and the true nature of educational goals. The demand is strong for concrete educational objectives that are measurable, so that their attainment can be demonstrated.

Following, or more accurately, coinciding with the stress on accountability has come a different type of education for school administrators—one that emphasizes precision and performance measurement, advancing such techniques as programmed budgeting, management information systems, planning-programming-budgeting systems, management-by-objectives, cost-benefit analyses, the "systems" approach, and other models for the businesslike treatment of educational affairs. There is an underlying unanimity in all these techniques, and five common assumptions can be identified:

1. A program or an organization is made up of many elements.
2. All these elements are interdependent.
3. Objectives for each element can be clearly stated and measured.
4. The final result is an amalgamation or summation of the measured results of each of the elements.
5. The process is continuous.

Educational management has become more of a science and less of an art. Decision-making is more frequently quantitatively based. The result is an increased demand for information on processes and procedures, on cause and effect, on the ability to predict results, and on performance measurement and evaluation. This demand from the top of the organization and from outside the organization has permeated the entire field of education, causing all of us within to analyze our activities with a view to predicting their consequences and to look for instruments that will help us do this.

Another outside factor pressuring us toward systematic evaluation of our performance is the scarcity of financial resources. Education became big business in the 1960's. The Federal Government, state and local governments, foundations, and other granting agencies "discovered" education. Grant money poured in and with this largesse came visibility—a spotlight on the expected accomplishments that all those dollars would certainly produce. And then the rub! Education, like the library, was a "good thing." The techniques of specifying objectives in precise terms and measuring their attainments did not exist. Toward the end of the decade, research, like the Coleman report (1966), which found only limited correlation between small classes, amount of education of teachers, numbers of books in the library, and the performance of students, and the Jencks report (1972), which found only a limited relationship between amount of education and earning capacity in adult life, seemed to indicate a flaw in the beautifully simple American belief that more money spent on education necessarily equaled better education. With the questions came an inevitable retrenchment. The expansive sixties have been replaced by the cautious and uncertain seventies.

In times when resources are scarce and competition is high for the budget dollar, those unconcerned with the budgetary process are at a disadvantage. As a matter of self-preservation, and in order that those programs that we believe in are permitted to continue, it behooves us to articulate the specific connections between dollars spent and benefit incurred, so that it may become apparent to others that the public investment of dollars in school library programs is worthwhile. A corollary of this is the importance of being able to translate our school library program, describing its contribution in terms that nonlibrarians will understand and, in so doing, to justify the library. Teachers, administrators, children, and parents need to acquire the same perception we have of the role of the library and what its unique contribution is within the school and within our society.

B. Internal Pressures

There are three major internal problems faced by all school librarians. The first problem is that of operationalism. The school librarian gets caught up in busy work, in everyday activities, in the pressure of time and events. By the end of the day, or the week, or the month, there is nothing tangible to show that the library program is any better than it was yesterday, or last week, or a month ago. School librarians, no less than all humans, need some milestones of progress, some method of measuring the effects of actions taken and time spent. These measurements can become useful indicators that time spent in some activities has a bigger return than time spent in others and thus can be a guide to more effective time budgeting.

A second problem facing the school librarian is that of professional perspective. School librarians need to shift their perception of their jobs from that of service attendants to that of media managers. The school librarian's job has changed radically over a relatively short period of time. A tremendous variety of multimedia material and equipment has been added. The scale of the task has also increased. Less and less are school libraries small, one-room, hole-in-the-corner places. Collections are increasing rapidly, and the role of the school librarian is also increasing in complexity. The growing responsibility of the school librarian combined with ever-present scarcity of time and staff means that the school librarian must continually make choices about how to spend his or her time, which programs to set in motion, how to allocate resources across not only the range of subject material but the range of formats within each subject area as well. All this means that the school librarian, willy-nilly, has become a decision-maker—an administrator managing a highly complex activity. As is true for any decision-maker/manager, the school librarian needs accurate management information. Measurement techniques can help in the transformation of the school librarian from a bureaucrat following prescribed routines to a professional decision-maker selecting a flexible course of action designed to maximize resources (both time and money).

A third problem for the school librarian is caused by our society's emphasis on upward mobility, on advancement and progress. School librarianship offers little in the way of vertical advancement. The promotion ladder is short and not available to many, yet the responsibilities of the job increase with each year. The opportunity for horizontal job enhancement is probably greater for school librarianship than for any other position within the school. Sometimes, however, this is overlooked and the daily routine becomes overwhelming and the job attitude becomes time-serving. Cynicism replaces the first fine enthusiasm. There is a tendency to disassociate from the day-to-day happenings in the library. This is unhealthy for the individual and for the organization. The presence of one individual school librarian can make a substantial difference, not only in the lives of the students in the school but also for the faculty, the parents, the administration, and, in due time, for the community and for our entire society. With the proper measurement tools the librarian on the job can measure his individual impact on the immediate community and assess from that his ultimate impact on the larger environment. Our culture has imbued us with a step-by-step belief in progress. To measure whether there be progress or retrogression, we need finite points, milestones of our achievements.

House (1973, p. 127) has commented, "Evaluation becomes desirable when you think you are doing well but feel unappreciated; when you are in serious trouble; or when someone with authority over you insists that you be evaluated." In the final analysis, the external and internal pressures toward measurement blend together. We need to satisfy the external demand for accountability and also to be accountable to ourselves. We need to justify our budget requests and also to allocate our internal resources more rationally. We need to be able to explain to other people our library's contribution to the educational program and we also need to understand and to take pride in our knowledge of the importance of the professional role of the school librarian. These are good reasons to set goals and objectives that can be attained and to develop methods of determining whether, and to what degree, we are attaining these ends.

III. WHAT IS PERFORMANCE MEASUREMENT?

A. Definition and Relationship to Evaluation

Performance measurement and evaluation are two large umbrella-like terms that are closely related, although not quite identical. Performance measurement is necessary for evaluation. Scriven (1967, pp. 40–41) says the process of evaluation involves asking questions such as:

How well does _____ perform (with respect to such and such criteria)?

Does it perform better than _____?

What does _____ do? (What is the effect of application?)

Is the use of _____ worth what it costs?

Each of these questions requires one or more measures of performance.

There is no real purpose in measuring performance unless some form of evaluation is going to follow. For many years, librarians (not only school librarians, but all types of librarians) have counted the number of items circulated as a performance measure. Knowing that the library has circulated 5,000 books in March is a useless piece of information by itself. That circulation figure must be evaluated with other pieces of information (such as the nature and quality of the collection, the hours of accessibility, the distance clients have to travel to reach it, the availability of other libraries in the area, the noncirculating use of materials within the library) before it becomes relevant information, either reinforcing the present policies and procedures of the library or suggesting that those policies and procedures need revision.

Thus, measurement involves the process of ascertaining the extent or quantity of something while evaluation refers to the process of determining its worth or value. Rothstein (1964) in an early article on measurement and evaluation of reference service makes the same distinction. "Measurement is description in quantitative terms; evaluation is the rating or assessment of effectiveness and worth." He continues, "Evaluation presupposes measurement against a specific standard or yardstick or goal."

Performance measurement is a process, not a one-time event. It includes a number of activities that occur and recur over time. Performance measurement is a means by which the character of an enterprise can be explored and expressed. In this review, performance measurement will be discussed in the context of the entire process of management, including analysis of the present performance of the librarian, the task of setting goals and objectives for the future, the development of techniques to measure the attainment of these goals and objectives, the evaluation of the results, and the revision of the goals and objectives on the basis of the information obtained.

B. The Search for Goals

The Talmud says, "If you do not know where you are going, any road will get you there." Goals and objectives are ways of looking ahead and planning a future. Broader and more general in scope than objectives, goals are the philosophy or the conceptual framework within which specific objectives are fashioned. An objective is a description of what is to be accomplished. The emphasis is on a desirable future with a specified course of action to be undertaken now to achieve that future.

In any task, the first step is a goal-setting activity, or perhaps we should say goal-affirming activity, for it is relatively easy to specify some general goals for school librarians that are acceptable to all. In part, we take these goals from already existing, socially determined goals for education; in part from similar social goals for all libraries regardless of type; and in part from goals designated specifically for school media libraries.

The three principal aims of education, as summarized by Stake and Gooler (1973, p. 287) and paraphrased here, are: (1) the career purpose—to prepare young people for their life work; (2) the knowledge purpose—to help young people know about their world and to build skills for understanding and discovering new knowledge; (3) the human purpose—to enable young people to examine what man is and to provide an opportunity to be participants in the human experience.

The school library's goal, as part of the formal education process, is to assist the school in the achievement of these three broad purposes.

An example of a goal statement that would be acceptable for all libraries regardless of type is one formulated by Kenneth Beasley (1974, p. 391). "The effectiveness of a library is a function of the ability of the library to supply information under conditions which encourage still further use." School libraries would doubtless agree that this is an epigram expressing a primary goal for all libraries.

As an example of a goal designated specifically for school media libraries, the new national media program guidelines state that: "Programs of media services are designed to assist learners to grow in their ability to find, generate, evaluate, and apply information that helps them to function effectively as individuals and to participate fully in society" (American Association of School Librarians, 1975, p. 4).

It is important to note that, in large part, these broad goal statements are *not* measurable. They provide direction and express belief in desirable futures. To move from these larger goals down the ladder of generality to objectives and further down to the measurement of performance is a process that refines out a certain transcendental quality. Nonmeasurable goals are not cast from the picture entirely, however, but will, and should, continue to serve as important guiding principles. The psychologist–philosopher Rokeach (1968, p. 160) makes a distinction between terminal and instrumental values that underlines the distinction made here between goals and objectives. He asserts that a terminal value is a belief that "transcendentally guides actions and judgements across specific objectives and situations, and beyond immediate goals to more ultimate end states of existence. The instrumental value is a belief that a prescribed action will lead to a desired end state." The overall goals that we subscribe to for our school media programs are those that involve terminal values. The objectives that we set involve instrumental values. When we specify objectives to be accomplished, it is important to realize that they will invariably fail to represent the sum total of what is desired.

The subjective element of the individual school librarian's personal value commitments is another important factor to be considered in objective formulation. A growth job is one where the needs and desires of the individual are coincident with the requirements of the job. Usually there is a process of shaping the job to fit the individual's personal needs and values, which are, in turn, being shaped by the requirements of the job. Because of the tremendous variety of tasks that confront the school librarian and the physical inability of being able to accomplish them all, the school librarian has a great deal of choice in how and where to make his contribution. This means that school librarianship is a field that offers considerable adaptive maneuverability for librarians. The unification of job values and personal life values encourages the development of self-actualization and the harnessing of total work commitment in a mutually beneficial relationship.

No two school media programs will ever be exactly alike, because of the impact of the librarian's personal style. Each library will share the common goals of the profession, but each will differ according to the individual school librarian's particular values.

Since the process of bringing student and faculty together with material and information is a highly complex one, we are often striving to satisfy many different objectives at the same time. In some ways our goals seem conflicting and contradictory, but to serve *all* students and faculty in the school, we must accept a pluralistic viewpoint. In the inevitable reduction process of sharpening objectives and specifying performance measurements, we must exercise great care not to abandon a multivalued framework for a more simplistic one.

C. Norms, Standards, and Library Statistics

1. THE COURSE OF SCHOOL MEDIA CENTER STANDARDS

One way to measure is to compare to existing standards or norms. Published national library standards have always been an important source of normative statements about the qualitative and quantitative aspects of the library program. Blackman (1967, p. 4.34), in a discussion of the meaning and use of standards, notes that of the three definitions for the term "standard"—(1) a uniform measuring unit, (2) a prevailing practice or average level of attainment, (3) a goal or statement about what ought to be—the most appropriate for published professional standards is the latter. They do not describe what is, but what ought to be.

A statement in the preface to the 1969 school library standards corroborates this acceptance of standards as goal pointers. It states "there is often a time lag between the appearance of national standards and their achievement on a wide scale. . . ." (*Standards for School Media Programs,* 1969, p. 4). Baughman (1973, p. 274) notes that a standard "states a criterion level for elementary and secondary schools in developing, expanding and implementing a media center program" and that standards "should allow an institution to achieve a higher level of performance in carrying out its responsibilities and meeting the needs of its patrons."

Much could be (and has been) written about the course of national school library standards. The first standard, "Standard Library Organization and Equipment for Secondary Schools of Different Sizes" (Certain, 1917), was published as a final report of a committee appointed by the National Council of Teachers of English to study the appalling conditions of school library programs. It was later approved by the Education Committee of the American Library Association. It is frequently referred to as the "Certain Standards" after the name of the Chairman. Certain also chaired a committee that helped develop *Elementary School Library Standards* (American Library Association, 1925).

These standards were primarily quantitative in nature. Subsequent standards added qualitative statements and increased the scope of concern. *School Libraries of Today and Tomorrow*, the 1945 standard, combined both qualitative and quantitative statements and included both elementary and secondary school library programs (American Association of School Librarians, 1945). The 1960 standards were prepared by a committee whose membership included twenty professional organizations representing the many groups with an interest in the school library. The resulting work emphasized the importance of the school library's relationship to the overall goal of the school (American Library Association, 1960). These standards, according to Francis Henne (1972, p. 236) "constituted a landmark in the history of standards."

The 1969 standards were the first to combine standards for school libraries with standards for audiovisual services in a unified media center program (*Standards for School Media Programs*, 1969). A major contribution of this document was its movement to standardize terminology. The terms "media specialist" and "media center" were used throughout the work in an attempt to shift from the bookish connotation of "librarian" and "library." (This change set off a furious debate and a plethora of other suggestions for terminology. An example: Because a librarian deals with learning resources, he might be called a "resourcerer." And presumably if he had an aide, the aide would become the "resourcerer's apprentice.") The fine philosophic statements of the 1960 standards are missing from the 1969 work, and there is a too heavy emphasis on the quantitative aspects of equipment and material necessary to create a media program. Still, as a first attempt at coordination by the two major professional associations dealing with learning resources in schools, the American Association of School Librarians and the Association of Educational Communications and Technology (formerly Department of Audiovisual Instructions, National Education Association), it was successful.

These two associations continued to collaborate to produce in the 1975 publication a smoothly coordinated document that provides the working school librarian with well-stated, integrated guidelines for creating a strong media program (American Association of School Librarians, 1975). An interesting feature of this new publication is the rejection of the term "standards" in favor of "guidelines" or "criteria." This action seems to reflect a general social movement away from rigid, prescriptive requirements to a more flexible, democratic approach based on choices.

Media Programs focuses on qualitative goals, describing programs designed to respond to both district and school objectives. For each aspect of the total program, the document provides a definition, some guiding principles, and several criterion statements for programs on the district and on the school level. Quantitative statements follow and provide guidelines for the numbers and kinds of staff, collections, and facilities necessary to implement the programs. The guidelines recognize alternative choices that may better serve certain individual program needs. The work is impressive and every school librarian should become familiar with its provisions. It will be a powerful aid in articulating program requirements and in formulating goals and objectives.

In addition to national standards, nearly every state has its own school library standard, the work primarily of state educational agencies but usually involving state professional associations or special committees. Every school librarian should, of course, be thoroughly familiar with his own state standard. In addition, he might find it helpful to examine some particularly fine examples from other states.

Maryland's *Criteria for Modern School Media Programs* (Maryland.

State Department of Education, 1971) is an attractive and innovative handbook stressing new educational approaches and a service orientation. There are few quantitative statements. Rather, the emphasis is on the responsibilities and interrelationships of all the parties involved. The objective of the media program as described here is "to place the learner in communication with other peoples, places, cultures and times."

Several of the state standards provide a phased approach to the achievement of their standards. Two examples are the *Standards for Educational Media (Library and Audiovisual) Programs in Illinois* (1972) and Iowa's *Plan for Progress... in the Media Center* (Iowa. Department of Public Instruction, 1969). The *New Jersey Blueprint for School Media Programs* (1969) provides a checklist of the quantitative standards so that a self-evaluation can be made easily. Pennsylvania's *School Library Standards* (Pennsylvania, Department of Education, 1972) includes the legal requirements for school libraries and the certification requirements for school librarians as determined by the State Board of Education. Sometimes there is a separate state standard for audiovisual services but more often all these standards are combined in one integrated publication.

States also sponsor or publish other valuable material for the school librarian. *School Libraries in Missouri* (Missouri. State Department of Education, 1972) is a publication from the Missouri State Department of Education summarizing the results of a statewide assessment of school libraries. *An Instrument for the Qualitative Evaluation of Media Programs in California* (California. Bureau of Audio-Visual and School Library Education, 1972) is intended as a guide for evaluation team members and, despite its name, is more quantitative than qualitative in nature. Ohio's *Spotlight: Media Solution* (Ohio. Association of School Librarians, 1973) is a handbook for the media specialist offering a three-level plan for developing the services of the media center. Wisconsin's *Learning to Use Media* (Wisconsin. Department of Public Instruction, 1972) is a K–12 sequential instructional plan for the development of instructional media center skills.

There are regional standards and regional publications also. Further exploration of the literature on standards may be undertaken by examining a selected, annotated bibliography on standards for all types of libraries, although only three of the 138 entries are directly concerned with school libraries (Ottersen, 1971). In addition, the entire October 1972 issue of *Library Trends* (Standards for Libraries, 1972) is devoted to various aspects of library standards.

It is important that the practicing school librarian become familiar with those standards, guidelines, and auxiliary publications that relate to his or her particular situation. Standards are generally widely accepted, authoritative, and persuasive in obtaining support. They are useful in the goal-setting, objective-stating process as one source of criterion statements against which to measure the performance capability of the library.

2. THE MEANING AND USE OF LIBRARY STATISTICS

Statistical information about school libraries is collected by the local school system, by the state, and by the Federal Government. What is collected on the state and local level has differed considerably. However, current movement on the national level will no doubt ensure more uniformity on the state level in the future. Almost certainly, in time, this will also affect what is collected on the local level.

Since 1971, a national library statistics program known as the Library General Information Survey (LIBGIS) has been working on a rational and systematic way of collecting statistical information, for use first at the state level by state agencies, after which it is forwarded to the National Center for Educational Statistics (NCES) for aggregation on the national level (Palmer, 1970). Several demonstration projects have been conducted. The first serious data collection was scheduled to begin in 1974. This national data-gathering effort is of great importance to school librarians since the statistical picture created will influence the Federal Government's posture with regard to continuation of such beneficial programs as the Elementary and Secondary Education Act, Title II School Library Resources.

This statistics gathering effort was preceded by a number of others. Since the 1870's the U.S. Office of Education has collected data on public, school, and other types of libraries, using it to infer the condition and the progress of education in the United States. The most recent Office of Education publication for the school library sector is *Public School Library Statistics, 1962–63* (Darling, 1964), although each year since 1970, a new survey has been announced as "in preparation."

The statistical data collected by type of library for the Library General Information Survey will be assembled in seven broad categories—population served, library resources, expenditures, income by source, library use, personnel, and physical facilities—with some further breakdowns in each section. A publication entitled the *Library Statistics Operation Handbook*, being prepared under the auspices of the American Library Association, will describe the statistics project and the categories in more detail. The best summary of this work to date may be found in the *Bowker Annual* [Library statistics (1974): see also Childers (1975) review on "Statistics that Describe Libraries and Library Service."]

These national efforts are intended to produce descriptive statistics only; simple summaries of what exists, for as Prentiss (1970, p. 39) expressed it, "Library statistics of today . . . deal almost exclusively with the library's capacity to perform rather than its actual performance." These statistics are in no way to be confused with standards which describe what ought to be or with any performance measurement in which expressions of value are assigned to the results of data-gathering. They will affect the school librarian in a number of ways. The Federal Government, and perhaps state governments also, will use them in decision-making concerning programs that affect school librarianship. They will also be used to present to the general public an overall sense of the conditions of school libraries. And finally, they will require the school librarian to maintain records in the categories defined by LIBGIS.

IV. LIBRARY PERFORMANCE MEASURES— STATE OF THE ART

Research on library performance has been frequently undertaken in the technical services area where things and processes exist that are easily countable and thus lend themselves to statistical manipulations. In the public service area, and for the library as a whole, far fewer measures have been developed. Not only has library performance research concentrated on particular areas within librarianship, it has also concentrated on certain types of libraries more than others, particularly university and special libraries. Public and school libraries have received much less attention.

Santayana once wrote, "All problems are divided into two classes, soluble questions, which are trivial, and important questions which are insoluble." Perhaps library performance research can be thought of in the same way. At any rate, the measures developed can be put on a continuum from the least to the most rigorous. The least rigorous performance measures are the checklists and the inventories which sometimes tend to be trivial. They are relatively easy to generate and to apply, but more difficult to use as decision-making tools. The information generated lacks directional clarity and the data gathered are not really comparable, even when obtained from the same institution at different times. More sophisticated measures apply mathematical and statistical techniques and become more difficult to generate and to apply, but correspondingly easier to use as decision-making tools, since the information gathered is hard data in numerical form and easier to compare from one situation to the next.

A. Inventories and Checklists

Most of the evaluative work in the school library field has involved the use of inventories and checklists. Fulton's (1969) evaluative checklist for an educational media program is nationally known and has been heavily used in its original form and in various modifications. This checklist is noteworthy for including criterion statements for each of six areas: commitment of school to program, curriculum and instruction involvement, availability and accessibility of media, adequacy of physical facilities, budget and finance, and media staff. Each area includes a number of statements describing possible conditions. The school's program is evaluated against these statements and rated on a scale of one to nine. A profile sheet graphically portrays the "peaks and valleys" of attainment. Fulton's checklist was created as part of an Office of Education grant for the Department of Audiovisual Instruction of the National Educational Association. This group, now the Association for Educational Communication and Technology, has had a committee working for the past two years to produce a new evaluation instrument which should be available by the latter part of 1975.

A number of studies in the school library field, also using inventories and checklists, have attempted to clarify and categorize the myriad activities of the school librarian/media specialist. Four recent and important studies are the School Library Manpower Project, the Jobs in Instructional Media Study, Gaver's Services for Secondary School Media Centers, and Liesener's Process for Planning School Media Programs.

1. SCHOOL LIBRARY MANPOWER PROJECT

The School Library Manpower Project, a five-year (extended to a sixth year in 1974) study on the recruitment, training, and utilization of school library personnel, funded by the Knapp Foundation of North Carolina and conducted by the American Association of School Librarians, has produced a number of valuable publications. Three of them are of particular concern to us in the context of evaluation and performance measurement. The *School Library Personnel Task Analysis Survey* (American Library Association, 1969) was part of the initial information gathering work of the School Library Manpower Project. The study involved the identification of superior school library media centers in each of the fifty states and a survey of this population to learn the types of personnel employed and their respective tasks and responsibilities.

The instrument used for the identification of these superior programs, called the "Criteria of Excellence" checklist, has been printed and reprinted a number of times since school districts have found it an effective way of doing an initial evaluation of individual school library programs (Case, 1969). The checklist itemizes twelve statements that describe the superior school library program: the staffing at both school and district level, the collection variety, physical facilities, organization of materials, guidance in instructional use, curriculum planning contribution, in-service teacher training, consultative services to teachers, variety of learning opportunities, and continuous evaluation of the library program. These are the criteria. Nine columns are provided on the right-hand side under three broad headings: Program, Research, and Implementation. The evaluator is to check one of the three columns under each of the three categories. Under Program, the choices are: fully operational, partially operational, or nonoperational; under Research: presently under study, planned for study, or no study planned; under Implementation: expect achievement in one or two years, expect achievement in three to five years, or do not expect to achieve.

For the School Library Manpower Project, once superior school library programs were identified, a checklist of three hundred task statements was developed in order to provide information on the differentiation of tasks performed in the elementary and secondary library media centers by heads, assistant librarians, audiovisual specialists, technicians, clerks and aides, and district or contract personnel. Twelve standard categories were used in analyzing the responses beginning with development of educational programs and ending with clerical and secretarial tasks. Summarizing the tasks performed by heads of library media centers in the 296 superior school centers, the highest percentage of tasks were reported for three categories—administration, selection, and development of educational programs. From this work came the 1971 publication of occupational definitions for the school library media specialist, the head of a school library media center, the district school library media director, and the school library media technician (American Library Association, 1971).

In 1973 the American Library Association published the *Behavioral Requirements Analysis Checklist* (BRAC) (Case and Lowrey, 1973). This special inventory of competencies for school library media personnel is to be used in educational program development and also to test the performance of librarians on the job and to assess the capabilities of an educational program to produce competent school library media personnel. The competencies necessary to carry out the functions to reach these three goals of recruitment, task analysis, and education are organized into seven major areas:

1. Human behavior (knowledge of human behavior processes and application of this knowledge to interactions with people)
2. Learning and learning environment (knowledge, abilities, and attitudes associated with curriculum, learning theories, strategies for teaching and learning)
3. Planning and evaluation (program design and methods of achieving goals)
4. Media (printed and nonprinted forms of communication and associated technologies)
5. Management (operational direction and leadership exercised)
6. Research (the process of searching, documenting, evaluating, and applying information)
7. Professionalism (conduct of qualified people who render a service, engage in continued study, and maintain high standards of achievement and practice)

Each of these areas is broken down into job functions with task statements in behavioral terms.

In addition to the approximately seven hundred tasks included, response questionnaires are included to provide a predictable measurement of task competency and a judgment as to the value and need for that competency. The four response questionnaires are available for four different evaluation purposes. The questionnaires for the school library media director and the program developer permit an assessment of what is being accomplished or omitted from the education program. Actual on-the-job performance can be evaluated through the use of the questionnaires for the school library media specialist and the media director. As an example, the questionnaire directed to the working librarian asks five questions about each of the tasks included. (The selection of which tasks to evaluate depends on the situation.) The respondent is asked if the task has been performed during the past six to eight months, to judge his capability of performing the task, to judge the degree to which his formal library education prepared him for the task, to judge the importance of the task to his overall job, and to indicate where, in his opinion, is the best place to learn the task.

The School Library Manpower Project has had, and continues to have, a major impact on the school library field. Many of the inventories and checklists, particularly BRAC, will be useful to the school librarian in mounting a program of measurement and evaluation.

2. JOBS IN INSTRUCTIONAL MEDIA STUDY

Coincident with the beginning of the School Library Manpower Project was the Jobs in Instructional Media Study (JIMS) (Bernotavicz and Wallington, 1970; Wallington, 1972). This study examined the tasks of audiovisual personnel using a functional job analysis technique based on Department of Labor techniques and a model of the instructional media field, called the Domain of Instructional Technology [DIT] (Silber, 1970). Tasks were looked at from two directions—"what gets done" and "what people do to get things done." The latter tasks were analyzed to determine whether they related to data, people, or things. These tasks were then further classified according to their degree of complexity and according to the level of educational development required to perform them. The purpose of the JIMS study was to enable an organization to regroup separate tasks into jobs on a more rational basis, to use current trained personnel more efficiently, and to design training programs for new personnel entering the field, in other words, similar to the goals of BRAC—task analysis, recruitment (or job reclassification in this case), and education. The concluding effort of the study was to produce a data bank of tasks which could be reclustered into any number of job descriptions either by function or by difficulty of tasks or skills required (Jobs in Instructional Media, 1970).

Oglesby (1971) compared the JIMS study, the School Library Manpower Project, a Media Guidelines project at the Teaching Research Division of the Oregon State System of Higher Education (Hamreus, 1970), and the 1969 *Standards for School Media Programs* and came to the conclusion that the occupational definitions for the media specialists were essentially the same in all four documents, a conclusion not totally supported by the spokesmen from the JIMS study and the Media Guidelines study (*Reactions*, 1972).

3. SERVICES FOR SECONDARY SCHOOL MEDIA CENTERS

The final two inventories or checklists worthy of note in the school library field are less concerned with occupational definitions and more directly focused on evaluation of media center programs. Mary Gaver (1971) examined the variety and balance of services offered as a means of evaluating the media center program of secondary schools. A checklist of 110 services was used. The instrument, Gaver emphasizes, "measures the services which staff members *think* are given to faculty and students, but in no way measures the *impact* or *output* on faculty or students" (Gaver, 1971, p. 27). Quantity of services is the goal, and participants are not given the opportunity to specify the depth, extent, or quality of a service provided. The checklist is useful for its presentation of a substantial array of services possible.

4. FROM CHECKLIST TO EVALUATIONAL TOOL—PROCESS FOR PLANNING SCHOOL MEDIA PROGRAMS

Liesener and Levitan (1972) took a different tack from Gaver in their concern with service outputs rather than inputs. Liesener developed a means of measuring and quantifying school media program outputs through a comprehensive inventory of services identified from the user's viewpoint rather than the operational viewpoint usually held by the practicing librarian. His work was an outgrowth of attempts to measure effectiveness based on the ultimate test of user satisfaction first performed in the medical library field (Orr et al., 1968).

Services were first classified into six service areas with opportunity for specification of service depth on a continuum from the most effort required from the user and the least from the librarian to the opposite (Liesener, 1974). Public relations, once a separate area, was largely combined with reference services. The five areas are:

   I. *Access to Materials, Equipment, and Space*. Provision of materials and equipment plus the facilities and staff necessary for proper use of the collection. Includes circulation policies, reserves, special collections, copying services and provision of material not in the collection.
  II. *Reference*. Provision of a reference collection, provision of specialized searches and bibliographic products. Also publicizing media center events, activities and acquisitions and providing information on relevant services and activities outside the school.
 III. *Production*. Graphics, photography and reprography. Services range from providing materials for self-help to providing finished products, e.g. transparencies, charts, photographs.
  IV. *Instruction*. Directional services, formal instruction and orientation, in-service training, information, instruction and guidance in reading, viewing and listening.
   V. *Consulting*. Includes services offered to teachers and school staff on selection and use of print and non-print materials for current planning and for achieving desired educational objectives.

Using the inventory, Liesener then demonstrates a means of applying cost-accounting techniques to determine costs of specific services in terms of both resources and staff time required. A form for collecting data and a program costing matrix is included to aid in the allocation of costs to services, as is a form to assist the media specialist in determining service priorities with the participation of the faculty, administration, and students in the school. This report is thus a practical package for the practicing librarian who wishes to analyze his program in systematic fashion and to develop a budgetary planning process based on program, planning, and budgeting system (PPBS) techniques. A preliminary outline of Liesener's conceptual framework and processes for media program planning is provided in a recent issue of *School Media Quarterly* (Liesener, 1973). A more detailed and comprehensive planning program will be available with the publication of his book *A Systematic Planning Process for School Media Programs* (Liesener, 1976).

B. The Application of Mathematical and Statistical Techniques

With Liesener's development of data-gathering instruments as part of the overall planning process for the school library, the evolution of the simple checklist into a useful evaluational tool becomes apparent. Other methods of measurement have been developed that involve much more elaborate and complex statistical approaches. No attempt will be made to explain these techniques in detail here but we will point out their objectives, the assumptions that they make, and comment on their usefulness in the school media area.

1. OPERATIONS RESEARCH AND THE UNIVERSITY LIBRARY

Operations research techniques have been applied to certain areas of librarianship with some important results. An overview of operations research work in the library field was published as the Proceedings of the Thirty-Fifth Annual Conference at the University of Chicago Graduate Library School (Swanson and Bookstein, 1972). Operations research uses a systems orientation and identifies all the individual functions of an organization and the point at which they interact. It then uses mathematical models and simulations to evaluate the combined impact of all the interactions. All data are quantified insofar as possible, sometimes rather arbitrarily. Operations research attempts to optimize some activity or procedure, whether journal use or selection, number of copies of a book, loan periods, network design, or cost. Bookstein and Swanson (1972), in their introduction, summarize the feelings of most librarians about this highly mathematical technique with a story from Peanuts. Lucy asks Charlie Brown why he doesn't like mathematics since, after all, she says, "It's a very precise subject." Charlie answers, "That's just the trouble, I'm at my best in something where the answers are mostly a matter of opinion."

One book, explaining operations research in the library field, that approaches intelligibility for the lay reader willing to work is Philip Morse's *Library Effectiveness* (1968). In the first half of his book, he describes four techniques and their application to librarianship: probability distributions to predict average behavior of the library user (browsing, borrowing, use of catalog, use of study space, length of stay, etc.), the Poisson distribution to predict the number of persons in the library at any time of day, queueing theory and its application to the circulation procedure, and the Markov process to predict the variations for book use with age and subject matter. The latter half of the book demonstrates the application of these techniques to the Massachusetts Institute of Technology library. A paper by Morse on measures of library effectiveness is included in an issue of the *Library Quarterly* (Morse, 1972).

The Industrial Engineering School at Purdue University, under the direction of Ferdinand Leimkuhler, has experimented with the application of operations research to library problems since 1963, resulting in a substantial number of theses, books, and articles on the subject. In these studies, the library is viewed as a warehouse. The focus is primarily on selection, use, and storage problems, although a few papers have been produced on behavioral aspects. One of the best of these is a paper by Baker (1968) on the interactions between librarians, users, and funders. A summary of the work at Purdue is provided in Leimkuhler's discussion of library operations research (Leimkuhler, 1972).

The University of Lancaster in England has had a Library Research Unit, under the direction of Michael Buckland (1970, 1972) which has concentrated on loan and duplication policies. A computerized simulation game on library management is one outcome of this work. For those interested in purusing the applications of operations research to library performance measurement further, Slamecka's bibliography (1972) is recommended.

The research studies in large university libraries described in the preceding paragraphs would seem to have little application to school librarianship at the present time. A more familiar approach, using the inventory/checklist method, is a comprehensive tool for university library self-evaluation developed by the Association of Research Libraries called the Management Review and Analysis Program [MRAP] (Webster, 1974). This is a guide to conducting a complete internal evaluation of library management policies and activities through a systematic investigation of top management functions. Although the process advocated is a major undertaking far beyond the scope or need of the school library, the approach, the questions posed, and the framework provide useful suggestions.

2. COST EFFECTIVENESS, "UTILITY" THEORY, AND THE SINGLE INDEX CONCEPT

Special librarians have been concerned for some time with the question of justifying costs and demonstrating benefits. Wessel (1968) summarizes a number of approaches and techniques (most involve a considerable degree of mathematical and statistical knowledge) employed by special libraries to measure their library effectiveness.

Morris Hamburg, of the Wharton School, University of Pennsylvania, has analyzed the problem of developing performance measures for public libraries (Hamburg *et al.*, 1972, 1974). He initially examined the stated objectives of libraries and found them not sufficiently explicit in most cases. Where they were specific enough to be useful they were too interrelated with other societal objectives to be measured in isolation. "The real outputs for library services are the stimulated school teacher, the informed voter, the successful businessman, etc." (Hamburg *et al.*, 1972, p. 110). He concludes that the one measurable item that demonstrates the library's contribution is "exposure of individuals to documents of recorded human experience" (Hamburg *et al.*, 1972, p. 111). Documents are used here in the largest sense of any library material regardless of form. The objective then becomes to maximize document exposure per dollar expended to obtain those exposures. Hamburg excludes from measurement the use of the library for study or reading one's own materials, for socializing, or for classes. He proposes a method for measuring document exposure called exposure count and adds two variations for increased accuracy—item use-days and exposure time.

Exposure counts are obtained by totaling library usage in all categories—each circulation, renewal, direct in-library use, interlibrary loan, each time a library employee provides information in person or over the telephone, and each storytelling session for children. The latter two categories are examples of "indirect exposure" as opposed to the first four which are considered "direct exposures". Item use, suggested by Meier (1961), adds to the count a weighting for the days of use per circulation or interlibrary loan. Exposure time is also based on exposure count but is an attempt to estimate the actual amount of time spent for each document circulated. Checkout and return times for in-library use items would also be monitored to estimate exposure time.

Using document exposure time, Hamburg constructs two types of performance measures. The first is a ratio of benefits to costs, obtained by dividing total estimated exposure hours for a year by the total library costs for that year. Division of exposure hours by cost results in exposure hours per dollar. The second performance measure is that of difference between benefits and costs. To obtain this measure, an imputed monetary value for each exposure hour is developed, which is then multiplied by the total exposure hours. The costs are subtracted and the balance is a monetary estimate of the benefits accruing from library service for that year. The imputed monetary value of document exposure is derived as follows: The value of any governmental investment is expected to yield a return equal to that of a private investment (approximately 10 to 15 percent). It is assumed that the government investment in a public library meets that expectation. Based on this assumption, the monetary value is estimated to be 10 percent greater than the cost.

Hamburg describes in detail how his measures were applied to the Philadelphia Public Library system and how he derives his estimations of each of the parameters involved. For the 1969–1970 fiscal year, he estimated there were 6.94 exposure hours per person. The cost estimate involved current operating expenditures plus depreciation costs for the collection, buildings, equipment, and furnishings and was estimated at $4.60 per person, resulting in 1.51 exposure hours per dollar. Using an imputed monetary value of 10 percent greater than cost, each exposure hour was estimated to be worth 72 cents or approximately 46 cents per person. The major value of this technique lies in the comparability of the figures from year to year and from library system to library system.

3. OTHER USEFUL TECHNIQUES

In another public library study, Lipsman (1972) examines the problem of program impact measures in her fine study, *The Disadvantaged and Library Effectiveness*. She suggests "proxy" measures, such as the absolute or relative change in the number of users, following the institution of a particular program and the overall consensus among informed members of the community as to the value of special programs. Neither of these measures directly attacks the question of the impact of library services on the individual. To attempt this, Lipsman used a case study approach to evaluate four basic relationships: program objectives to user requirements, activities to objectives, achievement (output) to objectives, and cost to achievement. From the case studies, five key factors were isolated as critical to program effectiveness: staff effectiveness, community involvement, autonomy in decision-making, user involvement in activity, and effectiveness of publicity.

Other public library use studies are discussed in a state-of-the-art review of evaluation for adult public services by Monroe (1972). She recommends more attention to "library impact" on practical problems or needs, rather than measures of inputs (books added, bibliographies compiled) or outputs (attendance, books circulated).

The majority of the measures described, plus one more to be described in some detail in Section VI,C, have been aimed at some sort of comprehensive evaluation of total library services. A variety of measures have been developed for particular aspects of library service, for example, circulation, processing, reference services, and quality of collection, with probably more attention to the latter area than to any of the others. A brief examination of specialized measures for each area follows.

a. Measures of Circulation. Gross external circulation figures are usually kept for comparison purposes over different years or with different libraries. An estimate of in-library use based on an hourly count of items being used plus materials left on tables, could be added to that for internal library circulation (cf. Hamburg's "exposure count"). Circulation statistics can also be broken down by type of user (faculty or student, grade of student, or by course), by subject class (by tens division of Dewey, or by assigning groups of Dewey numbers to curriculum areas), by type of material (reference, reserve, audiovisual, book, periodical), by date of material, and so on. Simmons (1971) analyzed computer-produced circulation records at the University of British Columbia to find the extent of use of heavily demanded material, use by particular groups of borrowers, and use of materials in relation to loan policy, in order to provide management data for recommended changes in selection policies.

b. Measures of Technical Processing. Processing operations have been measured extensively in time and cost studies. Dougherty and Leonard (1970) provide an extensive bibliographic review of this area. Their 853-item review (some entries are duplicated in more than one place) is classified by subject and includes material on work simplification, work standards, standard times, performance standards, and cost effectiveness studies. Tesovnik and DeHart (1970) supplement this work with a bibliography of unpublished studies.

Hines (1974) notes that the smaller library is unable to perform time-and-motion studies or to keep an accurate count of the man-hours spent on given tasks. He suggests instead that the best technique for evaluating processing services in small libraries might be to examine the extent to which the library is complying with a number of recommended methods and procedures relating to processing services where broad professional consensus exists. Hines provides five exemplary statements to use as criteria against which to measure the library's performance. These are:

1. The use of standardized, externally provided catalog cards or information without change is significantly cheaper and better than either original cataloging and classification or the attempt to review, edit, or adapt externally provided copy or cards.
2. For school and public libraries in particular, ... centralized or cooperative acquisitions, cataloging, and processing, or the use of commercial cataloging and processing, are cheaper and better than the alternative of trying to carry out these tasks on the individual small library level.
3. ... there has been substantial consensus that the acquisition of materials to meet user needs should not be limited by form of publication. Indeed, the literature has laid increasing stress upon the need to acquire, provide proper bibliographic access, and proper processing and servicing facilities for films, filmstrips, audio and video tapes, and other nonprint media for an increasingly media-conscious and media using culture. [Here Hines notes that:] The school library indisputably holds the lead today in welding all forms of media to meet user needs—a position of leadership for which other types of libraries have yet to give due credit and the sincere flattery of imitation.
4. ... it is wise to avoid the use of professional educated staff to carry out

clerical or subprofessional tasks such as typing, filing, searching, or comparing Library of Congress cards or copy to books.
5. There should be a true network of nationwide resources in which each library unit aggressively and positively carries out a program of informing its users that it will locate or get any required information item for its users within a reasonable time, and carries out that program.

To this end, evidence of cooperative acquisitions, interlibrary loan, union lists, consortia, and other cooperative activities would be indications of a superior performance.

Cooperative loan activity among schools in an area can be effective. Altman (1972) conducted a feasibility study on establishing secondary school interlibrary loan networks. She found substantial title diversity and less collection overlap than had been previously assumed, indicating strong support for interschool networking.

c. Measures of Reference. On the subject of measurement and evaluation of reference services, Rothstein's article (1964) is still the best. The most common way of measuring reference service is to count the total number of questions asked. This gives a rough measure of the volume of reference work. Some public and academic libraries classify reference questions into type of question (informational and directional, short answer, search, and bibliography), source of question (in person or by telephone, student or faculty), subject area, and/or reason for asking the question (school, work, or personal).

Beasley (1964) suggests that a better measure than number or kind of reference questions would be the total staff time spent on reference work in comparison with other activities. In 1964, Rothstein reported that only between 6 and 8 percent of the total staff time was dedicated to reference service. Ten years later, Weech (1974, p. 322) reports, "Recent studies have indicated that the proportion of staff time devoted to reference service ranges from 11 percent to 20 percent."

Other performance measures of reference work include user opinions relative to their satisfaction with reference service, evaluation of reference collections (by date, by use, or against a standard list), and measurements of the ability of the library to respond correctly and effectively to simulated test questions or to questions actually asked by observed library users. Crowley and Childers (1971), among others, have used unobtrusive measurement techniques for reference service evaluation by posing a number of questions to librarians in such a way that the inquirers and questions appear to be "real." Their findings indicate that most librarians are able to answer correctly only slightly more than half the questions posed.

School librarians rarely have the time to do much direct reference work, and it may be that performance measurement in this area might be confined to an evaluation of the library's reference collection, although it might prove valuable to do a small study of the volume and kinds of reference questions asked by students in the nearest public library with a follow-up to determine whether or not the school library contains the resources to answer these questions.

d. Measures of the Collection. Techniques of evaluating the collection are discussed in a detailed, state-of-the-art review by Bonn (1974) in an issue of *Library Trends* devoted to evaluation of library service. He groups the methods for evaluating library collections into five categories: "(1) compiling statistics on holdings, use, expenditures; (2) checking lists, catalogs, bibliographies; (3) obtaining opinions from regular users; (4) examining the collection directly; and (5) applying standards (using various of the foregoing methods) plus testing the library's document delivery capability and noting the relative use of several libraries of a particular group."

Statistics relating to the collection can be compiled by counting total items or counting separately by type of material, counting volumes added, using collection formulas, comparing the existing collection to that of other times or to other comparable libraries, examining subject balance, checking the number and kinds of unfilled requests or interlibrary loan requests, and determining the optimum size of the collection on the basis of circulation and budget.

Recently, attention has shifted from measuring adequacy of resources as attested by shelf list or catalog entries to determining whether or not the material desired is actually available. A somewhat sarcastic, but amusing, article by Gore (1975) stresses the importance of measuring availability and describes the findings of a number of studies in this area. He asks, "What happens after people leave the catalog, call numbers in hand, and go to the shelves to fetch the books?" Studies show that users find what they are looking for less than half the time. Although part of the reason may be poor inventory control, many of the books will not be available because they are in use. Trueswell (1969) found that, in general, 20 percent of a library's collection accounts for 80 percent of its outside circulation and that 70 percent or more of the books lent on any given day will have circulated at least once in the previous year.

If "shelf failure" is high, remedies may include better shelving procedures, tighter security controls, shorter loan periods, greater use of interlibrary loan, review of selection criteria, and addition of duplicate copies of some material. On adding duplicates of heavily used material rather than more individual esoteric titles, Gore (1975) suggests, "Too many unreadable books may mean too few copies of those that are read."

This display of various techniques and methods of measuring library attributes is intended to provide the school librarian with a range of possibilities for further exploration. There remains one more comprehensive approach to performance measurement to be discussed in some detail in the next section.

C. A Comprehensive Tool for Performance Measurement

DeProspo *et al.* (1973) have produced a substantial study of performance measurement in public libraries that seems to have tremendous potential for application to other library situations, particularly to school libraries. Their approach is pragmatic but all-inclusive, using variations of many of the techniques already discussed. Unlike many of the researchers in this area, they selected for their target audience the practitioner rather than other researchers.

The greatest contribution of their Public Library Measurement Study may well be in the demonstrated use of statistical sampling techniques in ways the practitioner will find easy to understand and apply. A nice clarity of explanation is evident in this short passage from an article describing the study: "Sampling, (in brief) means that you select a portion of the whole (the universe) for detailed study. However, the portion selected must accurately reflect the characteristics of the whole. Findings about the sample are then used to infer things about the universe" (DeProspo and Altman, 1973).

Measurement formulas are provided in three areas—the availability of materials, the use of facilities, and the nature of staff and user interaction. Results of the measures are reported in probability terms ranging from absolute success as 1 to absolute failure as 0. Thus, for materials availability, it is possible to compute the probability that a library will own a particular title and the probability that the title will be available on the shelf. Facilities' use is measured by building use (time spent in the library reported as effective user hours), circulation (both in library and outside), furnishings and equipment use (also reported in probability terms so that actual use can be compared with potential use).

Perhaps a detailed example of the latter type of measure would be illustrative of the techniques developed. Suppose an elementary school library has its usual odd assortment of audiovisual equipment and wants to begin compiling some statistics so that the use of the equipment can be measured. We could, and we have, set up systems for counting uses. This is (1) terribly time-consuming, (2) usually inaccurate, and (3) does not really provide much information because it is not related to anything.

Using the techniques supplied in the Public Library Measurement Study, first, a sampling procedure is developed so that counting takes place only at certain specified and controlled times; second, the use of equipment is measured against an absolute standard of total possible use; third, use of any one type of equipment can be compared to any other type of equipment; and fourth, equipment use can be measured in comparable terms year by year, since differences in inventory are controlled by a built-in device in the formula.

As a first step, data are collected on the type and number of the different pieces of equipment. Let us assume our school has ten overhead projectors, six 16mm motion picture projectors only five of which are operable, twenty record players, five 8mm film loop projectors, five slide projectors, and five filmstrip projectors.

According to the formula, B = the sum of all the equipment found by adding the sums of all the different types. The different types are represented by subscripts. Thus

B_1 = Overhead projectors = 10
B_2 = 16mm projectors = 5 (not counting the one inoperable one)
B_3 = Record players = 20
B_4 = Film loop projectors = 5
B_5 = Slide projectors = 5
B_6 = Filmstrip projectors = 5
or, $B = B_1 + B_2 + \ldots + B_6 = 50$.

The next step is the sampling procedure. A typical day is selected to check on equipment use. Suppose the school day is divided into six periods and there is library use time before and after school. Equipment use could be sampled eight times during the day—once ten minutes before first period, once at midpoint of each of the six periods, and once ten minutes after school.

According to the formula, H = the total number of hourly counts of equipment use. In the example, $H = 8$, there will be eight counts of the use of six different types of equipment for a total of fifty pieces of equipment. The maximum possible use would be 50 multiplied by 8 or 400 uses during the collection period. The maximum possible use of the five working 16mm projectors would be forty; of the ten overhead projectors, eighty; and so on. This use figure is symbolized in the formula by a U.

The third step is to collect the information on use. On the sample day, the school librarian could send out a small team of fifth- or sixth-grade students eight times during the day. (They wouldn't have to be the same students each time, of course.) Each student might have a specific task. For instance, Johnny is to count the number of record players that are actually in use at 7:50 in the morning. Mary is to tally the overhead projectors, and Susan the filmstrip and slide projectors, etc. "In use" might be broadly defined and include equipment set up and ready to use before the end of the period.

By a matter of simple addition at the end of the day, the librarian could calculate that for item B_1, the overhead projectors, there were eighteen uses during the day from a maximum possible of eighty. This is represented in the formula by the use of a subscript. Thus, U_1 = the number of uses of the overhead projectors; U_2 = the number of uses of the 16mm projectors, etc. The total number of uses would be the sum of all the uses of each type of equipment.

Some imaginary figures might be as follows:
  The overhead projectors, U_1 were used 18 times (80 possible)
  The 16mm projectors, U_2 were used 10 times (40 possible)
  The record players, U_3 were used twice (160 possible)
  The film loop projectors, U_4 were used 7 times (40 possible)
  The slide projectors U_5 were used 3 times (40 possible)
  The filmstrip projectors, U_6 were used 10 times (40 possible)
  The total number of uses in $U = U_1 + U_2 + \ldots + U_6 = 50$.

All of these figures are then put into the total formula for equipment use (EQ) which is as follows: $EQ = U/HB$ where U = the number of actual uses, H = the total number of hourly counts of equipment, and B = the total of all the equipment. If U equaled 400, the highest possible value, then EQ would be 1 or 100 percent. This is the absolute standard. In our hypothetical case,

$$EQ = 50/400 = .125$$

In like manner each individual piece of equipment could also be scored

EQ_2 (Equipment use of 16mm projector)/(8 × 5) = 10/40 or .25
EQ_3 (Equipment use of 20 record players)/(8 × 20) = 2/160 or .0125

If the equipment count is taken on more than one day, as would be recommended, then H would be increased. For a typical week, if counts were taken eight times a day, then H would equal 56 and would be a more accurate reflection of use. Because of the power of sampling, however, at some point far short of counting each day the results obtained are more accurate than essaying a total count.

This is one measurement, perhaps one of the more complex because of the formulas and the subscripts, but on examination not beyond the powers of any school librarian.

The final group of measures, from the Public Library Measurement Study, for nature of staff and user interaction includes patterns of reference use—providing a ratio of number of questions asked per hour of staff time and other similar ratios, number of programs held (films shown, exhibits, book talks, in-service workshops, lectures, storytelling, etc.), variety of programming, and different groups within the community (substitute school) served by the program.

V. MEASUREMENT AS A PROCESS

A. Rubrics of Measurement

This concludes a short survey of measurement techniques and methods. It remains only to make a few summary remarks on the process of measurement itself and to suggest a step-by-step continuing plan for the school librarian/media specialist. First, there are five important rules relating to measurement that must be kept in mind.

1. *Measurement is a process, not a product.* It is an ongoing activity involving analysis, planning, implementing, and evaluating in a continuous cycle.

2. *Measurement requires value judgments.* Not everything of worth can be measured. The selection of what to measure and the interpretation of the results of measurement require professional and personal value judgments.

3. *Measure only where it makes a difference.* If there is no possibility of correcting, changing, or reinforcing a particular aspect being measured, it probably is a waste of time to measure it.

4. *The most important resource of the librarian is time.* Financial resources are important, but the school library is a labor-intensive activity. The choice of where and how the librarian spends his time will affect the overall direction of the program more than anything else. Time spent on planning will ultimately have a bigger impact than time spent on repetitive clerical tasks.

5. *The most useful tool for the librarian is knowledge.* This means knowledge of the range of alternatives and their anticipated consequences, of the experiences and considerations of others faced with similar problems, of the operational effectiveness of the particular library in question, and of the managerial perspectives and techniques to administer that library. In the face of continuing change, we realize that education is a lifelong process in all fields of endeavor and that yesterday's knowledge is only the base of tomorrow's knowledge requirements. As Thomas Jefferson once remarked, "To expect to be ignorant and free is to expect what never was and never will be."

B. Building Blocks for Measurement Capability

1. THE SYSTEMS APPROACH

The development of measurement capability should be undertaken using a building block concept. Simple methods of measurement can be essayed first. By combining single measures and improving them, more comprehensive and sophisticated methods can evolve. A wealth of evidence suggests that a systems approach can provide a serviceable framework within which to proceed. This approach allows one to take an overall view while analyzing in detail each element of a program and its relationship to other elements. There is an insistence on clear definition of goals and objectives but the systems approach also allows for the fact that there is often no one "best" way of achieving most objectives. A systems term used to express this concept is *equifinality*, defined in Webster's Third International as "the property of allowing or having the same effect or result from different events." In colloquial terms another way of saying this is: "There's more than one way to skin a cat."

The systems approach stresses the importance of searching for alternative ways of solving a problem. Finally, a systems perspective introduces a logical cycle to the activities of the organization: (1) goal articulation, (2) objective formulation, (3) analysis of operations, (4) search for alternatives, (5) selection and implementation, (6) measurement and evaluation, (7) feedback from any of the previous activities, and back through the cycle again and again, each time modifying and improving the program.

2. THE USE OF SAMPLING TECHNIQUES

The one statistical technique that seems to have the most immediate application for the school librarian is that of sampling. It is a technique that can be applied with a minimum of mathematical sophistication at first. With increasing experience it can provide a wealth of information with a small degree of effort. Without the power of sampling, the only measurement possibilities are checklists, which lack specificity, and counting things, which usually results in too much data on too few elements. As DeProspo and Altman (1973) put it, "Counting only a portion of what is being studied has a number of advantages over counting everything. Data can be collected quickly and cheaply. Working with a smaller amount of data allows the study of more variables and their interrelationships. Sampling counts are frequently more accurate than universal tallies as the proportion of error increases with the number of items counted."

3. THE NEED FOR GREATER STATISTICAL SOPHISTICATION

Beyond sampling, the area of inferential statistics offers a whole new world of powerful ways of measuring and evaluating. The new breed of librarian will do well to develop a basic knowledge of statistics so that he or she can become an efficient consumer of the articles describing research in relevant areas and so that he or she can develop a working level competence to undertake or supervise the collection of data in meaningful categories and to analyze and interpret the results of data collection in management/decision-making terms. Perhaps this is an area where library education has been remiss, particularly so for the school librarian.

Since there has been little direction for the practicing school librarian in measurement and evaluation, it would seem important that workshops be developed for the practicing librarian and for the supervisory librarians at the regional and state levels. The employment of consultants might also be encouraged to assist the practitioner in the initial process of analysis and establishing direction. Pooling of efforts on the local and state levels by discussion and presentation in association and other professional meetings is another useful method of acquiring confidence and a growing expertise in the area.

4. THE IMPORTANCE OF A MANAGERIAL ORIENTATION

Probably the greatest change that must take place is for the school librarian to acquire a managerial orientation. The collection of data and the process of performance measurement are empty exercises without intelligent use of the end products. A collection of data becomes information through its interpretation within the context of the total environment, and information becomes knowledge when it is used for informed decision-making.

VI. A STEP-BY-STEP PLAN FOR THE SCHOOL LIBRARY/MEDIA CENTER PRACTITIONER

Five discrete stages can be discerned for the task of developing and carrying out a plan for measuring performance and incorporating the results in a continuing plan of improving performance. The first stage is that of exploration and experimentation. Stage two is a planning period. Stage three is programming time. Stage four is the implementation stage. The fifth stage is the review and evaluation of the program. Then the cycle is repeated, beginning with a new planning period. A hypothetical example of the way this plan might work is described in the following paragraphs.

A. **Stage 1—Exploration and Experimentation**

It is spring. The year is drawing to a close. Much has been attempted. It is difficult to say what has been accomplished. Tasks have been identified, some have been started, few have been finished. Each day the backlog of unfinished activities grows. The librarian decides it is time for stocktaking and systematic planning.

Now begins a period of reading, thinking, and discussing. It is a preplanning time, a time of preparation. It may be possible to try out one or two measurements of tasks, activities, library use, collections, or other areas before the school year ends. A time diary would be helpful. It is a time to collect the supportive material required and to do some preliminary sketching of a comfortable and complete design for the coming year. This period lasts throughout the summer. The return to the school marks the end of this exploratory stage.

B. **Stage 2—Planning**

The first concrete task is the most difficult. Written goals, objectives, and priorities must be developed with the assistance of the entire school, if possible. Active participation from the leaders among the teaching faculty must be sought. Students and staff must be involved. The principal and supervisory librarian are key people in this process. A Committee of the Future might be organized to define the needs of the school in light of forecasts of future events. The charge to the committee is to develop a master five-year plan for the school. Subcommittees dealing with each functional area of the school are charged with preparing objectives that will become part of the master plan.

It may or may not be possible for the librarian to set in motion a master planning process for the entire school. The librarian does, however, have control and responsibility for planning the direction of the library program and its development. A preliminary step here will be to use the national *Media Programs* guideline in conjunction with the standards for the particular state as background to create a statement of the overall goals and objectives of the media program. This statement should be widely distributed.

Following the broadcasting of this statement of purpose, Liesener's plan (1973), or an adaptation of it, can facilitate the difficult process of involving the users in selecting service alternatives. Liesener presents a nine-step planning process. The first three steps are particularly germane. Step one requires the librarian to apply the "Inventory of School Library/Media Center Services" to his situation so that "one can begin to consider what services from the total array are more needed in a given situation." In step two, some of the teachers and students are asked to complete the same "Inventory." This has several purposes: it establishes the accuracy of their perceptions of the services offered; it increases the awareness of the range of potential services; it is a mechanism involving them in a systematic assessment and planning process. Not least in importance, it creates a client-centered posture on the part of the media center.

The determination of service preference and priorities in relation to local needs is Liesener's step three. The technique advocated involves using a "Form for Determining Preferences for School Library/Media Center Services." This form, an abbreviation of the "Inventory" provides a forced choice method of selecting from the service alternatives those most important to the local situation. The form is completed individually by a sample of students, teachers, and administrative staff and then, through group discussions, a consensus on a single statement of priorities is reached. This is then reported back to the entire school population for their ratification and approval. Liesener (1973, p. 283) points out several advantages to this technique. Since resources are always limited, "services must also be limited to what can be provided reliably and dependably if user benefit rather than frustration is to be achieved." The forced choice method provides the necessary "real-world" limitations. A major advantage of the use of this method is the development of an informed and supportive constituency with increased service appetites.

By the middle of the fall semester, this procedure, if begun at the outset of the school year, should result in a strong base of agreement with which to enter the next phase.

C. Stage 3—Programming

This stage covers the transformation of the service alternatives selected into a total program. Measurement of the present service capabilities against the criteria established by the group selection of priorities (with the help of state standards and media program guidelines) is prerequisite to developing a detailed program. The program plan details the boundaries of concern, the assessment methods used, and the time frame.

Collection assessment, as a whole or in part, will, no doubt, be one necessary requirement. The DeProspo–Altman (1973) method of determining the probability of ownership and the subsequent probability of availability based on a sample of the whole is an effective means of assessing the collection. One possible scenario follows.

In January, draw a random sample of perhaps five hundred titles from a tool such as *The Elementary School Library Collection* (Gaver and Van Orden, 1973) by selecting every twentieth title from the title listing.* Check the list against the catalog to determine the number of items owned and convert to a percentage. This is the probability of ownership. Check the items owned against shelf to determine the probability of availability. For those items not available, categorize reasons for unavailability—regular circulation, long-term loan, bindery, mending, in process, or missing.

If the collection is large enough to warrant it, or if there is a particular need to know, other smaller samples (no more than 20 percent of total collection) might be examined to check the reference collection, perhaps using Wynar's *Guide to Reference Books for School Media Centers* (1973); the media collection, for which one might suggest McDaniel's *Resources for Learning* (1971), or Greene and Schoenfield's *A Multimedia Approach to Children's Literature* (1972); new books, using *Children's Books of the Year* (Annual); paperbacks, using *Paperback Books for Children* (American Association of School Librarians, 1972) or *Paperback Books for Young*

---

*Other suggested tools: the Wilson catalogs—*Children's Catalog* (1972–1975), *Junior High School Library Catalog* (1970), *Senior High School Library Catalog* (1972); Bowker's *Children's Books in Print* (Annual); the National Association of Independent Schools' *Books for Secondary School Libraries* (1971); Sutherland's *The Best in Children's Books,* includes a "curricular use index" (1973); ALA's *Books for Elementary School Libraries* (Hodges, 1969).

People (Gillespie and Spirt, 1972); or in a particular subject area, for example, for science, using *The AAAS Science Book List for Children* (Deason, 1972); or any other aspect for which some tool exists which identifies the universe to be measured and can serve as a selection pool from which to draw a sample. In each subsequent year, another five-hundred-title sample (or however many were in the first sample) is to be drawn from the latest edition of whatever tool was used or from the same edition (recognizing the bias toward older material) by beginning the every twentieth title selection in a different place. After the second year, comparative figures would be available.

In addition to collection evaluation, no doubt circulation also requires regular assessment. For example, for one day each week (Monday the first week, Tuesday the second, and so on) the total outside circulation might be counted, categorizing the collection into three or four broad curricular areas (such as, science and mathematics, social studies, language arts, humanities, recreational reading-listening-viewing, and miscellaneous) using Dewey class numbers and knowledge of teachers' assignments as rough guidelines for the groupings. At periodic intervals during the day when the library is being set in order (perhaps once in midmorning, once after lunch, and once at the end of the day), a count by categories of all items left on tables and currently in use in the library is to be undertaken. The combined total of these two counts multiplied by five provides a weekly close approximation of total circulation. Charting the amounts for each category across the school year, week by week, will begin to demonstrate usage patterns. After one year of this type of sampling, the data may suggest that less frequent intervals (once every two weeks perhaps) will yield approximately the same information.

Other regular performance measures might be as follows: A measure of equipment use for the budding media center, such as that described in detail in Section IV,C, would also be included in the program plan. Hines's (1974) suggested criteria for processing might be applied to the library's situation. Those that could not be answered positively would become objectives for the following years. Once a year the percent of time spent in reference work during one typical week in the school year might be sampled for annual comparisons. Some attempt to collect typical questions at that time would produce information helpful in collection development and/or in library network planning. The nearest public library should be contacted for estimates of volume of use by students, heaviest times of use, types of questions posed, and other relevant information. If the library is on flexible scheduling, a time study of independent library use—again using a sampling technique to estimate the whole—could be instituted. If a library were not on flexible scheduling, an objective to achieve this might be included in the program plan.

With the use-of-facilities measure, or independent of it, a survey of the users could be instituted using a simple questionnaire to ascertain their satisfaction/dissatisfaction with the library on a scale of one to five. An opportunity to provide reasons for dissatisfaction (and for satisfaction, too, for that matter) will furnish useful information.

In addition to an annual, continuing, measurement program, a series of specific objectives for meeting the service priorities will also be drawn up. The program plan is less a participative effort than was the setting of service priorities, although there is a continuing need to inform users of the ways their priorities have been translated into an action program. The approach advocated here for the programming stage is modeled on that of the Planning, Programming, Budgeting System (PPBS), described by Hannigan (1972) as a methodology that "requires specification of goals; demonstrates utilization of manpower, resources and facilities; delineates priorities among multiple alternatives; and focuses on evaluation of output."

D. Stage 4—Implementation

This stage entails following the plan put together in the previous stage. It is important that expectations are realistic and that a flexible approach is used. Allow room for intuition. Also be prepared to adapt the ideality of the program plan to the reality of the situation. Implementation of the plan involves careful monitoring of activities and data collection for the subsequent stage.

E. Stage 5—Review and Evaluation

By this stage, if careful planning, programming, and implementing have taken place, there should be a wealth of data available for review. All the once-a-year measurements should be compiled for an annual report along with one-time measurements of specific objectives. Careful consideration must be given to the results of these measures, examining each by itself and as it relates to all the others in the total program plan for the library. The meaning of the data and future implications to be derived from this examination should be written down and organized into a coherent report that describes past achievements, highlights deficiencies, suggests causes, and provides direction for the future. This annual report is then used as the input for a new planning stage initiating the cycle anew.

Because the school librarian operates in an environment that largely works within a September-to-June time frame, it is suggested that the planning cycle follow this also. For the first year, the schedule will be:
1. Planning through the mid-fall semester
2. Programming through the end of the fall semester
3. Implementation in the spring semester
4. Review and evaluation at end of school year culminating in the annual report

For subsequent years, implementation would extend throughout the school year. The other activities would continue to be cyclical, although review, evaluation, and planning will be closely interwoven.

VII. SUMMARY AND CONCLUSIONS

Measurement is difficult. Not long ago there was a film that graphically portrayed the difficulties of measurement. This film, produced by the Arizona Department of Education, was set in a school media center and showed its range of activities. In one scene a group of fourth-grade students were trying to measure a snake with a yardstick. Five students were actively involved. One would straighten the tail, another tackled the front, the rest worked with various parts of the middle. Through it all, the snake, who seemed to be enjoying the whole business, would coil around one child's arm or another's leg, hump up in the middle, and wave his tail happily to and fro. Needless to say, a yardstick is not the appropriate tool to measure a live snake.

This review has tried to demonstrate that there are appropriate tools to measure the performance of the school library and that careful selection and modification of the number of possible measurement techniques already developed are an important part of the school librarian's job.

REFERENCES

Altman, E. (1972). Implications of title diversity and collection overlap for interlibrary loan among secondary schools. *Library Quarterly* 42, 177–194.

American Association of School Librarians (1972), "Paperback Books for Children." Citation Press, New York,

American Association of School Librarians (1975). "Media Programs: District and School." American Library Association, Chicago, Illinois.

American Association of School Librarians. Committee on Post-War Planning (1945). "School Libraries for Today and Tomorrow: Functions and Standards." American Library Association, Chicago, Illinois.

American Library Association (1960). "Standards for School Library Programs." American Library Association, Chicago, Illinois.

American Library Association (1969). "School Library Personnel Task Analysis Survey." American Library Association, Chicago, Illinois.

American Library Association (1971). "Occupational Definitions for School Library Media Personnel." American Library Association, Chicago, Illinois.

American Library Association. Joint Committee on Elementary School Standards (1925). "Elementary School Library Standards." American Library Association, Chicago, Illinois.

Baker, N. R. (1968). A descriptive model of library user/funder in a university environment. *Drexel Library Quarterly* 4, 16–30.

Baughman, J. C. (1973). The meaning of the standards for school media programs. *School Media Quarterly* 1, 274–277.

Beasley, K. E. (1964). "A Statistical Reporting System for Local Public Libraries." Pennsylvania State University, Institute for Public Administration, University Park, Pennsylvania. (Pennsylvania State Library Monograph No. 3.)

Beasley, K. E. (1974). Commentary. *Library Trends* 22, 387–393.

Bernotavicz, F. D., and Wallington, J. (1970). Act I of JIMS. *Audiovisual Instruction* 15 (May), 25–30.

Blackman, A. (1967). The meaning and use of standards. *In* "Notes on Comprehensive Health Planning" (H. L. Blum, ed.), pp. 4.33–4.40. American Public Health Association, Western Regional Office, San Francisco, California.

Bonn, G. L. (1974). Evaluation of the collection. *Library Trends* 22, 265–304.

Bookstein, A., and Swanson, D. R. (1972). Introduction. *Library Quarterly* 42, 1–5.

Buckland, M. K. (1970). "Systems Analysis for a University Library." University of Lancaster Library, Lancaster, England.

Buckland, M. K. (1972). An operations research study of a variable loan and

duplication policy at the University of Lancaster. *Library Quarterly* **42**, 97–106.
California Bureau of Audio-Visual and School Library Education (1972). "An Instrument for the Qualitative Evaluation of Media Programs in California." California State Department of Education, Sacramento, California.
Case, R. N. (1969). Criteria of excellence checklist. *School Libraries* **18**, 43–46.
Case, R. N., and Lowrey, A. M. (1973). "Behavioral Requirements Analysis Checklist; A Compilation of Competency-Based Job Functions and Task Statements for School Library Media Personnel." American Library Association, Chicago, Illinois.
Certain, C. C. (1917). Standard library organization and equipment for secondary schools of different sizes. *Educational Administration and Supervision* **3**, 317–338.
Childers, T. A. (1972). Managing the quality of reference/information service. *Library Quarterly* **42**, 212–217.
Childers, T. A. (1975). Statistics that describe libraries and library service. *In* "Advances in Librarianship" (M. J. Voigt, ed.), Vol. 5, pp. 107–122. Academic Press, New York.
"Children's Books in Print" (Annual). R. R. Bowker, New York.
"Children's Books of the Year" (Annual). Children's Books Committee, Child Study Press, New York.
"Children's Catalog" (1972–1975). 12th ed. with supplements. H. W. Wilson, New York.
Coleman, J. S. (1966). "Equality of Educational Opportunity." U. S. Office of Education, Washington, D. C.
Crowley, T., and Childers, T. A. (1971). "Information Services in Public Libraries: Two Studies." Scarecrow Press, Metuchen, New Jersey.
Darling, R. L. (1964). "Public School Library Statistics, 1962–63." U. S. Office of Education, Washington, D. C.
Deason, H. J. (1972). "The AAAS Science Book List for Children," 3rd ed. American Association for the Advancement of Science, Washington, D. C.
DeProspo, E. R., and Altman, E. (1973). Library measurement; a management tool. *Library Journal* **98**, 3605–3607.
DeProspo, E. R., Altman, E., and Beasley, K. E. (1973). "Performance Measures for Public Libraries." American Library Association, Public Library Association, Chicago, Illinois.
Dougherty, R. M., and Leonard, L. E. (1970). "Management and Costs of Technical Processes: A Bibliographical Review, 1876–1969." Scarecrow Press, Metuchen, New Jersey.
Fulton, W. R. (1969). Evaluation checklist; an instrument for self-evaluating an educational media program in school systems. *In* Davies, R. A. "The School Library; A Force for Educational Excellence," pp. 298–307. R. R. Bowker, New York.
Gaver, M. V. (1971). "Services of Secondary School Media Centers; Evaluation and Development." American Library Association, Chicago, Illinois. (ALA Studies in Librarianship, No. 2.)

Gaver, M. V., and Van Orden, P., eds. (1973). "The Elementary School Library Collection, Phases 1-2-3; A Guide to Books and Other Media," 8th ed. Bro-Dart Foundation, New Brunswick, New Jersey.

Gillespie, J. T., and Spirt, D. L. (1972). "Paperback Books for Young People; An Annotated Guide to Publishers and Distributors." American Library Association, Chicago, Illinois.

Gore, D. (1975). Let them eat cake while reading catalog cards: an essay on the availability problem. *Library Journal* **100**, 93–98.

Greene, E., and Schoenfield, M. (1972). "A Multimedia Approach to Children's Literature; A Selected List of Film, Filmstrips, and Recordings Based On Children's Books." American Library Association, Chicago, Illinois.

Hamburg, M., Ramist, L. E., and Bonner, M. R. W. (1972). Library objectives and performance measures and their use in decision-making. *Library Quarterly* **42**, 107–128.

Hamburg, M., Clelland, R. C., Brimmer, M. R. W., Ramist, L. E., and Whitfield, R. M. (1974). "Library Planning and Decision-Making Systems." MIT Press, Cambridge, Massachusetts.

Hamreus, D. (1970). Media guidelines. *Audiovisual Instruction* **15** (May), 31–34.

Hannigan, J. (1972). PPBS and school media programs. *American Libraries* **3**, 1182–1184.

Henne, F. (1972). Media programs in schools. *Library Trends* **21**, 233–248.

Hines, T. C. (1974). Evaluation of processing services. *Library Trends* **22**, 305–314.

Hodges, E. D. (1969). "Books for Elementary School Libraries; An Initial Collection." American Library Association, Chicago, Illinois.

House, E. R. (1973). The conscience of educational evaluation. *In* "School Evaluation; The Politics & Process" (E. R. House, ed.), pp. 125–145. McCutchan, Berkeley, California.

Iowa, Department of Public Instruction (1969). "Plan for Progress in the Media Center; Guidelines for Development of K-6 Media Centers or Libraries in Iowa's Schools." Iowa Department of Public Instruction, Des Moines, Iowa.

Jencks, C. (1972). "Inequality; A Reassessment of the Effect of Family and School in America." Basic Books, New York.

"Jobs in Instructional Media" (1970). Association for Educational Communications and Technology, Washington, D. C.

"Junior High School Library Catalog" (1970). 2nd ed. H. W. Wilson, New York.

Leimkuhler, F. F. (1972). Library operations research: a process of discovery and justification. *Library Quarterly* **42**, 84–96.

Library statistics (1974). *In* "Bowker Annual of Library and Book Trade Information," 19th ed., pp. 219–291. R. R. Bowker, New York.

Liesener, J. W. (1973). The development of a planning process for media programs. *School Media Quarterly* **1**, 278–287.

Liesener, J. W. (1974). "Planning Instruments for School Library Media Programs." University of Maryland, College of Library and Information Services, College Park, Maryland.

Liesener, J. W. (1976). "A Systematic Planning Process for School Media Programs." American Library Association, Chicago, Illinois.

Liesener, J. W., and Levitan, K. M. (1972). "A Process for Planning School Media Programs: Defining Service Outputs, Determining Resources and Operational Requirements, and Estimating Program Costs." University of Maryland, School of Library and Information Services, College Park, Maryland.

Lipsman, C. K. (1972). "The Disadvantaged and Library Effectiveness." American Library Association, Chicago, Illinois.

McDaniel, R., ed. (1971). "Resources for Learning: A Core Media Collection for Elementary Schools." R. R. Bowker, New York.

Maryland, State Department of Education (1971). "Criteria for Modern School Media Programs." State Department of Education, Baltimore, Maryland.

Meier, R. L. (1961). Efficiency criteria for the operation of large libraries. *Library Quarterly* 31, 215–234.

Missouri State Department of Education (1972). "School Libraries in Missouri; a Status Report." Missouri State Department of Education, Jefferson City, Missouri.

Monroe, M. E. (1972). Evaluation of public services for adults. *Library Trends* 22, 337–359.

Morse, P. M. (1968). "Library Effectiveness; A Systems Approach." MIT Press, Cambridge, Massachusetts.

Morse, P. M. (1972). Measures of library effectiveness. *Library Quarterly* 42, 15–30.

National Association of Independent Schools (1971). "Books for Secondary School Libraries." 4th ed. R. R. Bowker, New York.

"New Jersey Blueprint for School Media Programs" (1969). New Jersey State Library, Public and School Library Services, Bureau, Department of Education, Trenton, New Jersey.

Oglesby, W. (1971). A reason for peace. *Audiovisual Instruction* 16 (June), 70–72.

Ohio Association of School Librarians (1973). "Spotlight: Media Solution; Handbook for Media Specialists." Ohio Association of School Librarians, Audiovisual Committee, Springfield, Ohio.

Orr, R. H., Pings, V. M., Pizer, I. H., and Olson, E. E. (1968). Development of methodological tools for planning and managing library services. *Medical Library Association Bulletin* 56, 235–267, 380–403.

Ottersen, S., comp. (1971). A bibliography on standards for evaluating libraries. *College Research Libraries* 32, 127–144.

Palmer, D. C., ed. (1970). "Planning for a National System of Library Statistics." U. S. National Center for Educational Statistics, Washington, D. C.

Pennsylvania Department of Education (1972). "School Library Standards." Pennsylvania Department of Education, Bureau of General and Academic Education, Division of School Libraries, Harrisburg, Pennsylvania.

Prentiss, S. G. (1970). State overview. *In* "Planning for a Nationwide System of

Library Statistics" (D. C. Palmer, ed.), pp. 39–41. U. S. National Center for Educational Statistics, Washington, D. C.

Reactions ... from Robert N. Case, ... from Dale G. Hamreus, ... from Jim Wallington, ... from David C. Myers (1972). *Audiovisual Instruction* 17 (Jan.), 36–43.

Rokeach, M. (1968). "Beliefs, Attitudes and Values; A Theory of Organization and Change." Josey-Bass, San Francisco, California.

Rothstein, S. (1964). The measurement and evaluation of reference service. *Library Trends* 12, 456–472.

Scriven, M. (1967). The methodology of evaluation. *In* "Perspectives of Curriculum Evaluation" (R. W. Tyler, R. W. Gagne, and M. Scriven, eds.), pp. 39–83. Rand McNally, Chicago, Illinois.

"Senior High School Library Catalog" (1972). 10th ed. H. W. Wilson, New York.

Silber, K. (1970). What field are we in anyhow? *Audiovisual Instruction* 15 (May), 21–24.

Simmons, P. (1971). "Collection Development and the Computer: A Case Study in the Analysis of Machine Readable Loan Records and Their Application to Book Selection." University of British Columbia Press, Vancouver, British Columbia.

Slamecka, V. (1972). A selective bibliography on library operations research. *Library Quarterly* 42, 152–158.

Stake, R. E., and Gooler, D. D. (1973). Measuring educational priorities. *In* "School Evaluation; The Politics & Process" (E. R. House, ed.), pp. 279–290. McCutchan, Berkeley, California.

"Standards for Educational Media (Library and Audiovisual) Programs in Illinois" (1972). Office of the Superintendent of Public Instruction, Illinois Audiovisual Association, and the Illinois Association of School Librarians, Peoria, Illinois.

"Standards for Libraries" (1972). (Issue ed: Felix E. Hirsch.) *Library Trends* 21, 159–355.

"Standards for School Media Programs" (1969). American Library Association, Chicago, Illinois, and National Education Association, Washington, D. C.

Sutherland, Z. (1973). "The Best in Children's Books." University of Chicago Press, Chicago, Illinois.

Swanson, D. R., and Bookstein, A. (1972). "Operations Research: Implications for Libraries." University of Chicago Press, Chicago, Illinois. [Also published in *Library Quarterly* 42, 1–160 (1972).]

Tesovnik, M. L., and DeHart, F. E. (1970). Unpublished studies of technical service time and costs: a selected bibliography. *Library Resources and Technical Services* 14, 56–67.

Trueswell, R. W. (1969). Some behavioral patterns of library users: the 80/20 rule. *Wilson Library Bulletin* 43, 458–561.

Wallington, J. (1972). Act II of JIMS. *Audiovisual Instruction* 17 (Jan.), 29–32.

Webster, D. E. (1974). The management review and analysis program: an assisted self-study to secure constructive change in the management of research libraries. *College Research Libraries* 35, 114–125.

Weech, T. L. (1974). Evaluation of adult reference services. *Library Trends* 22, 315–335.
Wessel, C. J. (1968). Criteria for evaluating technical library effectiveness. *ASLIB Proceedings* 20, 455–481.
Wisconsin Department of Public Instruction (1972). "Learning to Use Media." Wisconsin Department of Public Instruction, Division for Library Services, Madison, Wisconsin.
Wynar, C. L. (1973). "Guide to Reference Books for School Media Centers." Libraries Unlimited, Littleton, Colorado.

Productivity Measurement in Academic Libraries

THOMAS J. WALDHART

University of Kentucky

and

THOMAS P. MARCUM

Vanderbilt University

I.	Introduction	54
	A. Growth and Productivity in Libraries	54
	B. The Meaning of Productivity	55
II.	Productivity Measurement	57
	A. Measures of Productivity	58
	B. Productivity Measurement in Libraries	62
III.	Productivity Measurement: A Hypothetical Example	66
	A. Introduction	66
	B. Measurement of Output	67
	C. Measurement of Input	68
	D. Labor Productivity	72
	E. Total Productivity	73
IV.	Conclusions	74
	References	75

I. INTRODUCTION

With the completion of two major studies on the economics of libraries (Baumol, 1967; Baumol and Marcus, 1973) and the current financial crisis precipitated by reduced budgets and the double-digit inflation of the first half of the decade of the 1970's, the academic library community has become increasingly concerned about the continued economic viability of college and university libraries (De Gennaro, 1975).

Although present economic conditions are not likely to persist forever, and libraries can expect to realize some relief from the financial problems which they now face, the long-term implications of the economic studies cited in the preceding paragraph are unmistakable. Baumol and Marcus (1973) argue that the growth rate observed in library costs "is not a fortuitous phenomenon whose effects can be expected to be transitory nor one ascribable to peculiar circumstances within one or a few activities." Either academic libraries will have to secure additional funding to match the growth in costs or devise a method for slowing the growth in library costs while retaining existing levels of service. Failure to accomplish one or the other, or perhaps both, will almost assuredly result in the systematic deterioration of library services.

A. Growth and Productivity in Libraries

The magnitude of the long-term economic problems facing academic libraries is demonstrated by annual percentage growth rates identified by Baumol and Marcus (1973): book expenditures, 11.4 percent; total library expenditures, 10.5 percent; salaries and wages, 9.7 percent; volumes added, 6.6 percent; nonprofessional staff, 6.3 percent; expenditures per student, 6.1 percent. To illustrate the severity of the problem created by the compounding of growth rates, a growth rate of 6 percent per year results in a doubling of costs in twelve years and a quadrupling of costs in twenty-four years (Baumol and Marcus, 1973).

The observed rates of growth in library costs result from the complex interaction of a number of factors: increasing volume of publications; development of new library services; the expansion of existing library services; expanding user population; expansion of institutional programs and development of new programs which the library is expected to support; effects of inflation in the economy as a whole; and a limited, or nonexistent, increase in productivity in libraries. It is presently unclear what relative weights should be assigned to each factor in attempting to determine its contribution to the rate of growth in library expenditures.

Some of the factors enumerated are essentially beyond the direct control of individual libraries (e.g., inflation) and attempts to resolve the economic problems of libraries by attacking the other factors (e.g., by reducing the rate of acquisition of new materials or by limiting the development of new or expanded services) have the undesirable effect of depressing the quality or availability of library services.

Assuming that significant annual increases in library support are unlikely, given the financial condition of universities and colleges, one factor—increasing productivity—seems to hold the greatest potential for slowing the rate of growth in library costs and at the same time allowing libraries to maintain a reasonable level of library services. Warheit (1972) supported this conclusion when he observed that "the basic problem of improving librarian productivity still remains the only real approach for slowing down the accelerating rise in library operating costs."

B. The Meaning of Productivity

Productivity refers to a comparison of the quantity of products and services produced by an organization and the quantity of resources employed in the production process. When the same resources previously employed result in the increased production of products and services, it is said that productivity has increased (Fabricant, 1969). It is this potential of increasing productivity which has attracted the attention of individuals interested in controlling the rate of growth in library costs. Productivity may be increased by improving the quality of labor, increasing tangible capital, increasing efficiency in the use of labor or capital, or a combination of these factors (Fabricant, 1969). For example, if an individual library increases the number of volumes added to its collection in 1974 by 4 percent and the acquisitions department of the library acquires these volumes by employing the same level of resources which were expended in 1973 (with the value of the resources adjusted to a common base year), the productivity of the acquisitions department will have risen 4 percent in 1974 as compared with 1973.

Various types of ratios have been employed in libraries to determine levels of performance. These include unit cost ratios, cost-effectiveness ratios, cost-benefits ratios, ratios of response time, ratio of book budget to users, and ratio of holdings to total user population (Evans et al., 1972). Greenberg (1973) cautions that these operating or performance ratios should not be confused with productivity ratios because they "often fail to meet one important criterion of a productivity ratio, namely, that the output and the input be expressed in constant terms over the selected time period."

While, in theory, productivity is a simple ratio between output and input which specifies no individual class of input or output, until recently students of productivity have concentrated almost exclusively on a specific class of input—human labor (Smith, 1973). The use of labor productivity as *the* measure of productivity has led to some confusion in the literature of librarianship. Kilgour (1969) stated that "output per man hour of labor input is the generally accepted measure of productivity," and at the same time argued that technological change based on computer technology represents the library's best opportunity for resolving its economic problems through increased productivity. Mason (1972), however, is not convinced that automation of library activities will necessarily be accompanied by an increase in productivity. He argues that "if it costs more to do essentially the same things, productivity will decrease." The concept of *total productivity*, rather than *labor productivity*, is implicit in Mason's argument. Kilgour and Mason are talking about two very different kinds of productivity and within the limits of their definitions of productivity both may be essentially correct in their conclusions. The important question in this context is: What concept of productivity is most appropriate when considering the economic contribution of computers to libraries? In large part the answer depends on the perspective and motivation of the individual asking the question.

In reality there is no generally accepted single measure of productivity. It may be expressed as a ratio between output and total input, output and labor input, output and capital input, or output and any other identifiable class of input (Fabricant, 1969). Two distinct types of productivity ratios have been employed in the past, *partial productivity* (e.g., labor or capital productivity) and *total productivity* (sometimes called total factor productivity). In the first case, total output is compared with partial input; in the second case, total output is compared with total input (Craig and Harris, 1973).

II. PRODUCTIVITY MEASUREMENT

Considering the importance of productivity to the continued economic stability of libraries, it is interesting to note that no studies of library productivity have been identified in the published literature, although there have been some articles published which recognize the concept of productivity and speculate as to its role in libraries. Part of the explanation of its general lack of application in libraries may lie in the complexity of the concept itself, part in the difficulties of measuring productivity in a service-oriented, nonprofit institution such as a library, and part in the lack of explicit guidelines which would provide librarians with some direction in conducting productivity studies at the library level.

Although the measurement and systematic improvement of productivity has received little attention from academic librarians to date, a recent policy of the State of Wisconsin provides some insight into the role which productivity measurement and improvement might play in libraries in the future. A rule, referred to as a base budget cut for productivity, was introduced as part of the University of Wisconsin's legislative appropriation. It reduced the base budget by 2.5 percent in the first year of the biennium and 5.0 percent in the second (Lampman, 1974). Governor Lucey (1972) explained that the cut of the base budget meant that "as a matter of public policy, all State agencies will be required to improve their management efficiency in the 1973–75 budget years, maintaining essential public services but cutting service delivery costs by at least 2.5 percent annually." This unique budget rule is based on the fact that since productivity increases at an average yearly rate of 2.5 percent in the private economy, there is reason to believe that public service agencies realize, or can be expected to realize, comparable productivity gains (Lampman, 1974).

Management in commodity industries has long recognized the importance of increasing productivity to the economic viability of our nation's businesses. The Wisconsin Rule, however, represents a first application of this philosophy to the public service sector of our economy. While use of such a productivity rule is not presently common practice, the Wisconsin Rule emphasizes the importance which some public administrators place on productivity and reinforces the need for librarians to become familiar with productivity measurement and improvement as well as with the potential uses and abuses of productivity measures.

A. Measures of Productivity

1. PARTIAL PRODUCTIVITY: LABOR

Partial productivity compares the relationship between a specified class of input and total output in terms of products and services. The most common partial productivity measure is that of labor productivity, where the total output is compared with the simple, unweighted sum of all hours of labor spent in production, to give output per man-hour of labor input (Fabricant, 1969).

Occasionally the occupational mix of an organization changes for reasons which may relate to increasing productivity. For instance, a higher rate of output per man-hour may be achieved only by the addition of new technology which necessitates a work force that possesses special skills or training (e.g., library automation). Under such circumstances management may be interested in examining the librarian's productivity in terms other than unweighted man-hours. If this is desirable, labor productivity can be based on man-hours which are weighted to reflect the change in the value of labor (Greenberg, 1973). Such procedures complicate the calculation of labor input and are not normally undertaken in the determination of labor productivity.

The rate of growth of total personnel costs in academic libraries has been estimated at 5.3 percent per year (Baumol and Marcus, 1973). This rate of growth is composed of two elements, increased personnel costs due to inflation and increased personnel costs due to the addition of staff (both professional and nonprofessional) to support expanded and new programs of library service. Such a rate, combined with the fact that 50–60 percent of the total library expenditures for academic libraries is attributed to salaries and wages (Baumol and Marcus, 1973), has led a number of individuals to concentrate heavily on methods of increasing the productivity of *librarians* (i.e., increasing labor productivity) as a means of controlling the growth of library costs (Kilgour, 1969; Shoffner, 1970; Warheit, 1972).

Some economists contend that for a special sector of the economy—the service sector—inflation in the general economy and the increased levels of activity within an organization or industry are insufficient to explain the unusual rates of growth in unit costs within these fields. In simplified form, conventional wisdom assumes that, because of the technological structure of some service industries, increases in productivity are negligible or nonexistent. This inability to increase productivity is largely because some service industries are characterized by relatively inflexible labor content activities, where the quality and the quantity of the products and services which they produce are directly related to the level of labor input (Baumol and Marcus, 1973; Bradford *et al.*, 1969; Katz, 1973; Lampman, 1974). Baumol and Marcus (1973) summarize this position as follows:

> The implication of the analysis for the cost behavior of the service and manufacturing sectors is straightforward. With costs of labor rising at comparable rates, but labor requirements falling cumulatively and steadily in the one sector (manufacturing) while remaining fairly constant in the other (service), a differential in cost behavior becomes inevitable. Costs of the service sector must rise steadily and cumulatively relative to those in the remainder of the economy at a percentage rate directly related to the differential in their productivity.

To illustrate the impact which the limited growth in labor productivity could have on the operation of libraries, consider the following example. If salaries and wages in the general economy rise at a rate of 5 percent per year and productivity increases by 4 percent per year, the cost of goods and services in the general economy will grow at an annual rate of 1 percent. In contrast, if the salaries and wages of librarians cataloging books rise at a rate of 5 percent per year and the productivity of these librarians remains essentially unchanged, cataloging costs per unit will grow at an annual rate of 5 percent—4 percent above the annual rate of growth observed in the economy as a whole. Baumol and Marcus (1973) conclude that "the difference in the technologies of the two sectors forces this differential upon them, and, with occasional exceptions, we can expect such a differential to persist year after year."

The general conclusion that service industries, be they profit or nonprofit in orientation, realize little or no increase in labor productivity is not universally accepted by economists. Recently some economists have expressed the opinion that the relative lack of increase in productivity in the services is very likely the result of our inability to accurately detect changes in productivity where the quality and quantity of output are difficult to identify and measure, rather than to any limitation inherent in the service industries (Fuchs, 1966; Newburn, 1972; Rockart, 1973). One economist (Denison, 1973) has concluded that, on the basis of existing data, concern about advances in labor productivity, or lack thereof, in the service sector of the economy is exaggerated.

2. PARTIAL PRODUCTIVITY: CAPITAL

In theory, capital productivity is a partial productivity measure which characterizes the relationship between capital investment as input and the products and services of an organization or industry as total output. Capital may be categorized as *intangible* when the capital is invested in activities which improve the quality of labor. *Tangible* capital is that capital which is invested in physical plant, equipment, inventories, research and development, and other identifiable elements which contribute to the production process (Fabricant, 1969). Craig and Harris (1973) noted that:

> Of all the terms involved in productivity measurement, capital historically has been the most difficult to define. At the same time, capital also is one of the most important resources of any firm. Most previous work in productivity measurement has recommended that capital input be considered as the physical use of the equipment. Depreciation generally is used as the approximation of the capital consumed in the production process.

Since capital productivity is not commonly employed in practice and capital input is usually measured as a component of total productivity, capital and its role in library productivity are discussed in the next section, which deals with total productivity.

3. TOTAL PRODUCTIVITY

The second major class of productivity commonly measured is that of *total productivity*, where total output of an organization or industry is compared with total input employed in production with each input appropriately weighted (Fabricant, 1969). Unlike partial productivity which examines a special class of input, usually labor,

Smith (1973) feels that total productivity is particularly suited to the needs of top-level management because it "admits the full complexity of the production system which is concerned with the relationship between all outputs and, particularly, all inputs." In effect, total productivity provides management with a measure of the efficiency with which *all* organizational resources are employed in the production of products and services (Craig and Harris, 1973).

Total productivity in the library can be calculated as follows (Craig and Harris, 1973):

$$P_t = \frac{O_t}{L + C + R + Q}$$

where

P_t = Total productivity
L = Labor input factor
C = Capital input factor
R = Raw materials and purchased parts
Q = Other miscellaneous goods and services
O_t = Total output

A simplified example illustrates the importance of total productivity from the viewpoint of management. Assume that a library becomes a member of a computer-based processing network. As a result of membership, cataloging output per man-hour of labor input rises 25 percent since an individual cataloger can now produce more of the same product in less time. Using labor productivity as an index of performance, one would realize a clear and significant increase in productivity. However, the magnitude of the productivity gain may be misleading in terms of the consumption of resources by the organization as a whole. This becomes evident when one considers the impact of membership in the processing network on the total productivity of the cataloging system. Assume that while labor input requirements for the cataloging system of the library have been reduced by 25 percent, the library must expend $40,000 a year to realize that 25 percent reduction in labor input. The $40,000 may consist of membership fees, costs of purchasing new equipment, a processing fee, a fee for maintenance of equipment, communication costs, costs of retraining cataloging staff, and other costs.

It should be evident that the *real* gain in productivity, in this example, depends on the dollar value of the 25 percent reduction in labor input. If it is equal to $40,000, no change in total productivity has been realized. If it is less than $40,000, the library has realized a loss in total productivity; and if it is more than $40,000, the library has realized a gain in total productivity. "Gains indicated by increased labor productivity may not actually be gains at all. *The cost of generating the increased labor productivity must be considered*" (Craig and Harris, 1973).

It should be emphasized that the preceding example is simplified for illustrative purposes. The determination of productivity gains in libraries becomes considerably more complex if membership in the hypothetical processing network results in the provision of *new* products and services or if the *quality* of the existing products and services is significantly altered as a result of such membership.

B. Productivity Measurement in Libraries

Prior to the development of the hypothetical example of productivity measurement in a library, a number of practical and conceptual issues should be examined.

1. LEVELS OF PRODUCTIVITY MEASUREMENT

The majority of existing studies of productivity have been conducted at the national level, on an industrywide basis. Craig and Harris (1973) feel that this tendency can be explained by the motivation of economists who "are concerned with productivity because they feel that its movement is integrally related to the nation's general economic health." Less attention has been given to the measurement of productivity at the institutional or firm level, and that which has been completed relates primarily to commodity producing industries. The direct application of this work to libraries is somewhat limited because, unlike commodity industries, libraries are typically nonprofit, service-oriented institutions.

A program of productivity measurement in libraries must begin with a decision on the level at which the measurement is to be accomplished. Because of the unusual problems presented by productivity measurement in libraries, it would appear preferable to conduct initial studies of productivity at the system level (e.g., circulation, acquisitions, cataloging), rather than at the national or institutional (i.e., the library) level. Early work should concentrate on those systems which are most amenable to productivity measurement, for instance, cataloging and acquisitions, gradually expanding to systems of increasing complexity once a methodology has been formalized and some of the problems of productivity measurement in libraries have been resolved.

A practical problem associated with the measurement of productivity in libraries is that the product of such measurement tells management little about the efficiency with which library resources are employed in the production of intermediate goods and services (Anderson, 1970), and thus contributes little to management control at the system level. In contrast, measurement of productivity at the system level creates the problem of what to do with costs relating to products which "flow" through the system. For instance, does the cost of purchasing books and journals represent input costs to acquisitions, cataloging, reference, or some other system in the library? Should these costs be prorated among the various systems of the library, assigned to a given cost center, or disregarded? In the example presented in Section III, we have chosen to disregard such costs. Our basic rationale for doing so is that, in our opinion, the costs of these materials will have a negligible impact on the productivity movement of the system in question and thus are irrelevant to the costing of input for that system (Fisher, 1971). Another problem of measuring productivity at the system level is that such measurements tend to present a fragmented view of the organization, and the fragmented measures are not easily translated into a measure of productivity at the library level. The level at which productivity is measured will be determined by the needs of a given institution.

2. PARTIAL PRODUCTIVITY

A change in output per unit of a given class of input, for instance labor or capital, provides management with information relative to the rate of change in the efficiency with which labor or capital input is converted to output (Fabricant, 1969). A rise or fall in efficiency may result from the influence of a number of factors acting singularly or synergistically. These factors include changes in available technology (Atkinson and Stiglitz, 1969; Nordhaus, 1969; Porter, 1968); the size of the organization (Fleming, 1970) or the manner in which the organization is structured (Lundberg, 1972; Ross and Murdick, 1973); the number of hours worked (Levenson, 1967);

supervisory style (Sales, 1966); existing knowledge (Besen, 1968; Denison, 1974; Diwan, 1971; Dudley, 1972; Gintis, 1971; U. S. National Science Foundation, 1971; Welch, 1970); capital invested (Denison, 1969; Diamond, 1965; Domar, 1963; Griliches and Jorgenson, 1966; Gupta and Steedman, 1971; Jorgenson and Griliches 1967); and a multitude of other factors. The change in efficiency in the use of the total resources of an organization cannot be determined by comparing a change in output with a change in labor alone or capital alone (Fabricant, 1969).

For this reason, partial productivity measures suffer from an inability to reflect the combined impact of a complex mix of resources which contribute to the production process, and should be used with some caution in libraries. Where partial productivity measures, like labor or capital productivity, are considered appropriate, their nature should be clearly understood, their limitations acknowledged, and they should be supplemented by measures of total productivity.

3. TOTAL PRODUCTIVITY

The major problem which libraries must face when attempting to determine total productivity is the added complexity introduced by the necessity of measuring, within a weighted framework, total input factors. Labor productivity, the most common measure of partial productivity, represents a relatively straightforward calculation of unweighted labor input and, in contrast to total productivity, can be accomplished with little difficulty. The problems that are encountered when measuring total input factors will be discussed in detail in the context of measuring input.

4. MEASUREMENT OF INPUT

In the calculation of a productivity index, all of the output and input elements of concern must first be identified and then expressed in a common unit of measure. The most common unit of measure employed in commodity industries is that of dollar value. In addition, in order to permit the comparison of productivity indices from one time period to another, each index must be adjusted to a base period value. This process of adjusting each index is referred to as deflating the output and input factors (Craig and Harris, 1973).

Greenberg (1973) provides a detailed description of the process of calculating unweighted labor input as an element in the determination of labor productivity. When it is necessary to establish a weighted labor input, e.g., when determining total productivity, the weight normally assigned is the compensation per man-hour. One problem which may be encountered when calculating labor input is that some positions in the current year may not have been in existence or may not have been filled in the base year. This problem can usually be resolved by estimating the base year wage rate for these positions (Craig and Harris, 1973).

The measurement of other input factors, which is essential for total productivity, includes raw materials and purchased parts, miscellaneous other goods and services, and capital (Craig and Harris, 1973). Of these remaining elements of input, capital is the most troublesome to identify and measure.

Intangible capital, invested to improve the quality of labor, is considered to be reflected in the wage differential used for weighting wages. The basic assumption in such measurement is that the difference in wage rates is based on differences in skill level, education, experience, and other factors (Fabricant, 1969). A number of alternative procedures for measuring tangible capital input are discussed at length by Craig and Harris (1973) and Greenberg (1973). For the purposes of the example of productivity measurement presented in Section III, tangible capital input is assumed to be reflected in the physical use of equipment and buildings, with depreciation employed as an approximation of the capital consumed in the production process (Craig and Harris, 1973).

5. MEASUREMENT OF OUTPUT

The measurement of output, even in commodity-producing industries, is a complex process because of changes in the quality of products and services which occur over time and because of the introduction of new products and services. In the commodity industries, output is usually defined as the "summation of all units produced times their selling price" (Craig and Harris, 1973).

Organizations and industries which exist in the service sector of the economy are faced with an added complication in developing productivity indexes, since it is often extremely difficult to adequately identify and measure changes in output. Some of the conceptual problems at issue in the measurement of output in service industries are discussed by Marimont (1969), Treadway (1969), and Reder (1969). Tentative recommendations for dealing with some of these problems are offered by Newburn (1972) and Rockart (1973).

Not only do libraries fall into the service sector of the economy, making identification and measurement of output especially difficult, they further represent a special segment of the service sector—the nonprofit segment which in 1966 accounted for approximately 30 percent of the employment in the services (Fuchs, 1966). As such, the concept of "selling price" has little validity for measuring output in libraries.

Although not without its problems, the most appropriate measure of output for libraries seems to be the number of units produced. Where the quality of the output remains fairly homogeneous, such a measure would appear justified. Where there is considerable variability in the quality of the output or a number of different kinds of products are generated, some method of weighting units of output must be employed as a means of equating for product differences (Dudick, 1972). Methods commonly used to weight output are man-hours per unit of output or cost per unit of output. Until refined measures of library output can be devised to deal with output of a "service" nature, the production-oriented systems in libraries, which are engaged in the generation of tangible, discrete, relatively homogeneous units of output, appear the most amenable to productivity measurement.

Given the desirability of introducing productivity measurement to libraries, the complexity of the problems surrounding its application in practice, and the absence of working examples of productivity measurement in libraries, it is useful to consider a hypothetical system. Lacking precedence, the methods utilized in the example must be viewed as tentative, subject to modification and refinement to accommodate local circumstances. The example is offered to illustrate some of the problems which libraries are likely to encounter in productivity measurement and to consider possible solutions to these problems.

III. PRODUCTIVITY MEASUREMENT: A HYPOTHETICAL EXAMPLE

A. Introduction

The cataloging system of a medium-sized university library, which possesses a staff of 17 and processes 25,000–30,000 new titles per year, was chosen to provide the context for the example of productivity measurement. It is assumed that the library is "average" in the sense that it processes a typical mix of new titles: serials–monographs; original cataloging–cataloging from copy; English language–foreign language. A cataloging system was selected because the output of cataloging (i.e., card catalog cards) represents discrete, easily identifiable, and relatively homogeneous products.

Three generalizations relative to the structure of the model are appropriate. First, all input costs for the period examined (1970–1974) have been held constant at base year dollars, relieving us of the necessity of adjusting 1971–1974 costs to 1970 base year dollars. Second, for simplicity, the output of the cataloging system is assumed to be card catalog cards only. Depending upon the structure of the system, other output is possible (e.g., book labels and pockets, new book lists), however, selection of additional output would needlessly complicate the example. Third, regardless of the units which constitute output of the system, they must be combined into a single scale of measurement. In the example, constant dollars were chosen as the measure of output although physical units of output (e.g., the number of titles processed, or the number of cards produced) could just as easily have been employed.

During the first two years of operation (1970–1971) the cataloging system functioned in a conventional manual mode. In 1972 the cataloging system implemented a computer-based system which permitted cataloging on-line via a computer-based processing network. The primary cataloging output of the processing network is card catalog cards. The network provides additional products and services; however, they are not relevant to the cataloging function and are not considered in the example.

B. Measurement of Output

The output of the cataloging system could be measured in terms of constant dollars, dollars adjusted to the base year, unweighted physical units, or weighted physical units (Table I). Where the output consists of a single product of homogeneous quality, either constant dollars, adjusted dollars, or unweighted physical units may be used. If the system produces a number of different products varying in value, it is usually desirable to establish a weighting system which reflects that variation. Common measures employed in such circum-

TABLE I
Cataloging Output, 1970–1974

(1) Year	(2) Number of titles acquired	(3) Number of titles processed	(4) Average No. cards per title processed	(5) Total No. cards produced (3 × 4)	(6) Constant dollar value per card produced	(7) Total output in dollars (5 × 6)
1970	29,100	30,000	7	210,000	.05	10,500
1971	29,600	29,500	7	206,500	.05	10,325
1972	22,800	22,000	7	154,000	.05	7,700
1973	27,089	27,000	7	189,000	.05	9,450
1974	28,130	30,000	7	210,000	.05	10,500
	136,719	138,500	–	969,500	–	48,475

stances are man-hours per unit of output or cost per unit of output. In the example, a constant dollar value of five cents per card was used. Changing the magnitude of the constant dollar value per card (e.g., to ten cents per card) has no effect on the movement of the productivity index, as along as that value remains constant throughout the period of study.

C. Measurement of Input

1. LABOR

To facilitate the computation of labor input, employees have been identified with corresponding compensation as indicated in Table II. The annual compensation for each individual includes all wages paid, retirement benefits, leave time paid, and other fringe benefits. The total fringe benefits were estimated at 25 percent of base wages. Through this weighting process the quality of labor is implicit in the annual compensation and need not be accounted for by means of a separate measurement of intangible capital.

In addition to the direct labor costs, an administrative overhead of $25,000 has been assumed for the model. This overhead is expressed in constant base year dollars, giving a total labor input for the cataloging system of $182,000 for the base year 1970.

Under most operational conditions the activities of some individuals may be fragmented among a number of different systems, thus

TABLE II
Labor Input for Base Year, 1970

Staff	Number of employees	Annual compensation[a]	Total labor input in dollars
Professional	4		60,000
A	—	19,281	
B	—	14,218	
C	—	13,595	
D	—	12,906	
Paraprofessional	5		45,500
A	—	10,719	
B	—	9,869	
C	—	8,857	
D	—	8,432	
E	—	7,623	
Clerical	8		52,000
A	—	7,761	
B	—	7,183	
C	—	6,394	
D	—	6,184	
E	—	6,184	
F	—	6,184	
G	—	6,055	
H	—	6,055	
Administrative overhead	—	—	25,000
	17	157,500	182,500

[a] Annual compensation includes wages, contributions to retirement, sick leave, vacation, and other leave pay. Fringe benefits were estimated at 25 percent of base wages.

making it necessary to allocate the annual compensation of such individuals among the competing demands, either on the basis of the individual's estimation of the amount of time devoted to a particular system (usually adequate for most purposes) or through more formal work measurement procedures.

The labor input costs for the full five-year period are presented in Table III. It is assumed that no changes in the staffing of the cataloging system occurred during 1971. However, in 1972, as a result of the library's joining the computer-based processing network, the staff of the cataloging system was reduced by one professional,

TABLE III
Labor Input,
1970-1974

Year	Total labor input in dollars
1970	182,500
1971	182,500
1972	139,500[a]
1973	139,500
1974	139,500

[a]Total labor input reflects the reduction in the cataloging staff of professional D, paraprofessional E, and clericals D, E, F, and two-thirds G.

one paraprofessional, and three and two-thirds clericals. This change in staffing level represented a reduction in labor input of approximately 25 percent ($43,000) over 1971. During 1973 and 1974 the staffing level of the cataloging system remained essentially unchanged from the 1972 level.

2. CAPITAL AND RAW MATERIALS, PURCHASED PARTS, AND MISCELLANEOUS SERVICES

Table IV presents capital input costs and a combined category for raw materials, purchased parts, and miscellaneous services. While in practice it would be necessary to identify the individual elements which contribute to these input costs, it is not essential for the purposes of this example.

Items that may be categorized as raw materials and purchased parts include blank catalog cards, supplies for duplicating machines, pencils, paper, and other materials. Miscellaneous services include subscriptions to the *National Union Catalog* and a service which provides cataloging copy in microform. The costs of these subscriptions are prorated among those library systems which utilize them. Other miscellaneous services include equipment maintenance fees, telephone costs, and fees and dues of the computer-based processing network. The base year dollar input for the combined category of raw materials, purchased parts, and miscellaneous services was estimated at $110,000. This input cost changed in 1972 with the introduction of the computer-based processing network. Membership dues and fees for services represented an additional input cost; cancellation of the microfilm service represented a reduction in input cost. In addition, changes observed in 1973 and 1974 reflect increases in fees charged by the processing network.

Capital has traditionally represented a difficult input to define and, consequently, to measure. Items which may be included in this category of input costs are chairs, desks, building space, tables, duplicating equipment, and computer terminals. The most common measure of capital input has been the cost of an item (equipment or building) appropriated over the useful life of that item. This computation yields a yearly sum (called depreciation), which can be thought of as capital input costs for that year. The base year dollar estimate for capital input was $190,000.

The change observed in capital input during 1972 is attributed to costs which were incurred as a result of joining the computer-based processing network. It was assumed that four terminals were purchased at a cost of $4,000 per terminal. The useful life of the terminals was estimated to be five years, with no salvage value at the end of that time. Employing a straight-line depreciation, it was estimated that the terminals represented a capital input cost of $3,200 per year.

TABLE IV
Capital and Raw Materials, Purchased Parts, and Miscellaneous Services Input, 1970–1974

Year	Capital input	Raw materials, purchased parts, and miscellaneous services input
1970	190,000	110,000
1971	190,000	110,000
1972	193,200	137,000
1973	193,200	143,520
1974	193,200	147,824

D. Labor Productivity

The indexes of labor productivity for the years 1970–1974 are presented in Table V. The labor productivity index is determined by dividing the current year production by the base year production and multiplying the quotient by 100.

The slight decrease in labor productivity in 1971 is assumed to be attributable to the displacement of staff time from production functions to planning and preparation for membership in the processing network which would go into effect beginning in 1972. However, while total output dropped significantly in 1972, labor productivity showed less of a decline than would have been expected because of the 25 percent reduction in labor input. Obviously, if the reduction in staffing level had not been accomplished during 1971 the loss in labor productivity for 1972 would have been considerably greater than was observed. The gradual increase in output and the steadily increasing gains in productivity realized in 1973 and 1974 reflect the increased efficiency of the cataloging staff in the use of the computer-based system, as well as a number of other factors.

The introduction of the computer-based system clearly resulted in a significant gain in labor productivity for the cataloging system, after a brief period of adjustment and accommodation during which labor productivity dropped slightly. However, to demonstrate how partial productivity measures such as labor productivity may in fact

TABLE V
Index of Labor Productivity, 1970–1974

(1) Year	(2) Total labor input	(3) Total output	(4) Production (3 ÷ 2)	(5) Labor productivity index[a]
1970	182,500	10,500	.0575	100.00
1971	182,500	10,325	.0566	98.43
1972	139,500	7,700	.0552	96.00
1973	139,500	9,450	.0677	117.74
1974	139,500	10,500	.0753	130.96

[a]The index of labor productivity is equal to the current year production divided by the base year production multiplied by 100.

be misleading, total productivity for the cataloging system is presented in the following section.

E. Total Productivity

Total input in this example includes the sum of labor input, capital input, and raw materials, purchased parts, and miscellaneous services input. In effect, total productivity is a measure of the efficiency with which the organization utilizes these resources in the production of products and services.

Table VI provides the indexes of total productivity for the years 1970–1974. It is calculated in the same way as labor productivity except that total productivity employs a summation of all input factors rather than a given class of input.

After a slight decline in total productivity in 1971, a significant loss of approximately 25 percent was observed in 1972. This loss in total productivity corresponds closely with a 24 percent decline in total output, which was observed for 1972 as compared with that for 1971. What the index of total productivity demonstrates then is that the savings which were realized in labor through the introduction of the computer-based system were simply displaced costs. These costs

TABLE VI
Index of Total Productivity, 1970–1974

(1) Year	(2) Total factor input[a]	(3) Total output	(4) Production (3 ÷ 2)	(5) Total productivity index[b]
1970	482,500	10,500	.0218	100.00
1971	482,500	10,325	.0214	98.17
1972	469,700	7,700	.0164	75.23
1973	476,220	9,450	.0198	90.83
1974	480,524	10,500	.0219	100.46

[a] The total factor input includes labor, capital, and raw materials, purchased parts, and miscellaneous services input.

[b] The index of total productivity is equal to the current year production divided by the base year production multiplied by 100.

are reflected in increased capital input, and increased raw materials, purchased parts, and miscellaneous services input which are required by the computer-based system. While labor productivity rose approximately 30 percent in 1974 as compared with 1970, total productivity, after a period of fluctuation, rose to a level in 1974 which was essentially equal to that achieved by the manual system in 1970.

IV. CONCLUSIONS

During the 1960's academic libraries, along with the colleges and universities which they support, experienced a period of unprecedented growth. Whereas periods of rapid growth in most organizations are marked by an emphasis on innovation and change, periods of more stringent economic conditions are characterized by organizational retrenchment and an emphasis on increasing productivity. Although academic libraries can hardly expect to maintain the rates of growth that have been characteristic of recent years, the ability of the academic library to sustain a significant portion of the growth in quality and variety of library services initiated during the last decade will depend upon the ability of librarians to increase the efficiency with which the resources of the library are employed in the production of these services—*on their ability to increase productivity*.

The actions which individual academic libraries take to minimize the effects of inflation and limited budgets on library services will vary, as they should, depending on local circumstances. Nevertheless, improving library productivity should represent a management goal which is central to efforts directed at maintaining the economic viability of academic libraries. In 1969 Kilgour identified a continuously increasing labor productivity as the economic goal of library automation. In 1975 such a goal is perhaps too limited. Improving labor productivity through automation or any other means will not resolve the overall economic problems of academic libraries, *unless* the cost of introducing improvements in labor productivity is significantly less than the savings in labor costs. This is not to say that increasing labor productivity is unimportant or insignificant. It may be critical, especially where it is difficult to secure an adequate labor supply or where it is demonstrated that the library's inability to increase labor productivity is endangering its ability to provide necessary services. In any case, improvement in labor productivity must represent an integral element in any program of productivity improvement. What is important, from an economic standpoint, is that improvements in labor productivity be viewed within the broader framework of improving total productivity.

Productivity measurement is in essence a method of economic analysis. Almost certainly its application in academic libraries will result in the identification of a number of difficult choices relative to the allocation of scarce resources. Raffel (1974) argues convincingly that although economic analysis can be extremely helpful in decision-making, it has limitations, and that these limitations should be recognized by the decision-maker.

The introduction of productivity measurement and programs of productivity improvement to academic libraries will require that management recognize the importance of increasing productivity to the long-term economic stability of academic libraries. With some refinements, existing methods of productivity measurement are adequate for use in those library systems which are production-oriented. Implementation of a broad-based program of productivity measurement in academic libraries, however, is contingent upon the development of more sophisticated methods for adequately measuring total library output, particularly where the principal output of the system is a service rather than an identifiable product.

REFERENCES

Anderson, W. H. L. (1970). Production scheduling, intermediate goods, and labor productivity. *American Economic Review* **60**, 153–162.

Atkinson, A. B., and Stiglitz, J. E. (1969). A new view of technological change. *Economic Journal* **79**, 573–578.

Baumol, W. J. (1967). "On the Economics of Library Operations." National Advisory Commission on Libraries, Washington, D. C. (ED022 525.) (Reprinted in part as: Baumol, W. J. (1969). The costs of library and information services. *In* "Libraries at Large: Tradition, Innovation, and the National Interest" (D. M. Knight and E. S. Nourse, eds.), pp. 168–227. R. R. Bowker, New York.)

Baumol, W. J., and Marcus, M. (1973). "Economics of Academic Libraries." American Council on Education, Washington, D. C.

Besen, S. M. (1968). Education and productivity in U. S. manufacturing: some cross-section evidence. *Journal of Political Economy* **76**, 494–497.

Bradford, D. A., Malt, R. A., and Oates, W. E. (1969). The rising costs of local public services; some evidence and reflections. *National Tax Journal* **22**, 185–202.

Craig, C. E., and Harris R. C. (1973). Total productivity measurement at the firm level. *Sloan Management Review* **14**, No. 3, 13–29.

De Gennaro, R. (1975). Austerity, technology, and resource sharing: research libraries face the future. *Library Journal* **100**, 917–923.

Denison, E. F. (1969). Some major issues in productivity analysis: an examination of estimates by Jorgenson and Griliches. *Survey of Current Business* **49**, No. 5, Part II, 1–28.

Denison, E. F. (1973). The shift to service and the rate of productivity change. *Survey of Current Business* **53**, No. 10, 20–35.

Denison, E. F. (1974). "Accounting for United States Economic Growth 1929–1969." The Brookings Institution, Washington, D. C.

Diamond, P. A. (1965). Technical change and the measurement of capital and output. *Review of Economic Studies* **32**, 289–298.

Diwan, R. K. (1971). Impact of education on labor productivity. *Applied Economics* **3**, 127–135.

Domar, E. D. (1963). Total productivity and the quality of capital. *Journal of Political Economy* **71**, 586–588.

Dudick, T. S. (1972). Rises in productivity. *Management Adviser* **9** (Nov.), 19–24.

Dudley, L. (1972). Learning and productivity change in metal products. *American Economic Review* **62**, 662–669.

Evans, E., Borko, H., and Ferguson, P. (1972). Review of criteria used to measure library effectiveness. *Medical Library Association Bulletin* **60**, 102–109.

Fabricant, S. (1969). "A Primer on Productivity." Random House, New York.

Fisher, G. H. (1971). "Cost Considerations in Systems Analysis." American Elsevier, New York.

Fleming, M. C. (1970). Inter-firm differences in productivity and their relation to occupational structure and size of firm. *Manchester School of Economic and Social Studies* **38**, 223–245.

Fuchs, V. R. (1966). The first service economy. *The Public Interest* No. 2, 7–17.

Gintis, H. (1971). Education, technology and the characteristics of worker productivity. *American Economic Review* **61**, No. 2, 266–279.

Greenberg, L. (1973). "A Practical Guide to Productivity Measurement." The Bureau of National Affairs, Washington, D. C.

Griliches, Z., and Jorgenson, D. W. (1966). Sources of measured productivity changes: capital input. *American Economic Review* **56**, No. 2, 50–61.

Gupta, S., and Steedman, I. A. (1971). An input-output study of labor productivity in the British economy. *Oxford University Institute of Economics and Statistics Bulletin* **33**, 21–34.

Jorgenson, D. W., and Griliches, Z. (1967). The explanation of productivity changes. *Review of Economic Studies* **43**, 249–284.

Katz, D. A. (1973). Faculty salaries, promotions, and productivity at a large university. *American Economic Review* 63, 469–477.
Kilgour, F. G. (1969). The economic goal of library automation. *College & Research Libraries* 30, 307–311.
Lampman, R. J. (1974). Reflections on a productivity rule for a university. *Monthly Labor Review* 97, 30–32.
Levenson, I. F. (1967). Reduction in hours of work as a source of productivity growth. *Journal of Political Economy* 75, 199–204.
Lucey, P. J. (1972). Wisconsin's productivity policy. *Public Administration Review* 32, 795–799.
Lundberg, E. (1972). Productivity and structural change. *Economic Journal* 82, Supplement, 465–485.
Marimont, M. L. (1969). Measuring real output for industries providing services: OBE concepts and methods. *In* "Production and Productivity in the Service Industries" Vol. 34, Studies in Income and Wealth (V. R. Fuchs, ed.), pp. 15–52. National Bureau of Economic Research, New York.
Mason, E. (1972). Automation or Russian roulette. *In* "Proceedings of the 1972 Clinic on Library Application of Data Processing" (F. W. Lancaster, ed.), pp. 138–156. Illini Union Bookstore, Champaign, Illinois.
Newburn, R. M. (1972). Measuring productivity in organizations with unquantifiable end-products. *Personnel Journal* 51, 655–657.
Nordhaus, W. D. (1969). An economic theory of technological change. *American Economic Review* 59, No. 2, 18–28.
Porter, R. C. (1968) Technological change with unlimited supplies of labor. *Manchester School of Economic and Social Studies* 36, 69–74.
Raffel, J. A. (1974). From economic to political analysis of library decision making. *College & Research Libraries* 35, 412–423.
Reder, M. W. (1969). Some problems in the measurement of productivity in the medical care industry. *In* "Production and Productivity in the Service Industries" Vol. 34, Studies in Income and Wealth (V. R. Fuchs, ed.), pp. 96–153. National Bureau of Economic Research, New York.
Rockart, J. F. (1973). Approaches to productivity in two knowledge based industries. *Sloan Management Review* 15, No. 1, 23–33.
Ross, J. E., and Murdick, R. G. (1973). People, productivity and organizational structure. *Personnel* 50 (Sept.), 8–18.
Sales, S. M. (1966). Supervisory style and productivity: review and theory. *Personnel Psychology* 19, 275–286.
Shoffner, R. M. (1970). Economics of national automation of libraries. *Library Trends* 18, 448–463.
Smith, I. G. (1973). "The Measurement of Productivity: A Systems Approach in the Context of Productivity Agreements." Gower, London.
Treadway, A. B. (1969). What is output? problems of concept and measurement. *In* "Production and Productivity in the Service Industries" Vol. 34, Studies in Income and Wealth (V. R. Fuchs, ed.), pp. 53–94. National Bureau of Economic Research, New York.

U.S. National Science Foundation, Division of Science Resources and Policy Studies (1971). "A Review of the Relationship Between Research and Development and Economic Growth/Productivity." National Science Foundation, Washington, D. C.

Warheit, I. A. (1972). The automation of libraries; some economic considerations. *Special Libraries* **63**, 1–7.

Welch, F. (1970). Education in production. *Journal of Political Economy* **78**, 35–39.

Relevance: A Review of the Literature and a Framework for Thinking on the Notion in Information Science*

TEFKO SARACEVIC

Case Western Reserve University

I.	Preface: Where Lies the Importance of Thinking on Relevance? ..	81
II.	Introduction: How Relevance Is Involved in Controversy, the History of Science, and Other Fields	82
	A. Logic	83
	B. Philosophy	84
	C. Interaction	85
III.	How Information Science Became Involved with Relevance	85
	A. Orientations	85
	B. Scientific Communication	87
	C. Balancing Communication Ecology	88
	D. Information and Relevant Information	89
IV.	How to Construct a Framework for Viewing Relevance from Intuitive Understanding and Then on to More Elaborate Communication Models	90
	A. Intuitive Understanding	90

*This work was partially supported by NSF grant GN-36085.

		B. Communication	91
		C. Communication of Knowledge	91
		D. Information Systems	93
		E. Environment; Values	94
		F. Summary	94
	V.	How the "System's View" of Relevance Developed and How It Has Been Challenged	95
		A. Logic of Retrieval	95
		B. False Drops	96
		C. Completeness of View	96
		D. First Challenge	97
		E. Test and Evaluation	97
	VI.	How the "Destination's View" Emerged, Equating Relevance with Relevance Judgment, and How Experimentation Was Spurred	98
		A. Definitions	99
		B. Hypotheses	100
		C. Experiments	101
		D. Completeness of View	101
	VII.	How Bibliometrics Evolved and How It Is Related to the "Subject Literature View" of Relevance	102
		A. Distributions: Bradford, Lotka, Zipf	103
		B. "Subject Literature View" of Relevance	105
		C. Completeness of the View	106
	VIII.	How Splitting of the Notion Began and the "Subject Knowledge View" of Relevance Resulted	107
		A. The Concept of Information Need	107
		B. Pertinence	108
		C. Foskett's Public Knowledge—Private Knowledge	108
		D. Kemp's Pairs	109
		E. Two "Knowledge Views" of Relevance	109
		F. The "Subject Knowledge View" of Relevance and Its Completeness	110
		G. "Pertinence View" of Relevance and Its Completeness	111
	IX.	How the Disenchantment with Relevance Led to Another Splitting and How the "Pragmatic View" of Relevance Evolved	112
		A. Relevance Is "No Good"	112
		B. Cybernetics; Pragmatism	113
		C. Cooper's Utility	114
		D. Wilson's Situational Relevance	115
		E. Kochen's Utility Function	116
		F. Completeness of View	117
	X.	How Theories of Relevance Have Covered Different Aspects and Why They Are Important	119
		A. Maron-Kuhns' Relevance Number	119

	B. Goffman's Relevance as a Measure and the Epidemic Theory	120
	C. Hillman's Similarity Classes	122
	D. Cooper's Logical Relevance	122
	E. Completeness of Theories	124
XI.	Back to the Framework	124
	A. Summary of Different Views	126
	B. Speculation on Properties and Future Work	128
	Appendix: Synthesis of the Experiments on Relevance in Information Science	129
	References	135

I. PREFACE: WHERE LIES THE IMPORTANCE OF THINKING ON RELEVANCE?

From the small world of our everyday lives to the large world of mankind, of our civilization and our biosphere, the complexity, the interdependence between the spheres of our lives and worlds increases tremendously. Everything has become increasingly dependent on everything else. The imbalances in one sphere create serious imbalances in all. Improvements in some spheres have sometimes led to counterproductivity for the whole. The problems we have created are unlike any problems faced by prior generations. As Mesarovic and Pestel (1974) have pointed out, the current civilization of mankind and possibly even the whole of mankind are at a turning point.

Developed countries are undergoing a transition in their social order. In the words of Bell (1973), the postindustrial society is coming. Economy is changing from a goods-producing to a service economy. Knowledge is becoming the most important social force and "knowers" (professionals, technicians, managers, policymakers, etc.), the most important social group. Theoretical knowledge is becoming central as the source of innovation and of policy formulation for the society. The problems created by this transition are considerable. Not the least are the problems related to the communication and management of knowledge.

As individuals in a complex society, we face many complex problems and frustrations. The nature, the extent, and the rates of change in our lives have created problems in the quality of life and in our abilities to cope with it. We need and depend on many things to function, to survive—not the least of them is information.

The problems of mankind at this turning point of postindustrial society have one thing in common. To work toward their rational resolution, we need the resolve and the wisdom to act. Knowledge and information are not the only elements in this equation, but they are important elements. And the complexity of our present problems can only increase their value and general significance.

The effective communication of knowledge thus becomes a crucial requirement for the resolution of a variety of problems. For different problems different information systems (libraries included) have been developed or envisioned. Today, most, if not all, information systems have one common demand thrust upon them: to increase effectiveness of communication and of services. The emergence of new services, such as urban information and referral, and of new concepts in systems, such as information utilities, can be directly traced to such a demand and to attempts at resolving some of the above-mentioned problems. Behind the concept of information utilities is the need and demand for the dispersing of information to a wider populace of users with an increase in the effectiveness of communication.

Relevance has to do with effectiveness of communication. Underlying all information systems is some interpretation of the notion of relevance. The better we understand the meaning of relevance from different points of view, the better we understand various "systems of relevances" [a term borrowed from the philosopher Schutz (1970)], the better information systems could be built. In addition, the better we understand relevance, the better chance we have of avoiding failures and of restricting the variety of aberrations committed in the name of effective communication. In that lies the importance of advancing our thinking on relevance.

II. INTRODUCTION: HOW RELEVANCE IS INVOLVED IN CONTROVERSY, THE HISTORY OF SCIENCE, AND OTHER FIELDS

If I were to follow the tradition of much of the literature on relevance in information science, I would start with the statement that the understanding of relevance is fraught with controversy, that much of our thinking is muddled, philosophically imprecise, and that the talk about relevance uses a bewildering array of terminology. Indeed, all these statements have been made, but if we were to survey the history of science, we would find that such statements were consistently made about a great many of the phenomena and notions over which science and scholarship have struggled. That is, the evolution of thinking on relevance is not different from the evolution of thinking on so many other notions throughout the history of science.

A "paradigm" of the evolution of thinking on a notion in science can be made: recognition of a problem—first, simple definitions and statements; challenge—refinement and broadening; restatement—hypotheses, theories, observations, and experiments; synthesis; restatement; challenge; and so on until the thinking temporarily reaches a satisfactory level of consensus and resolution, a dead end, or abandonment. By 1975, the thinking on relevance in information science has reached one of the challenge stages (about the third). But, before examining how information science became involved with relevance, let us consider the involvement of other disciplines with the notion of relevance as a backdrop that should be and has to be taken into account by information scientists and librarians concerned with relevance.

A. Logic

For some two thousand years logicians and philosophers have been struggling with the notion of relevance. They have developed extensive theories and interpretations. In logic, the notion of relevance has been involved in specifying and explaining various relationships, chiefly in the works and theories that deal with relations, such as deduction, implication, entailment, and logical consequence, and also, but to a lesser extent, in induction and concept formation. Relevance is used to state a necessary condition, for the validity of an inference from A to B is that A be relevant to B. In modern times, Carnap (1950, and in other works), among others, has extensively discussed relevance and irrelevance, here in regard to probabilities and confirmation of conclusions from premises. Anderson and Belnap (1962) have vividly pointed out the fallacies of relevance and have provided, within the structure for a pure calculus of entailment, an "axiomatic system that captures the notion of relevance." Relevance exhibits the properties of identity, transitivity, permutation, and self-distribution.

B. Philosophy

Philosophers have involved, in a general way, the notion of relevance in the explanations of "aboutness" and in the theory of meaning. But, in a very specific way, relevance has been involved in explication of relations between different realities. In modern times the most powerful philosophical discussion of relevance was provided by Schutz (1970) in his posthumously published notes. Schutz was concerned with making it possible to understand "what makes the social world tick," that is, what makes it at once social and world. He contended that the social (or life) world is not simply one homogeneous affair, it is articulated or stratified in different realities; relevance turns out to be the principle at the root of the stratification of the life world. He elucidated three basic interdependent systems of relevance; topical relevances, motivational relevances, and interpretational relevances. He also considered the relation of the "stock of knowledge at hand" and considered relevance as that which effects changes in that stock. Schutz represented graphically the circular interrelationship between the three systems of relevances as shown in Fig. 1.

In topical relevance something is characterized as problematic in the midst of the unstructuralized field of unproblematic familiarity. In interpretative relevance one's personal stock of knowledge is

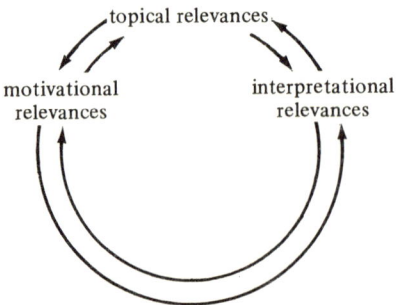

Fig. 1. Interrelation between systems of relevances.

combed to analyze or grasp the meaning of a newly perceived phenomenon. Motivational relevance is illustrated by a decision on how to act on an interpretive decision—thus the latter will determine the former. Schutz considered the "stock of knowledge at hand" and the "problem at hand" as that which effects changes in the system of relevances and vice versa.

C. Interaction

The thinking in logic has provided some information scientists (e.g., Cooper, 1971; Hillman, 1964) with a framework for their theoretical work on relevance. The thinking in philosophy, unfortunately, has not been directly recognized by information scientists to date, although philosophical work, such as that by Schutz, may have provided a framework for some of the views on relevance in information science (e.g., a framework to the work by Foskett, 1972; Kemp, 1974; Wilson, 1973) and generally avoided some arguments that were already argued out.

Some other subjects have dealt with relevance, but none as directly and extensively as logic and philosophy. These subjects are sociology (in the sociology of knowledge), psychology (in the studies of perception, learning, and capacity of memory), and linguistics (in the studies of semantics and pragmatics). It remained for information science to struggle with relevance in relation to communication and to emerge as the third subject that directly contributes to the thinking on that so elusive and so human a notion.

III. HOW INFORMATION SCIENCE BECAME INVOLVED WITH RELEVANCE

A. Orientations

Relevance was the key notion in the emergence of information science, and it has remained the basic notion in most of its theoretical constructs and all of its practice. Thus, a review of relevance should begin with a review of information science.

A field of activity and a subject of study are defined fundamentally by the problems attacked and operationally by the solutions offered and methods used, that is, by the work done. As problems and/or solutions change over time, specific definitions of a field or subject change as well.

Information science is a field and a subject that is concerned with problems arising in communication of knowledge in general and with records in such communication in particular, from both applied and basic points of view. It shares this concern with other fields, notably those of librarianship and of documentation; thus this sharing of concerns specifies the fundamental relationship between information science and librarianship. It follows that the thinking on relevance in information science should be of direct interest to librarianship and vice versa.

We may further define information science by enumerating the areas of applied (i.e., professional or practical) and of basic (scientific) concerns and work. Of major interest to practical applications of information science have been: (1) technical aspects of the communication of knowledge, which involve a variety of applications of information technology for information processing and transmission; (2) representational aspects, which involve the development of a variety of vocabularies, languages, and classifications for representing information, various types of file organizations and procedures, and logic for retrieval; and (3) systems aspects, which involve the design, development, and operation of a variety of information systems in general and information retrieval (IR) systems in particular, and also involve the development of complex information networks and of an information industry.

On the theoretical side, information science studies have dealt with the behavior and effects of information as a phenomenon and communication as a process; information users and uses; processes in, and evaluation of, information systems; and, finally, the various aspects of the ecological environment of information systems, such as the structure of scientific and other literatures and the structure and relations in scientific and other social communication. Quantitative studies involving characteristics and empirical laws in communication have created study areas of their own, under the names of bibliometrics and scientometrics (a more appropriate universal term may be "infometrics" in line with sociometrics, econometrics, psychometrics, etc.). Studies in the ecology of communication have carved out for information science a scientific problem area, which is contributing to the solidification of information science as a scientific subject.

But why has all this happened? Why has information science emerged on its own and not as part of librarianship or documentation, which would be most logical? It has to do with relevance.

Why, then, has relevance emerged as a central notion of information science?

B. Scientific Communication

All of it has to do with the nature of scientific communication. Although it now extends to other areas, information science has its roots in the problems encountered in scientific communication. To achieve an understanding of relevance and indeed of information science, as well as some understanding of relations (differences and similarities) between information science and documentation and between information science and librarianship, one has to achieve some understanding of scientific communication.

Modern science has developed a unique system of communication, which began with the appearance of the first scientific journals in the seventeenth century. The basis of this system has remained the same to this date. The system is based on the organized and selective publication of fragments of work, of items of knowledge related to a broader problem, rather than complete treatises; that is, on the selective derivation from, and selective integration into, a network of other works, and on evaluation before and after publication. All of this is ultimately designed to contribute to the creation of what Ziman (1968) calls "public knowledge," that is, "the aim of scientists is to create, criticize and contribute to a rational consensus of ideas and information."

Selectivity is present in every step of the scientific communication process. Knowledge is cumulated selectively. A very small proportion of published items are utilized in the formation of what Price (1965) has called a "research front."

It is this concern with fragments of knowledge, with "research fronts," with selective cumulation, and with networks and governance of science, that enables the functioning of science and that has led to the concern with relevance. That is, to be effective, scientific communication, and indeed science itself, has to deal not with any information, but with *relevant* information. And the history of science is the history of that effectiveness.

Price (1963), Ziman (1969), and others have pointed out that the invention of the mechanism for the systematic publication of fragments of scientific work may well have been the key event in the history of modern science. This invention has enabled science to grow much faster than the rest of scholarship. Science has even developed a governance of its own.

There are many other aspects that play a role in scientific communication (e.g., conferences, invisible colleges, professional societies). However, all follow from and end up in this particular selective mechanism.

C. Balancing Communication Ecology

Over the last three centuries, communication in science has developed into an ecological system with elaborately organized and interdependent subsystems or strata (Warren and Goffman, 1972). Periodically, there have been disruptions in that ecology caused by various factors. In the last seventy years or so, such disruptions have been caused by a combination of factors but result mainly from large quantitative increases in the number of scientists and the consequent increase in the number of publications, qualitative difficulties in selection, the breakdown of boundaries between subjects, and the increase in specialization. As a result of these ecological disruptions and imbalances, and the resulting problems and bottlenecks in scientific communication, there have emerged fields of activity directly and primarily concerned with the study and treatment of these problems. Thus, at the turn of this century, documentation emerged, a discipline which defined the problem as one of the organization of knowledge; thus, it developed a concern with classification, indexing, etc. Indexing and abstracting services emerged as documentation's "solution" to scientific communication problems. After World War II information science emerged, which defined the problem as one of providing the scientist with information; thus it developed a *concern with relevance,* for it was perceived that the "amounts" of nonrelevance endanger communication. Information retrieval systems emerged as information science's "solution" to the scientific communication problem.

Shera and Egan (1953) thought that the emergence of documentation was the result of the "failure of librarianship" to address itself to the problems of scientific communication. In turn, one might argue that the emergence of information science was due to the "failure" of documentation to address itself to the problems of the output of scientific communication. However, one should consider this failure theory quite cautiously, for fields do not really develop because of the failure of other fields, but because they define a problem area in a unique way and because they build a rational consensus of ideas and information about the problem that ultimately leads to solutions. The success or failure lies in the adequacy of defining and then addressing the problem. The success of information science, whatever there is, is due to the fact that it did address itself to the question of relevance and the failure, if we fail, will result from an inability to address relevance adequately.

D. Information and Relevant Information

Historically S. C. Bradford (1948) was probably the first to use the term "relevant" in the context utilized today in information science. In the 1930's and 1940's he talked about articles "relevant to a subject." In the forties and fifties development of information retrieval (IR) systems began. From the beginning, it was obvious that the main objective of IR systems was a provision of relevant information to users. A worldwide consensus emerged on this point.

The distinction between "information" and "relevant information" was made in recognition of the selective mechanism of scientific communication and as a means of underlining the user orientation of IR systems. However, the distinction between information and relevant information, although intuitively quite clear, became and has remained a major point of discord, a major stumbling block, because a consensus on meaning has not been reached. From the outset it was recognized that relevance indicates a relation. (Remember Bradford's "articles relevant to a subject.") But what relations does it involve? Between what elements? What factors affect the relation? The thinking, and resulting controversy, on relevance in information science evolves around these questions. To understand the thinking and possibly unravel the controversy, it is necessary to construct a framework within which the matter can be viewed. Such a framework may also advance our thinking on relevance.

IV. HOW TO CONSTRUCT A FRAMEWORK FOR VIEWING RELEVANCE FROM INTUITIVE UNDERSTANDING AND THEN ON TO MORE ELABORATE COMMUNICATION MODELS

A. Intuitive Understanding

Intuitively, we understand quite well what relevance means. It is a primitive "you know" concept, as is information, for which we hardly need a definition. When in a situation that involves communication (a contact and a sharing), we use our intuitive understanding of relevance *if and when* any productive contact is desired. When in communication with no particular outcome in mind (small talk, for instance), relevance plays little or no role. However, the moment we would like to have some result, some productivity, some degree of effectiveness (learn or teach, influence or be influenced, direct or be directed, know, enjoy, appreciate, etc.)—at that moment we encounter this intuitive notion of relevance. This affects the whole action, the whole process of communication, overtly or subtly. In other words, our intuitive understanding of relevance has something to do with productive, effective communication: how well the process was conducted, the extent to which our objectives were achieved. Relevance is a fundamental aspect of human communication, it is a part of everyday life.

We also understand intuitively that this effectiveness, this productivity, depends on a great many factors. Different criteria could be involved. And like so many other things in life, relevance is relative. Some things are more relevant than others (i.e., there could be a rank-ordering); some things are not relevant any more (i.e., time could have an effect); and some have a chance of becoming relevant (i.e., there could be an association). Relevance depends a great deal on what we already know and on what is generally known. We must admit that there are various aspects that at times predominate in determining relevance, such as what we think we want and how we ask for it; how we understand what is asked and what we think is *really* asked; what is wanted in contrast to what is *really* needed; who is asked, who is asking; what the situation is; what will be done with what is provided; etc. In other words, we know that we can look at relevance from different points of view. And the question of the relative nature of relevance poses a serious problem.

B. Communication

To create a framework for reviewing and relating the different views of relevance in information science, we have to consider the process of communication. Communication is a process (sequence of events) where something called information is transmitted from one object to another (Goffman, 1970, via Shannon and Weaver, 1949, via Aristotle). The first object can be called the source, the second, the destination; the objects can be people, organisms, machines, or systems. A dynamic feedback interaction can occur between a source and a destination; they can exchange roles (Wiener, 1961). Communication can be considered as a process on its own, as Shannon did in information theory, or, also, as a process affecting other processes, as Wiener did in founding cybernetics. That is, environment can be considered since it does play a significant role. We may not know what information is as a phenomenon any more than we know what energy, matter, gravity, or electricity is; but we can study its behavior and effects. Three levels of problems can occur in communication; (1) technical (accuracy—were signals received as sent?); (2) semantic (preservation—was the meaning understood the same way?); and (3) behavioral (effect—was the desired outcome achieved?). Semantic problems obviously also involve the technical, and the behavioral problems involve the other two.

In this context we can consider *relevance as a measure* of effectiveness of the contact between a source and a destination in a communication process.* A measure is a relation. Relevance is also a relation.

C. Communication of Knowledge

"Communication" is used in many diverse contexts, e.g., media, signal transmissions, speech and hearing, rhetoric, propaganda, advertising, medicine, psychoanalysis. Thus "communication" has related but different connotations. "Information" is used in Roget's *Thesaurus* in at least seven diverse senses; and when considering

---

*There is a great distinction between a measure (e.g., time), a measuring unit (hour), a measuring instrument (watch), and measuring (determining elapsed time between events). We can consider relevance as a measure without defining other aspects. In information science, a persistent confusion on these aspects exists, especially in test and evaluation.

synonyms, there are more than a hundred associated words. In Shannon's information theory, "information" is restricted to the context of signals: information is very specifically defined as a property of a collection of coded signals or messages which reduced the receiver's uncertainty about which message is sent. Information theory treats only the technical problem of communication.

In information science the connotation of "communication" and "information" is extended to and limited to the context of "knowledge" as used in the theory of knowledge. Information science attempts to treat all three levels of communication problems. For information science, to keep this context and connotation in mind, we use the term "communication of knowledge," although strictly speaking, it is not knowledge but data, information, or information-conveying objects, that are being transmitted.* In simple terms, the distinction is as that between "to know" and "to inform."

We may think of public knowledge as being organized into a structure of subjects, represented in a language, and recorded in literature. Elements of this literature can be called documents. Broadly speaking, then, subject knowledge is represented by subject literature; thus documents may convey information. The structure of subject knowledge and of subject literature, although related, are not the same. And the structure of linguistics or other symbolic representations is still different.

A source and a destination involved in the communication of knowledge both have, as one of the elements, a file (or files) where subject knowledge and/or its representations are stored in an organized manner (structured, associated, etc.). Examples of such files are: memory, library collection, catalog, computer file, data bank, and store of sentences. *Communication of knowledge is effective*

---

*For the explication of important distinctions and relations between data, information, knowledge, understanding, and wisdom, as well as between fact-retrieval, document-retrieval, and question-answering, which fall broadly within information retrieval, see Kochen (1974). For information science an applicable definition is given by Bell (1973): "Knowledge is a set of organized statements of facts or ideas, presenting a reasoned judgment or an experimental result, which is transmitted to others through some communication medium in some systematic form." And "public knowledge" as mentioned before is defined by Ziman (1968, 1969), as "a rational consensus of ideas and information."

when and if information transmitted from one file results in changes in another. Relevance is the measure of these changes.

Changes consist of additions to, deletions from, or reorganizations of the files of knowledge and/or the files of representations. One can take a much broader view and argue that communication of knowledge is effective when and if it results in actions or changes in behavior, or even when and if there is a directly observable result. The argument is grossly deficient in that such results are affected by a great many other variables in addition to, and unrelated to, the communication of knowledge.

In any case, since so many elements are involved in the communication of knowledge and in its effectiveness, relevance can be considered from different points of view, involving elements, e.g., of subject knowledge, of subject literature, of any representation of the source's file, of the destination's file, or of the processes. One can consider them separately or together in various combinations or in various hierarchies. And there are still other aspects to consider.

D. Information Systems

Embedded in the communication of knowledge may be various systems, called information systems, which are aimed at enabling, enhancing, preserving, or extending the communication process. Examples are libraries, IR systems, control and command systems, management information systems, and inquiry systems. Again associated with such systems are sources and files. An information system selects from existing subject knowledge, subject literature, and/or any of its representations; organizes the selections in some manner in its files; and disseminates or makes available the selections in some manner to given destinations. Embedded in, or associated with, information systems can be other communication systems, such as signal transmissions systems, graphic reproduction systems, or computing systems.

For a variety of types of communication of knowledge, for a variety of uses, for a variety of conditions and environments, for a variety of desires for effectiveness or efficiency, and for a variety of understandings of what are the information problems—a variety of information systems have been built. Underlying all of them, one can find explicitly stated, or implicitly assumed, some interpretation of the notion of relevance. Therefore, when considering relevance one may also have to involve aspects of information systems.

E. Environment; Values

Communication of knowledge and information systems can be considered by themselves, but they do not exist in vacuum. They operate within an environment, by means of the environment, and under constraints imposed by the environment. They affect and are affected by the environment. The same knowledge communication process, the same information system, can be related to a number of realities of an environment, to a number of environments, and can perform many functions. Change is the only stable factor.

Knowledge, information, communication, information systems—all are embedded in, all reflect some system of human values: ethical, social, philosophical, political, religious, and/or legal. Therefore, when considering relevance, one may also involve aspects of the environments, realities, and values.

F. Summary

Given that, in the context of information science, relevance is considered as a measure of the effectiveness of the contact between a source and a destination in a communication process; then in considering what factors and relations are involved in relevance, we can consider the following elements:
1. Subject knowledge
2. Subject literature
3. Any other linguistic or symbolic representation
4. Source, especially the file or files
5. Destination, especially the file or files
6. Information systems
7. Environments, realities, functions
8. Values

The majority of works on relevance in information science have concentrated on determining: (1) what factors or elements enter into a consideration of the notion of relevance; and (2) what relation does the notion of relevance specify.

The controversy stems either from insistence that *only* some of the enumerated factors or relations are *the* factors or relations or from the failure to recognize the existence of some other factors. The confusion stems from a very low adherence to the basics of semantic hygiene.

I wish to suggest that all the works, views, and ensuing conflicts on relevance that have emerged so far in information science can be interpreted within the previously described framework. Moreover, I suggest that when, and if, a complete theory of relevance emerges in the context of information science, it will have to emerge within this framework and incorporate at least the enumerated aspects.

V. HOW THE "SYSTEM'S VIEW" OF RELEVANCE DEVELOPED AND HOW IT HAS BEEN CHALLENGED

A. Logic of Retrieval

World War II spurred unprecedented scientific and technological activity, resulting in a mass of reports and literature. Computers were developed. The end of the War brought suggestions (as by Vannevar Bush, 1945) to apply computers to control the documents recording the advance of science and technology. The first information retrieval (IR) systems emerged in the late forties and early fifties, developed by such pioneers as Taube, Perry, Mooers, and Luhn. Principles of information retrieval that were posited then remain influential to this day.

It has been generally accepted that the main objective of an IR system is to retrieve information relevant to user queries. The logic of search and retrieval is based on the algebra of sets, Boolean algebra, which is well formulated and thus easily acceptable to computer manipulations. Inherent in the application of this logic is a fundamental assumption that those documents (answers, facts, data, etc.) retrieved are also those relevant to the query—those not retrieved are not relevant. In some systems documents can be ordered (evaluated, associated) as to their relevance and retrieved when some specified threshhold is reached and even presented in some ordered form; but even here the assumption that "retrieved/not retrieved" corresponds to "relevant/not relevant" still holds.

B. False Drops

The early pioneers quite correctly recognized that not all that will be retrieved will be relevant (Mooers, 1950; Perry, 1951; Taube, 1955). Their concern was with nonrelevance rather than relevance, with unwanted retrieval. They diagnosed that the "false drops," "noise," "false coordinations," and "extra tallies" were caused by internal malpractices, ineffectiveness of whatever representation (indexing language, coding scheme, classification) was used, and/or inadequacy in the way these were applied. The "system's view" of relevance was a result of the idea that relevance is mostly affected by the internal aspects and manipulations of the system. Relevance was conceived of in terms of indexing, coding, classification, linguistic manipulations, file organization, and, eventually, question analysis and searching strategies. This thinking led to an intense interest in the development of a myriad of schemes, the perfection of system organization and manipulation, and general attention to input and manipulative processes—almost to the total exclusion of other aspects. In theoretical works, linguistics has been subject to a great deal of attention, because it is believed that it will lead to better representation schemes.

C. Completeness of View

Clearly, the internal aspects of any system will affect its performance—but not to the exclusion of other variables. How a source manipulates information certainly influences the effectiveness of the contact with a destination, but it is not the only aspect that enters into considerations of relevance. Therefore, the "system's view" of relevance, although correct, is incomplete. However, the most glaring inadequacy of this view lies not in the fact that it does not recognize other aspects, but in the fact that it does not recognize selection to the system per se as one of the systems aspects that enters into relevance. As a result, to this date, selection to IR systems remains an aspect to which little attention is paid—articles on the topic of selection are scarce; investigations are few.

However, there is another school of thought, but it is not the prevalent view. In this school of thought, selection to the system is the most important aspect that enters into relevance (a view expounded chiefly by information scientists from Battelle Memorial

Institute). Information analysis centers have developed as a result of this view. Since this view has not received broader support among information professionals, relatively few information analysis centers are in existence.

D. First Challenge

The challenge to the simplicity of the "system's view" began with the historic 1958 International Conference on Scientific Information with its numerous spirited papers and discussions (National Academy of Sciences, 1959; cf. pp. 803–811, 855–886; 1275–1290; 1395–1409). Later more substantiated challenges were offered as part of the ongoing attempts to construct a theoretical framework for the study of relevance (Goffman, 1964; Hillman, 1964). Among others, these suggestions were offered:

1. The notion of relevance should be considered independently and prior to any particular method or representation or IR system.
2. There is a relevance to a subject.
3. Relevance is multivalued, a matter of degree, and not a simple yes/no decision.
4. Relevance of given documents may change as a result of other documents, as the stock of knowledge at hand changes.

As powerful as these arguments were, they did not appear to represent a serious challenge to the "system's view" of relevance. It remained for the debate surrounding the first attempts to test and evaluate IR systems to swing the pendulum to an opposite view.

E. Test and Evaluation

Pioneers of IR development were, by and large, engineers and scientists. It was thus logical for them to consider test and evaluation an important aspect of systems development. The first quantitative measuring units proposed were the familiar recall and precision*

Recall is the ratio of relevant answers retrieved to the total number of relevant answers in the file. *Precision* is the ratio of relevant answers retrieved to the total number of answers retrieved. Precision was originally called relevance, but the name was changed because of complaints of semantic confusion.

measures of Perry, Kent, and associates (Kent *et al.*, 1955). Although often challenged as to their adequacy, these or similar measuring units have remained in use to this day, and their use is now worldwide. There is a whole literature including many theoretical works on measuring units for IR systems, but they are not of direct interest to considerations of the notion of relevance. Underlying these measuring units is relevance as a measure, that is, as a criterion that reflects performance of IR systems. Relevance was selected as a result of the recognition of the notion that the prime objective of IR systems is to provide relevant information to user queries.

Testing of IR systems began in the 1950's as unverified claims and counterclaims mounted as investments rose. In the late fifties and early sixties large-scale tests conducted by C. Cleverdon at Cranfield (which were to continue throughout the sixties) attracted universal attention. The number of papers reporting results of the project was small (for a summary see Cleverdon, 1960), but the literature generated by the debate over the Cranfield Project was immense. This great debate continues to this date and remains concentrated on the methods utilized at Cranfield and other tests. The central issue was measuring methodology: How was the relevance of the answers determined? How should it be determined? Who are to be the relevance judges? How is the relevance judgment to be passed? The debate imperceptibly but completely shifted the problem of relevance from the system to the destination. At issue was relevance judgment. The idea that relevance is best connected to user judgment, or the "destination's view" of relevance, was born.

VI. HOW THE "DESTINATION'S VIEW" EMERGED, EQUATING RELEVANCE WITH RELEVANCE JUDGMENT, AND HOW EXPERIMENTATION WAS SPURRED

The great testing debate in the early and mid-sixties in large part turned into a relevance debate. As a result definitions of relevance proliferated and a few new hypotheses emerged. Eventually, two schools of thought developed.

One school has suggested that relevance is such an elusive and subjective property that it cannot serve as a criterion for performance testing (cf. Doyle, 1963). The other school took the view that while this may indeed be the case, further experiments are justified (Cuadra, 1964). Thus, psychology entered information science largely as a result of concern with relevance, or rather, with relevance judgments.

In 1964, the National Science Foundation (NSF) called an invitational conference of leaders in the field to assess the results of IR testing and to chart new paths. One of the conclusions reached was that the "major obstacle to progress in evaluation of IR systems is the lack of sufficient knowledge regarding . . . human assessments of the relevance of retrieved documents" (National Science Foundation, 1964). This spurred experimentation with relevance judgments, which in turn solidified the "destination's view" of relevance. Large-scale experiments were funded by NSF (Cuadra and Katter, 1967a; Rees *et al.*, 1967). Experiments were clearly affected by the definitions and hypotheses that emerged.

A. Definitions

Numerous definitions of relevance were offered in the sixties mainly as a result of the criticism of those who argued that it is not clear what relevance means. There was a rather naive belief that a "good" definition by itself would alleviate the controversy. (A good definition, in this context, referred to a paraphrase.) By themselves paraphrases, of course, do no such thing. However, relevance definitions were a form of hypothesis enumerating factors that entered into the relations. Thus, the definitions played an important role in setting the boundaries of experiments. Definitions fell into a general pattern:

Relevance is the A of a B existing between a C and a D as determined by an E.

In various definitions the slots were filled with terms such as these:

A	B	C	D	E
measure	correspondence	document	query	person
degree	utility	article	request	judge
dimension	connection	textual form	information used	user
estimate	satisfaction	reference	use of information	requester
appraisal	fit	information provided	point of view	information specialist
relation	bearing	fact	information requirement statement	
	matching			

As an aid to their experiments Caudra and Katter (1967a) established this definition: "Relevance is the correspondence in context between an information requirement statement and an article, i.e., the extent to which the article covers material that is appropriate to the requirement statement."

The most obvious criticism of these, as all other paraphrasing type definitions, is that they do not first establish primitive terms and then progressively and logically proceed to more complex definitions, using proofs or evidence where necessary; but instead they simply substitute terms that are as undefined or ambiguous as the term which they tried to define at the outset, e.g., what is appropriateness? satisfaction? utility? The most obvious advantage of paraphrasing definitions is that such definitions provide a preliminary context for further work and deliberation.

B. Hypotheses

The hypotheses offered in relation to experimentation with relevance judgments by and large concentrated on enumerating and classifying the factors that affect relevance judgments. For instance, Rees and Saracevic (1966) hypothesized on the variables and conditions under which the judgment would achieve a high degree of agreement. O'Connor (1967) concentrated on the reasons for relevance judgment disagreements and on conditions under which agreement may or may not coincide—relating these conditions to unclearness. Cuadra and Katter (1967a) provided us with the handiest classification scheme for factors affecting relevance judgment and with the largest enumeration of factors. They suggested the following general classes of variables that affect relevance judgment:
  1. Documents and document representation
  2. Queries (or as they said, "Information requirement statements")
  3. Judgmental situations and conditions
  4. Modes of expression
  5. People (judges)

None of the hypotheses have given direct consideration to the "system's view" of relevance. However, by acknowledging that documents and document representations (which, after all, come from a system) are one of the factors affecting relevance judgment, a relation between the system's view and the destination's view of relevance has been established.

The most obvious criticism of all the hypotheses offered is that they are not of the nature of rigid scientific hypotheses and thus can not be directly tested under controlled conditions. Instead, they are an elaborate extension of previous definitions and classifications. Still they represent a step in the right direction, for they have led toward experimentation and away from anecdotal evidence.

C. Experiments

The first experimental observations related to relevance were reported in 1961 (Rath *et al.*, 1961; Resnick, 1961). By 1970, about two dozen experiments had been reported. Their synthesis is presented in the Appendix at the end of this review. I could not find reports of any experiments directly concerned with relevance after 1970. The relatively small number of experiments and the evident moratorium on relevance experimentation after 1970 may look strange, but they should be put in the context of the activities in the field of information science. The field is highly pragmatic; funds are expended mostly for practical and technological achievements; research funding is not as readily available in the seventies as it was in the sixties; and research interests have shifted.

All of the experiments could be easily criticized for methodological deficiencies and some could be praised for their achievements [for a lengthy review, see Saracevic (1970a); the summary of results presented in the Appendix was taken from Saracevic (1970b)]. However, the experiments do offer important clues as to the nature of some of the factors that affect human relevance judgments. For some factors, the experimental results provide ballpark estimates of the comparative extent to which they affect relevance judgments. For practitioners and researchers, these experimental findings could be of interest by themselves.

D. Completeness of View

The destination's view of relevance has concentrated on factors that affect human relevance judgment. It has equated relevance with relevance judgment. Certainly human factors and human judgments affect relevance, but they are still only one of the aspects that influence the measure of the effectiveness (i.e., relevance) of the contact between a source and a destination in a communication process. The destination's view is not incorrect at all; like the "system's view," it is merely incomplete.

As mentioned, there were a few hypotheses suggested and a few experiments carried out. They were probings or, as Caudra and Katter (1967b) said, they were attempts at "opening the black box of relevance." Generally speaking, the hypotheses and experiments dealt only with selected factors and aspects related to human relevance judgments. Indeed, it could be argued that they just scratched the surface; the area is in dire need of further theories, hypotheses, and experiments.

One of the most obvious aspects in need of investigation is the effect of the limitations of human memory on relevance judgment. Miller (1956) and others discussed "the magical number seven" as describing limits of human information processing. The effect of selection from the subject has not been investigated from the system's view. The effect of another type of selection has rarely been investigated from the destination's view, namely the selection due to the limitation of human memory in information processing. Such limitation is fully recognized in the practice of providing information. The effectiveness of communication and this process of selection are closely related. It has not been looked into, and would appear to be a most promising and important area of investigation.

VII. HOW BIBLIOMETRICS EVOLVED AND HOW IT IS RELATED TO THE "SUBJECT LITERATURE VIEW" OF RELEVANCE

Up to the 1970's, most of the work directly concerned with relevance in information science has concentrated either on the system's or on the destination's view of relevance. However, chronologically speaking, both of these views were preceded by the "subject literature view" of relevance. As mentioned, S. C. Bradford was concerned in the 1930's and 1940's with articles "relevant to a subject." His work pioneered the area that later became known as bibliometrics, the "quantitative treatment of the properties of recorded discourse and behavior appertaining to it" (Fairthorne, 1969). Some bibliometric work was continued in the late forties and throughout the fifties. But it wasn't until the mid-sixties and late sixties that work in bibliometrics started attracting more people and more attention; and it was not until the early and mid-seventies that it started to blossom.

In bibliometrics a number of empirical laws have been uncovered, theories have been suggested, and quantitative observations have been made. But the strength of the work in bibliometrics lies in the direct connection between empirical laws and theories on the one hand and observation on the other. (Unfortunately, by the way, this is *not* usual in most areas of work in information science or librarianship, including relevance.) Several excellent reviews of bibliometric research have appeared, such as that by Fairthorne (1969), which concentrated on showing the relationship between various bibliometric and other distributions; by Brookes (1973), which summarized bibliometric applications of significance to information science and librarianship; by Line and Sandison (1974), which synthesized approximately one hundred and eighty studies that dealt with obsolescence and changes in use of literature over time. Admittedly, bibliometric research has not been concerned with relevance—not directly—but even if not mentioned or realized, fundamental to most bibliometric works is a concern with relevance. Let me elaborate further on this point and suggest the nature of the subject literature view of relevance.

A. Distributions: Bradford, Lotka, Zipf

Originally Bradford was interested in the rate at which given sources (such as journals) contributed items (articles) relevant to a given subject—he was interested in the pattern of a statistical distribution that would describe the relation between a quantity (journals) and a yield (articles). He did observe that the scatter of articles on a subject across journals, where they appeared, forms a regular pattern of diminishing returns and stated his law of literature scatter. Bradford (1948) formulated the law as follows: "... if scientific journals are arranged in order of decreasing productivity of articles on a given subject, they may be divided into a nucleus of periodicals more particularly devoted to the subject and several groups or zones containing the same number of articles as the nucleus, where the number of periodicals in the nucleus and succeeding zones will be as $1:n:n^2:n^3 \ldots$"

For a century or so a similar statistical relationship between quantity and yield was observed in many subjects, and similar patterns of diminishing returns were observed in relation to many phenomena (e.g., Pareto's distribution of income). Explanations and interpretations were derived according to the interests of the subject and the nature of the phenomena. In other words, a similar statistical distribution describes patterns of many phenomena (so does the normal distribution) without assuming proximity of causes. The distributions afford a method of description (be it conformity or nonconformity) and prediction. They do not describe the underlying causes and mechanisms. In information science, the family of these distributions was given the names of Bradford, Lotka, Zipf, and/or Mandelbrot (see Fairthorne, 1969).

Lotka (1926) investigated the productivity of authors in scientific subjects. He found that a large proportion of the literature is produced by a small number of authors and it is distributed so that the number of people producing n papers is approximately proportional to $1/n^2$. Zipf (1949) investigated distribution of words in a text, and arrived at a similar conclusion: a small number of words is used very often, distributed so that if the words are ranked by frequency then rank times frequency is constant. Price (1965) investigated the pattern of citation networks and found that the number of papers cited at frequencies above average is small, thus forming a "research front." Urquhart (1959) investigated the patterns of use of periodicals from a large scientific library: the use was heavily oriented toward a small portion of the collection. Saracevic (1970c) studied the distribution of documents retrieved as answers from an experimental IR system in response to more than one hundred questions from a number of users. He found that the distribution follows Bradford's law—taking all queries together, a small number of documents were repeatedly retrieved as answers forming a nucleus, and the rest were falling off in the expected Bradford pattern. Then the relevance judgments of users on the same retrieved answers were studied—many answers were judged not relevant, but the distribution of those documents that were judged relevant again conformed to Bradford's law. A small number of documents in the nucleus were repeatedly judged as relevant answers irrespective of queries, and the rest were falling off as predicted by the law. Numerous other studies could be cited on the same or similar aspects—studies related to the use of libraries and of literature, distribution of index terms in subject indexes, and citation patterns. The observed statistical distributions are similar.

B. "Subject Literature View" of Relevance

For a better understanding of both the preceding aspects studied in bibliometrics and the notion of relevance, it is significant to note that they are associated. In the Soviet Union, Kozachkov (1969) related the notion of relevance to the "process of scientific cognition" and described various aspects of scientific literature as growth, scatter, and obsolescence in terms of their relation to relevance. Saracevic (1970a, pp. 110–51; 1970c) synthesized a number of the distributions and findings in bibliometrics and interpreted them in terms of relevance calling them "relevance related distributions." The appearance of articles in journals, the contribution of authors to literature, the networks of citations, the changes in the use and the obsolescence of literature, and the use of literature from libraries or IR systems are all manifestations of the communication of knowledge. Sometimes it is not realized that these, and similar manifestations, are not independent of each other even though they may be viewed one at a time. They are manifestations of a larger whole; namely, they relate to the structure of subject literature. I submit that underlying all these manifestations of communication of knowledge is the notion of relevance. These manifestations form the "subject literature view" of relevance.

So far, research in information science has concentrated mostly on the statistical distribution patterns of these various manifestations. Obviously distribution patterns are but one aspect of the problem; so much more remains to be learned even in regard to distributions. Still, what is emerging is a picture of the structure of subject literatures, of the patterns of what went on and what is going on. Needless to say, a rational forecast of what may be expected to take place in the subject literatures, and with what probability, is dependent on the degree and the depth of familiarity with their structures. In that fact lies the great importance of works on the structure of subject literatures.

Of critical importance would be investigation of the mechanism that operates to form the given structure of subject literatures over time. As suggested by many, the mechanism underlying the investigated distribution is one of selection, a "success-breeds-success" mechanism, a Darwinian mechanism. Previously I suggested that the notion of relevance underlies the described manifestations. In generalizing, I suggest that the notion of relevance underlies all of the mechanisms that are forming the given structure of subject literatures. Therefore, the notion of relevance also underlies the structure of literature itself. The given mechanisms exist, and the given structures are found, because of the requirements of effective communications necessary for survival, procreation, and use of the subject knowledge. Therefore, relevance is suggested as the underlying notion.

C. Completeness of the View

Effectiveness of communication depends on many factors. Various views on relevance result from considering the effectiveness at different points in the communication process. Thus emerged different classifications of the factors and different assessments of priorities. None of the views is by itself incorrect, but accepting one results in an incomplete view. Along with the system's and the destination's view of relevance, we may add the "subject literature view" of relevance. This view can be built around considerations of the structure of subject literatures. The view has not been developed to any extent, but there is a start. It is premature to talk about the completeness of the view.

The importance of the subject literature view of relevance in relation to other views and to the total knowledge communication process, especially where information systems are involved, is great. For information systems, the process starts with subject literature. The aim of information systems is to enable and to enhance contact between subject literature and users (destinations). Therefore, subject literature affects all aspects. The system's view of relevance has to take into account that selection from the literature by the system affects the effectiveness of the source. The destination's view of relevance has to take into account that answers can be provided only within the subject knowledge and subject literature. This provides for a relationship among the three views.

VIII. HOW SPLITTING OF THE NOTION BEGAN AND THE "SUBJECT KNOWLEDGE VIEW" OF RELEVANCE RESULTED

In the early 1960's suggestions that relevance involved numerous relations and that a distinction should be made between various relations began to be voiced. Most often a distinction was made between relevance and pertinence. Originally, this distinction stemmed from the distinction made between a question and an information need.

A. The Concept of Information Need

Experience has taught us that at times, often unintentionally, a question does not exactly coincide with what a questioner had on his/her mind. At times it is difficult to verbalize a question even if it is in one's mind; and at times people tend to answer with what they think the questioner needs, rather than answer the question as formulated.

Operationally, in IR systems and libraries, question analyses, reference interviews, and the like are aimed at clarifying questions and reducing the differences, if any, between the question as asked and the question in one's mind. The questioner's stock of knowledge at hand and the intended use of answers are also often probed to help in the provision of the most relevant answer.

Out of these experiences, and out of the sociological concepts of "need" and "need-event," came the concept of information need in information science. Information need is a psychological state associated with uncertainty, with an unknown, and with the desire to know. "It is not directly observable ... but it has a definite existence in the mind of the user at least and so it is useful to have a term by which one may refer to it" (Cooper, 1971). But the concept of information need has had its fierce critics in information science just as the general concept of "need" has had in sociology: "Numerous explanations, all unclear ... sacred expression ... coverup for question negotiation..." (O'Connor, 1968). However, to this date the concept of information need remains in information science chiefly to distinguish between a state of mind and the subsequent representation in a question.

B. Pertinence

The concept of information need brought out the notion of pertinence. Numerous authors made this following or similar distinction (cf. Rees and Saracevic, 1963). The question-asking, question-answering process can be represented as:

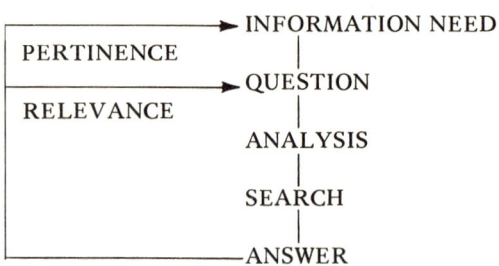

Relevance is the property which assigns certain members of a file (e.g., documents) to the question; *pertinence* is the property which assigns them to the information need (Goffman and Newill, 1966). Subsequently (as known from experience) some relevant answers are also pertinent; but there could be relevant answers that are not pertinent and pertinent answers that are not relevant. It has often been argued that, from the user's point of view, desirable answers are pertinent answers; but, in reality, an IR system can only provide relevant answers. That is, a system can only answer questions. It can only guess what the information need is. In practice, of course, there is often an intense effort to satisfy information need and not only answer questions.

C. Foskett's Public Knowledge—Private Knowledge

Although information need is a satisfactory concept from a practical point of view, from a more theoretical point of view the whole concept of "need" in explaining states of mind, stocks of knowledge at hand, and ensuing changes, is neither satisfactory nor comfortable. Given that a distinction between relevance and pertinence is to be made, many have felt that an explanation apart from information need is required. Cooper (1971), in defining logical relevance (see Section X), inspired a different explanation although he kept to the concept of an information need.

In a brief note, Foskett (1972) suggested an alternate distinction between pertinence and relevance. Taking Ziman's "public knowledge" and augmenting it with Kuhn's paradigm on the pattern of thinking in a given field of science, Foskett suggested that "relevance means being a part of a paradigm, or public knowledge, or consensus in a field; pertinence means related to the specific pattern of thought in a specific reader's mind."

D. Kemp's Pairs

Kemp (1974) goes beyond Foskett and discusses relevance and pertinence as related to public knowledge and private knowledge. He suggests that "relevance and pertinence each belong to a group of terms which have something in common—'public-ness' in one case and 'private-ness' in the other." These are the related groups of terms from different fields characterized by being public or private:

	Public	Private
Information science:	Relevance	Pertinence
Philosophy of science:	Public knowledge	Private knowledge
Psychology:	Denotation	Connotation
Linguistics:	Semantics	Pragmatics
Sociology of knowledge:	Formal communication	Informal communication

Kemp thinks that "relevance and pertinence are two different qualities, one capable of public objective assessment and the other being capable only of private subjective assessment." Pointing out similar distinctions from other fields, Kemp is providing an invitation to relate the knowledge on these other notions to the notion of relevance; an area certainly worth examining in great detail.

E. Two "Knowledge Views" of Relevance

Two "knowledge views" of relevance emerged from these delineations. In the suggested framework (Section IV) it was recognized that subject knowledge appears at the outset of the knowledge communication process and that the destination is an end user. The destination has a file—a mind in the case of a human being. There are a number of causes which can put the process into motion. One of them is the posing of a question by a destination. Although this cause is of special interest to IR systems and the reasoning stems from this interest, we shall not consider here any information system at all. In this case there are two pairs of relations, two pairs of contact points that can be considered in determining what constitutes a measure of the effectiveness of the contact. The first pair of relations is between *the question* (or rather the subject content or topic of the question) and the existing *subject knowledge*. This view corresponds, to some degree, to Schutz's "topical relevances" and to Kemp's concept of relevance as involving public knowledge. We may refer to it as the *subject knowledge view of relevance*.

The second pair of relations is between *the file* (or rather, the subject content of the file, the stock of knowledge at hand) and the existing *subject knowledge*. This view corresponds, to some degree, to Schutz's (1970) "interpretational relevances" and to Kemp's (1974) concept of pertinence as involving private knowledge. We may refer to it as the *destination's knowledge view of relevance*, or simply as the *pertinence view of relevance*.

Both of these views involve subject knowledge on one end of the relation, but they distinguish what is on the other.

F. The "Subject Knowledge" View of Relevance and Its Completeness

The "subject knowledge view" of relevance stresses the nature, structure, and extent of the subject knowledge on a topic given by a question. Subject knowledge and subject literature are obviously related, but they are not the same. As mentioned, each has a structure that is related but is also quite different. Each is dynamic but on differing parameters. Subject knowledge involves knowledge per se, including redundancy, association, organization, and sedimentation. Subject literature, as a representation, involves authors, documents, producers, and scatter, as well as redundancy, associations, and organization, which may differ from those of knowledge. Basically, because of the redundancy of knowledge, we can have more than one set of answers to a question; because of the redundancy of literature, we can have more than one set of documents containing answers to a question. All this, and obviously much more, including much that is not known on and about subject knowledge and subject literature, affects relevance. But one thing should be clear: relevance in the context of subject knowledge and relevance in the context of subject literature, although related, are not one and the same.

In the previous sections it was established that every view of relevance, if considered in isolation from other views, is incomplete by definition. Thus, let me consider only the completeness of further views within themselves.

In information science there has been no work that has tried to directly relate the structure, properties, and dynamics of subject knowledge to relevance. In philosophy this was attempted—e.g., the work by Schutz (1970) and that by some of the others referenced in his book. However, there are numerous works in information science (and in other subjects) on or about subject knowledge that either indirectly or directly refer to relevance, e.g., works by Goffman (1964), Price (1963), and Ziman (1968, 1969). Conversely, relevance could be considered in the explanation of the mechanism underlying the various observations on the structure and dynamics of subject knowledge.

In discussing the completeness of the destination's view of relevance, it was suggested that the limits of human memory may play a significant role in explanations of relevance. Harmon (1973) suggested the intriguing idea that the same limits of human memory affect the growth and formation of subjects and their breakup into specializations or related subjects. This may be a factor that plays a significant role in explanations of the "subject knowledge view" of relevance.

The subject knowledge view has not been formed as yet in any detail. But there already exists considerable material from which it could be formed. I submit that the *subject knowledge view of relevance is fundamental to all other views on relevance*, because subject knowledge is fundamental to communication of knowledge. In that lies the importance and urgency of the work on that view.

G. "Pertinence View" of Relevance and Its Completeness

The destination's knowledge or pertinence view of relevance stresses the content of the file of the destination. Since people are ultimate destinations in knowledge communication, the interest in people as destinations is of overriding importance. Thus, in the "pertinence view" of relevance, determining factors are the nature, structure, and extent of one's stock of knowledge at hand, the process and sequence of its sedimentation, and the process of the mind's selectivity.

The destination's view of relevance, discussed in Section VI, attempts to incorporate all factors that enter into human relevance judgment. The stress is on judgment. One of these factors is the stock of knowledge at hand, which, in turn, is the base of the pertinence view. Therefore, the destination's view does incorporate the pertinence view of relevance, but the latter is much more to the point. The pertinence view has a firmer base than the broad destination's view, because of a considerable number of philosophical and psychological investigations that have been devoted to the understanding of how we know what we know. These could be directly related to the pertinence view. In comparison, there has been much less research on human judgment; thus the broad destination's view has little to relate to.

Work on the pertinence view of relevance has not gone beyond providing a general framework for the view either in the concept of information need or in the contrast between public and private knowledge. There has been no enumeration of the specific elements and relations that are a part of either framework. Therefore, the view has only been broadly defined, and lacks clarity and precision. These inadequacies define the agenda for further research.

IX. HOW THE DISENCHANTMENT WITH RELEVANCE LED TO ANOTHER SPLITTING AND HOW THE "PRAGMATIC VIEW" OF RELEVANCE EVOLVED

A. Relevance Is "No Good"

Thinking on relevance probed in still other directions. Not surprisingly, there has also been some disenchantment and impatience with the notion of relevance. A lot of outspoken criticism has been leveled: "Not appropriate," "inadequate," "too confusing," "ambiguous," "overused," "nonmeasurable," "doesn't reflect X" (X being a myriad of factors enumerated by critics that, indeed, relevance does not reflect), "not a good criterion," etc. Such criticisms have been especially vehement when voiced by those concerned with practice and by others concerned with testing. How, indeed, does one run a system if one declares that it is aimed toward relevance, which is such an ambiguous notion? How, indeed, does one test systems using measures or criteria as elusive and imprecise as relevance? The criticisms do have validity but lose their force when put in a human context.

Relevance is a human notion. How does one do anything neatly and precisely and unambiguously with human notions? Twentieth-century science, in moving toward a study of human notions, found that reductionism to the "preciseness" of natural sciences does not work. The meaning of effectiveness in systems dealing with human notions is not the same as in engineering or business, and treating them in the same way leads to social dissatisfaction. These aspects have not been taken into account by critics of the use of the notion of relevance.

As a result of the disenchantment with the notion of relevance and the belief that relevance for practical purposes is not the appropriate notion, alternate terms have been suggested. "Usefulness," "appropriateness," "utility," etc. have been suggested and used as substitutes for relevance. Although the connotations of each of these alternatives are different, interestingly enough, the basic notion behind the use of the substitutions and of relevance is exactly the same. In these attempts the notion of relevance has not been abandoned, even if the word has been. Just as it was naive to think that a "good definition" (i.e., a paraphrase) of relevance would resolve the problem, so it is equally naive to think that abandonment of the word will lead to a solution. The history of science shows that a mere substitution of words for notions does not resolve a problem. However, it also shows that new avenues of thinking can be opened this way.

B. Cybernetics; Pragmatism

In a number of fields it has been realized that many processes can be looked at from the point of view of what happened to the results. The analysis of one whole and one set of processes can be looked at from this point of view: What effect did they have on other wholes and other processes? In information theory, Shannon looked at a certain aspect within the communication process. In cybernetics, Wiener looked at the governing effects of communication and, conversely, how the results of communication, through a feedback function, govern communication—he looked at how one process governs another.

In logic and linguistics, the study of pragmatics (use) emerged in addition to the traditional study of syntactics (rules) and semantics (meaning). Concern also developed over the interplay among the three. Starting in the nineteenth century in philosophy, the school of thought called pragmatism developed, suggesting that the meaning of an idea consists of the pragmatic consequences of the idea. Radical pragmatism of the twentieth century suggests that the activities of the consciousness, as actions in the outer world, have exclusively practical aims, in particular, aims designed to satisfy biological needs. In the fields of action—in manufacture, industry, production, and governance—pragmatic concepts (practical, utility, useful) are quite prevalent.

It is not surprising then, that a "pragmatic view" of relevance has developed. However, it did not develop from the notion of pragmatics in logic and linguistics, or the pragmatic philosophy, but rather strictly from the prevailing utilitarian, practical orientation of the fields of action. In addition, the demands and desire for justification, in terms of cost benefits, pervaded information science in the sixties and seventies as it pervaded other social, behavioral, and educational fields and enterprises.

The argument for the "pragmatic view" of relevance went as follows: it is fine for IR systems to provide relevant information, but the true role is to provide useful information—information that helps to directly resolve given problems; information that directly bears on given actions, that directly fits into given concerns and interests. Information systems should provide information that has utility. Thus, it was argued that relevance is not a proper criterion, a proper measure, for a true evaluation of IR systems. A true measure should be utilitarian in nature.

C. Cooper's Utility

A most eloquent (and the first in-depth) treatment of utility as a measure of retrieval effectiveness has been provided by Cooper

(1971, 1973). His argument is built on the assumption that "the purpose of retrieval systems is (or at least should be) to retrieve documents that are useful not merely relevant." With further elaboration: "The success of a retrieval system must ultimately be judged on the basis of a comparison of some kind involving costs and benefits." Cooper uses the suggested measure of utility in a complete neutral sense. "It is simply a cover term for whatever the user finds to be of value about the system output, whatever its usefulness, its entertainment, or aesthetic value, or anything else." In his 1971 study, Cooper defined "logical relevance" (see Section X, D) and made the following statement about the relation between relevance and utility: "... 'relevance' has to do with 'aboutness' (or 'pertinence' or 'topic-relatedness') and is ultimately defined in terms of logical implication, whereas 'utility' is a catch-all concept involving not only topic-relatedness but also quality, novelty, importance, credibility, and many other things."

As mentioned, in this review the concentration is on the notion of relevance and *not* on the evaluation of IR systems. Thus it is really of little or no interest here (or to any explication of relevance) to debate whether relevance, utility, or other specific measures should be applied to test and evaluate any specific IR system. However, Cooper's ideas on utility represent the beginning of the explication of still another view of relevance, that evolved—the "pragmatic view"—thus they are included here. Moreover, Cooper astutely notes a relation between his utility and relevance.

As in the pertinence view, in the "pragmatic view" the approach was to split the notion of relevance and to argue that relevance is one thing but X (X represents pertinence, utility) is another, even though they are related. Imperceptibly, the thinking on relevance moved in the late sixties and early seventies toward the belief that there are a number of "kinds" of relevances involving different relations. Different names started to be employed to characterize different "kinds" of relevance.

D. Wilson's Situational Relevance

Another and slightly different explication of the pragmatic view of relevance was provided by Wilson (1973). Wilson's explanation starts from the assumption that "relevance is not a single notion but many." He makes a basic distinction between psychological and logical relevance, the former dealing with actual uses and actual effects of information, while the latter is a double concept "of a relation between an item of information and a particular individual's personal view of the world and his situation in it; and it is a concept in which relevance depends on logical bearing on some matter on which he has preferences." To derive the notion of situational relevance, Wilson uses Cooper's definition of logical relevance, derived from deductive logic, and constructs a definition, using probabilities, of evidential relevance drawn from inductive logic. To specify the relations established by situational relevance, Wilson also uses the notions of an individual's (1) concerns, (2) preferences over ranges of alternatives (similar to the use in economic theories), and (3) stock of knowledge (information, belief). Situational relevance is defined as a relation between these three notions and an item of information established by inference either deductively (Cooper's logical relevance) or inductively (evidential relevance). "Situational relevance is relevance to a particular individual's situation—but to the situation as he sees it, not as others see it nor as it 'really is.' " Wilson suggests that situation relevance captures the "essentials of the vague popular notion of practical relevance ... that must bear on our actions."

E. Kochen's Utility Function

Kochen (1974) was the first to explicate rather than describe, theoretical principles of information retrieval, and make a distinction between "relevance as a relation between propositions and the recognition of relevance on its judgment by a user, which resembles a utility or significance judgment." This is the same distinction made by Cooper, but Kochen went further and formally defined the notion of utility.

Given a situation where a user abides by the following four axioms of utility theory, then Kochen has suggested that it is possible to assign for a given user with a given question a utility to each document in a collection:

Axiom 1. For *any* two documents, the user should be able to state unambiguously whether he prefers the first to the second, the second to the first, or that he is indifferent.

Axiom 2. If a user prefers the first document to the second, and the second document to the third, then he also prefers the first to the third.

Axiom 3. If a user prefers the first document to the second, and the second to the third, then he can specify a probability P such that for all three documents he is indifferent to the choice between the option of a search strategy that will retrieve the second document for sure and the option of using a method which retrieves the first document with probability P and the third with probability $1 - P$.

Axiom 4. If a user is indifferent toward two documents, then the user is indifferent to which document, the first or its substitution, is used in the strategy for retrieval given in Axiom 3.

From these axioms it follows that there exists a utility function which assigns a number to each document for a given user and question so that if a user prefers the first document to the second, then the number of the utility function for the first will be greater than for the second, and the expected utility of a strategy is the expected utility of the documents in it. Kochen recognizes that changes of preferences take place as learning takes place or as other variables intervene.

As in all utility functions, this one depends on the ability of users to assign preferences and associate probabilities, which is also its fundamental weakness. In many ways one can argue that this expectation, while at times realistic, is frequently inoperable. Without preferences there is no utility theory and subsequently there are no utility functions. But bringing the notions of preferences and the full strength of the utility theory to bear upon the notion of relevance is an important contribution. It opens a new area of study which should be followed.

F. Completeness of View

It is of general interest to note the power of a precise definition and the ensuing chain reaction which is often observed in the history of science. Although Cooper's definition of logical relevance was limited, it was precise enough to inspire other thinking such as that of Foskett, Kemp, Wilson, and Kochen.

As with other views, the "pragmatic view" of relevance is incomplete, but less so. It does recognize some of the different aspects of relevance not recognized by other views. Explicitly, it allows for the measurement of relevance at different points in the communication process. Significantly, there is a direct attempt (admittedly, barely a beginning) to establish a relationship between different views of relevance. However, in the "pragmatic view," immediate pragmatism of information in one form or another is the ultimate, definite, final criterion. What each individual does with information is superordinate to what the information is. A criticism of this view can be attempted from general criticism of pragmatism and cost-benefit approaches.

Pragmatism has been subject to serious criticism in philosophy. The chief criticism is that it applies to only one reality. It does not deal with the totality of human existence. It deals only with what is referred to as "paramount reality." And above all, it deals with that reality in an absolute manner—as being unquestionable.

In our times one of the operational reflections of pragmatism is the concept of cost benefits, which is also subject to serious criticism. Clearly, costs of a great many processes and actions can, and must, be related to the accrued benefits. But as many critics point out, a great many other processes and actions, especially those related to human problems, cannot, and should not, be judged on a cost-benefit basis—or at least not on that basis alone. Cost benefits cannot, and should not, be an omnicriterion for the evaluation of all human actions and enterprises. It is beside the point whether they can or cannot be estimated. At any rate, in the case of knowledge, costs can be estimated, but true cost benefits cannot.

The "pragmatic view" of relevance ushered in the concept of cost benefits. Yes, there are limited situations where cost benefits and relevance should be related. But if cost benefits were to be universally applied to the process of the communication of knowledge it would be the surest way to destroy its effectiveness. I wonder: Would the Alexandrian library ever have been built if cost-benefit studies were a criterion for a decision?

This should not be construed as a rejection of the "pragmatic view" of relevance. On the contrary, it is an important theory, deserving further attention, especially as to the factors involved in pragmatism of information and as to the relation to other views.

What is rejected is the idea that pragmatism is the only, or even the basic, aspect to apply to relevance.

In conclusion, let me relate the three views centering around destination. The "destination's view" concentrates on judgment, the "pertinence view" concentrates on the stock of knowledge at hand, and the "pragmatic view" on immediate application or on the problem at hand. If the pertinence view is related to some degree to Schutz's "interpretational relevance," then the pragmatic view can be related to some degree to his "motivational relevances." The pertinence view is fundamental to both views, for the stock of knowledge at hand is fundamental to a judgment and to a problem. Conversely, the pertinence view can be considered without involving the other two views; the destination's view has to involve the pertinence view, and it can, but does not have to, involve the pragmatic view; the pragmatic view has to involve the other two.

X. HOW THEORIES OF RELEVANCE HAVE COVERED DIFFERENT ASPECTS AND WHY THEY ARE IMPORTANT

I have reserved for last the discussion of the most significant work on relevance in information science: the attempts to formulate theories of relevance. Unfortunately, theories are few and far between. But they represent a significant step in the right direction. As few and as sketchy as they are, the theoretical works have resulted in (1) drawing methods and results from other, and more rigorous, subjects and focusing them on the study of relevance; (2) illuminating the nature of the notion more thoroughly and more beneficially than all the discussions combined; and (3) specifying the various relations involved, enabling the classification of relations and a more intense study of specific relations. Like other theoretical work in information science, theoretical work on relevance has had little discernible, direct impact on practice. The effects have been indirect.

A. Maron–Kuhns' Relevance Number

Maron and Kuhns (1960) presented one of the first detailed, formal theoretical treatises in information science. They were concerned with the derivation of a probabilistic measure that would enable the ranking of documents as to their relevance. Noting that the "problem of explicating the notion of relevance (which is the basic concept in a theory of information retrieval) is similar to that of explicating the notion of amount of information (which is the basic concept of Shannon's communication theory) . . . we approach the notion of relevance also in a probabilistic sense." Their conditional probability, which specifies the "relevance number," involves the relation between a user's *request*, the *subject area* of the request, designation by a given *representation*, and a given *document* provided by a *system*. Regardless of any applications, the significance of Maron–Kuhns' explication lies in (1) enumeration of the preceding factors affecting relevance; (2) envisioning that there is a relation between these various factors; and (3) introduction of the concept of probabilities in describing the relations.

The probabilistic approach has been successful in many subjects in relation to many complex phenomena. There exists a systematic, formal body of knowledge related to probabilities and to the treatment of measures as probabilities. However, formulating a measure in terms of probabilities is one thing, approximating probabilities (deriving numerical values) is another. Often this is a major problem in experimentation and practice, but, without formulation first, there is no approximation at all. Yet even though Maron and Kuhns and many others have tried to approximate probabilities related to relevance, this experimental and practical problem remains far from a satisfactory resolution.

B. Goffman's Relevance as a Measure and the Epidemic Theory

In the mathematical theory of measures, four axioms describe the properties that a measure has to satisfy to be a measure: (1) it is real-valued and nonnegative (expressed by a positive real number); (2) it is completely additive (the sum of the measures is the measure of the sum); (3) it has an order (a smaller set has a smaller measure); (4) it has an absolute zero. Goffman (1964) used these properties to prove that, given that relevance is determined solely on the basis of a query and the relevance of each document in a file independent of other documents (as is the prevailing practice in IR systems), then relevance does not satisfy all of the axiomatic properties of a measure—it is not completely additive. He also proved, in another theorem, that if relevance is determined not only on the basis of the query-document relation, but also on the relations among documents (i.e., documents to each other), then relevance satisfies all the axiomatic properties of a measure. To be a measure, relevance also has to take into account association, the effects of the items of knowledge on each other. This, of course, supports efforts in associative indexing.

Goffman and Newill (1967; elaborated in Goffman, 1970) developed an epidemic theory of communication, equating the process of the spread of ideas to the spread of diseases. The notion of effective contact is central to the theory. A population consists of infectives, susceptibles, and removals. The dynamics of epidemic processes (changes in infectives, susceptibles, or removals over time) are represented mathematically through a system of differential equations. A series of theorems prove the conditions under which the dynamics of the process changes over time in given populations. In the case of the information retrieval processes (a subprocess in a communication process), relevance is considered the measure of the effectiveness of the contact. The process is described as an interrogation procedure of a file of documents, "objects which convey information". Assuming that a general measure of relevance is probabilistic, a series of mathematical definitions and theorems provide various conditions under which a set of documents exhibit various relations. Among others, Goffman proved mathematically that relevance is not associated with a unique subset of documents as answers from a file and that more than one subset of answers is possible; that answers that were not initially relevant can become relevant in an appropriate sequence; and that relevance is an equivalence relation, which provides for a partitioning of a file in equivalence classes. It has been shown that "any measure of the effectiveness of information conveyed must depend upon what is already known . . . and [therefore, it is necessary to] introduce the notion of conditional probability of relevance."

The strength of the theory is that it provides for some of the dynamic aspects of communication and shows some of the complexity of relations of relevance as a measure using mathematical rigor. As a matter of fact, this is the only communication theory which has emerged in information science that attempts to show some of the dynamics of the process. It clearly shows the impact that the "interplay" among documents has on relevance.

One of the more interesting things remaining to be done is to relate the dynamics of this communication theory, where effectiveness of the contact is a central notion, to the so-called "relevance-related" distributions (as Bradford's law), which are essentially static in nature but involve relevance as well.

C. Hillman's Similarity Classes

As Maron–Kuhns introduced probabilities, as Goffman introduced axiomatic method and dynamics, Hillman (1964) introduced logic to the treatment of relevance in information science. In treating the basic problem in defining relevance, Hillman suggested the use of constructs from formal logic, particularly Carnap's concept formation theory. Assuming that the problem of mutual relevancies of queries and documents involves conceptual relatedness, Hillman critically examined various aspects in the theory of concept formation showing their applicability or nonapplicability to the definition of relevance. He suggested that to describe relevance relations in terms of similarity classes would be most appropriate. The theory is not complete, but its strength lies in the critical examination of a number of constructs in logic, accompanied by a judgment as to their applicability to the study of relevance. Especially valuable has been its ability to focus the attention of information scientists on logic.

D. Cooper's Logical Relevance

It remained for Cooper (1971) to employ the full weight of deductive logic in a carefully articulated definition of what he called logical relevance. He addressed the nature of inference involved in relevance. He assumed that relevance is a relationship "holding between pieces of stored information on the one hand and user's information needs formulated as information needs representation on the other ... both are linguistic entities of some kind." As in logic, Cooper takes a *sentence* to be the basic information-conveying unit of language. He also assumes that an information need and the data in an IR system can be represented by declarative sentences. And as a fundamental construct he takes the relationship of "logical consequence" (entailment, logical implication) from deductive logic, where a sentence (called "conclusion") is a logical consequence of a set of sentences (called "premises") when a set of conditions is fulfilled. Given these restrictions:

1. A search query is a yes–no type question, thus it can be transformed in a pair of yes–no *component statements* (e.g., Is hydrogen a halogen element?).

2. The data stored in a system are in well-formed sentences so that a *premise set* for the component statement can be derived by logical consequence; a *minimal premise set* is a set as small as possible—if a member is deleted the component statement would no longer be a logical consequence of the premise set.

3. The retrieval is inferential; it deduces direct answers to input questions.

Then Cooper provides his "restricted definition:"

> A stored sentence is *logically relevant* to (a representation of) an information need if and only if it is a member of some minimal premise set of stored sentences for some component statements of that need.

In generalizing from that definition, Cooper shows that the restricted definition could also be applied to fact retrieval systems and even to document retrieval systems (but not precisely), taking the strategy of transformation of whatever is stored into declarative sentences. The difficulties with this definition occur when dealing with induction (and inductive systems) rather than deduction, a problem fully acknowledged by Cooper—probabilities, degrees of relevance, simply cannot be accommodated.

The strength of Cooper's approach is that it defines, as fully and as precisely as deductive logic permits, one set of relations and one type of inference involved in relevance. As restricted as it is, Cooper's logical relevance has to be recognized as unique, inviting definitions of other possible types of inferences and providing grounds for differentiation. In his work on situational relevance, Wilson (1973) (see Section IX, D) attempted briefly to incorporate inductive logic and probabilities into a definition of evidential relevance.

"Logical view" of relevance concentrated on the *nature of relations* between elements rather than on *enumeration of elements* that enter into relevance. Coming from logic the nature of relation was treated as inferences. Two logical views emerged: (1) a "deductive inference view" drawing from deductive logic, and (2) a "probabilistic inference view" drawing from inductive logic and probabilities.

Since deductive logic is much more precise and complete than inductive logic, the first view is much more precise and complete than the second. The second view appears to be in particular need of further elaboration.

E. Completeness of Theories

All of the theories of relevance are incomplete in the sense that none of them incorporates all or most of the known, or intuitively understood, aspects of relevance. Each theory illuminates some aspect of relevance and provides a different tool, a different method, for describing the properties and relationships of the notion. No theory has, as yet, attempted to describe the mechanisms that account for the notion. In all probability the forthcoming theories on relevance will be of a step-by-step nature, further illuminating some particular aspect, painting a portion of the landscape at a time.

Why so much stress on theories? The answer is that there is nothing more practical than a good theory. The history of science provides numerous proofs that this is not just a cliché. Theoretical work on relevance has the potential of having great impact on the practice of information retrieval and librarianship in particular, and on the communication of knowledge in general. It can easily be demonstrated how different conceptions, views, and pseudo theories of relevance have led to the development of given systems and of given practices and standards in many types of information systems. Thorough and valid theoretical thinking on relevance has a potential of positive impact. Lack of it leads to uncertainty, with a reduced probability of positive impact and greater probability of negative results.

XI. BACK TO THE FRAMEWORK

This review is an inventory and a classification. On one hand, I have attempted to trace the evolution of thinking on relevance, a key notion in information science; on the other hand, I have attempted to provide a framework within which the widely dissonant ideas on relevance might be interpreted and related to one another. If the classification (the framework) is valid, it would seem to provide a potential for identifying gaps in knowledge and indicating possible directions for future work.

Information is a basic phenomenon, as basic and as puzzling as matter and energy. Communication is a complex process, as complex as transformation of matter and transmission of energy. Knowledge is considered the most complex human state and communication of knowledge the most complex human process. Since the notion of relevance is central to knowledge, information, and communication, it also involves the related complexities, puzzles, and controversies. Intuitively, it is generally understood and accepted that the notion of relevance has to do with the success of the communication process, the appropriateness of the results, the success of the relations. Therefore, we have taken the notion of relevance fundamentally to be a notion of the measure of the effectiveness of the contact between a source and a destination in a communication process.

In a slightly different context Weiler (1962) remarked that "the arguments about relevance are arguments about the framework of our discussion." And our analysis of the arguments about relevance in information science confirms his view. What aspect of communication, what relations, should be considered in specifying relevance? What factors are to be considered in determining relevance?

Some "formal" answers to these questions, answers that are above and beyond intuitive understanding, have been attempted in information science. Differences in answers have generated different views of relevance. As yet none of the views has achieved a stage of broad consensus. The thinking on the notion of relevance in information science seems to have reached a stage of perpetual challenge.

The process of communication of knowledge, which includes various elements, sequences, and relations, was suggested in Section IV, C as a framework for considerations of relevance and as a source of a scheme for classifying the various views of relevance which have emerged in information science. Even while measuring the same thing, a process can be validly measured at a number of different stages of the sequence of events, which involves different elements and relations—creating different viewpoints. This is exactly what has happened with the notion of relevance. Relevance can be, and has been, considered at a number of different points in the process of communication of knowledge; thus different elements and relations were considered and different viewpoints emerged. On a more specific level, relevance can be, and has been, considered in relation to specific types of knowledge communication.

Embedded in the communication of knowledge are information systems (libraries, IR systems, etc.) which aim at facilitating and enhancing the process. Different systems aim at enhancing different aspects of the process or are directed toward different uses or environments. Relevance can also be, and has been, considered with or without involving any of the information systems or their elements.

A. Summary of Different Views

Taking into account different elements and/or the nature of different relations in the communication of knowledge, the following views of relevance, arranged approximately by the sequence of events in the process, have emerged:

1. The *"subject knowledge view" of relevance* considered the relation between the knowledge on or about the subject *and* a topic (question) on or about the subject.
2. The *"subject literature view" of relevance*, closely related to the subject knowledge view, considered
   a. relations between the subject *and* its representation, the literature, or
   b. the relation between the literature *and* a topic (question) on the subject.
3. The *"logical view" of relevance* was concerned with the *nature of the inference* between premises on a topic and conclusions from a subject or subject literature. Two views have emerged:
   a. the *"deductive inference view"* considered the relation between premises *and* conclusions on the basis of logical consequence;
   b. the *"probabilistic inference view"* considered the relation between premises, information as evidence, *and* conclusions on the basis of degree of confirmation or probabilities.
4. The *"system's view" of relevance* considered the contents of the

file and/or the processes of a given information system *and* the relation to either
   a. a subject or a subject literature;
   b. a topic (question);
   c. a user or users.
5. The *"destination's view" of relevance* considered the human judgment on the relation between documents conveying information *and* a topic (question).
6. The *"pertinence" or "destination's knowledge view" of relevance* considered the relation between the stock of knowledge at hand of a knower *and*
   a. subject knowledge; or
   b. subject literature.
7. The *"pragmatic view" of relevance* considered the relation between the immediate problem at hand of a user (i.e., utility to a user or situation of the user) *and* the provided information in whatever form, involving preference as the base for inference.

The following can be ascertained: different views of relevance are not independent of each other. It seems that there exists an interlocking cycle of various systems of relevances (i.e., various systems of measures), systems that interplay with each other. Some views, some systems, may be considered as special cases or subsystems of other more general systems. In other words, there is not, and there cannot be, any *one specific view* of relevance, for there does not exist any single system of relevance in communication. Different systems of relevance may involve some different factors, but they are coupled in such a way that they can hardly be considered without attention to other systems of relevance. For instance, the "pragmatic view" cannot be considered without involving the "pertinence view" or the "destination's view" of relevance. None can be considered without the "subject knowledge view." Many practical problems in information systems (libraries included) and many cases of user dissatisfaction can now be explained as due to the existence of various systems of relevances.

Therefore, when considering relevance in a specific sense, one should be quite careful to indicate the elements and the nature of the relations between elements that are being considered. Different names can be given to the considerations of specific different sets of elements or different relations. This was started with names of "pertinence" and "logical relevance." However, it should always be realized that any specific consideration of relevance is tied to the larger question of systems of relevances. A most significant advance in thinking on relevance will be achieved with the illumination of the interplay between the systems of relevances.

B. Speculation on Properties and Future Work

It has been noted that different views of relevance have arisen because, in the communication of knowledge, there actually exists a number of dynamically interacting systems of relevances organized in some stratified, or perhaps hierarchical, fashion of complex systems—each view has concentrated on one system. If this explanation is valid, then we may postulate that there should exist some fundamental properties that are universal, common to all views or systems of relevance, and some unique properties that are specific to each system. Presently we can only speculate that among the universal properties are

1. *knowledge, knower*: all views assume prior existence of a body of knowledge or ideas; or a reservoir of knowledge, information, documents, data; or a knower; or some observables.
2. *selection*: implied by all views is a process of selection concentrating on elements or structure of above knowledge, etc.
3. *inference*: selectivity is based on some form of inference.
4. *mapping*: the aim is some form of mapping of selected elements or structure of knowledge onto something, at minimum, onto some other elements or structure of knowledge, etc.
5. *dynamics*: the dynamic interactions among properties are involved; changes in any property over time are possible.
6. *association*: the internal structure of elements of knowledge, etc., and other properties affect the dynamics, and vice versa.
7. *redundancy*: more than one set of elements of knowledge, etc., more than one pattern of association or structure, more than one form of inference, dynamics, or mapping may satisfy the criteria of any and all properties.

If these, or some similar, properties are indeed found to be universal to all views or systems of relevances, then an explication of each view will be incomplete if it does not in some way incorporate an explication of at least every one of the universal properties. Thinking on relevance can thus proceed in various directions:

1. taking a given view or system of relevance and proceeding to fully define all properties;
2. taking a given property in one or a number of systems and defining and contrasting the nature of the property; for instance, this was started with the explications of the nature of inferences—deductive, inductive, probabilistic, preferential, etc.;
3. taking a number of properties and explicating the interplay;
4. taking a number of explicated systems of relevance and explicating the interplay between them. The ultimate thinking on relevance will be that which explicates the interplay among all defined systems of relevances.

In summarizing the framework for considering relevance a number of elements or aspects have been enumerated. Information science deals with most of them, but not all of them. Most glaringly absent are considerations of the environments and human values involved in the communication of knowledge. Hopefully, future work on relevance will include these aspects as well.

Our understanding of relevance in communication is much better, clearer, deeper, broader than it was when information science started after World War II. But there is still a long, long way to go.

APPENDIX: SYNTHESIS OF THE EXPERIMENTS ON RELEVANCE IN INFORMATION SCIENCE

The experiments are organized and synthesized according to the five general classes of variables that affect human relevance judgment, as suggested by Cuadra and Katter (1967a) (reviewed in Section VI, B under "Hypotheses"). To derive conclusions I examined the data and results of the experiments rather than using the conclusions and claims of the authors.

A. Documents and Document Representations

Documents and their representations were the first, and most frequently treated, variable in the study of relevance judgments. Documents evoked early interest since they are the items provided by IR systems to users, and thus observations concerning their effect

upon the user and his judgment have direct practical implications for systems design and operations. Investigated were
1. Comparative effects on relevance judgments of titles, citations, abstracts and/or full texts (Rath et al., 1961; Rees et al., 1967; Resnick, 1961; Saracevic, 1969; Shirey and Kurfeerst, 1967)
2. Effects of stylistic characteristics of documents (Cuadra and Katter, 1967a)
3. Effects of degree of specificity and variations in document content in relation to queries (Cuadra and Katter, 1967a; Rees et al., 1967).

An analysis and a correlation of experimental results suggest several conclusions:
1. It may be expected with a considerable degree of certainty that documents, or objects conveying information, are the major variable in relevance judgments, in particular, and in relevance as a relation between sources and destination in a communication process, in general.
2. Although a number of factors are aligned with documents as variables, the most important of these factors affecting relevance appears to be the subject content of documents as compared to the subject content of the query. This finding relates to Schutz's (1970) "topical relevances."
3. Elements of style may also be expected to affect relevance judgment.
4. Highly specific subject content in a document appears to stimulate more relevance agreements.
5. Relevance judgments for the same article may be expected to differ from titles to full texts; titles should be utilized with considerable skepticism.
6. Relevance judgments for the same article may be expected to differ somewhat from abstracts to full texts, depending upon the abstract's type, length, detail, etc.

B. Queries

The query stimulates the generation of documents as answers and documents are judged for relevance in relation to the query. Experimental observations were made on the query–document relationship:
1. The effects on relevance judgments of query specificity (Cuadra and Katter, 1967a)

2. The effects on relevance judgments of judges' subject expertise at various stages of the research—the successive research stages were treated as enlargements of the queries (Rees *et al.*, 1967)
3. The relation between the wording and phraseology of queries and documents judged relevant or nonrelevant (Gifford and Baumanis, 1969)
4. The relation between disagreements in relevance judgments and unclearness of query statements (O'Connor, 1969)
5. The effect of judges' subject knowledge in relation to the subject content of queries (Cuadra and Katter, 1967a; Rees *et al.*, 1967).

The following conclusions may be drawn:
1. The more judges know about a query, the higher is the agreement among judges on relevance judgments and the more stringent the judgments become.
2. The more judges discuss the inference from query to answer, the higher the agreement on relevance judgments.
3. A close similarity and correlation seems to exist between texts of relevant documents, which cannot be found between texts of queries and texts of nonrelevant documents.
4. Document texts may be the most important factor in triggering relevance judgments in relation to stated queries; i.e., if one finds a statement in a document resembling a query statement, one is assured of a high probability that the document will be considered relevant by the user stating the query.
5. The less one knows about a query, the greater is the tendency to judge documents relevant. In specific terms, the less a system operator or user delegate knows about a query—its content, eventual use, or the problem in relation to which the query is asked—the greater the temptation to judge documents relevant. This finding relates to Schutz's (1970) "interpretational relevances."

C. Judgmental Situations and Conditions

This variable refers to the environment—real or constructed—within which relevance judgments are made. Two studies are examined:
1. The effect of aspects and definitions of relevance upon relevance judgments (Cuadra and Katter, 1967a; Rees *et al.*, 1967)
2. The effect of time and stringency pressures on relevance judgments (Cuadra and Katter, 1967a).

The results from these experiments are inconclusive and should be interpreted cautiously:
1. Not surprisingly, changes in experimental conditions may introduce changes in judgments.
2. Different definitions of relevance do not necessarily stimulate different relevance ratings; i.e., people tend to treat relevance as a primitive notion.
3. Greater pressure in the judgmental situations stimulates higher relevance ratings (i.e., "more" relevant). This finding relates to Schutz's (1970) "motivational relevances."

D. Modes for Expression

This variable refers to the instruments (psychometric devices) by which judges express relevance judgments. Since instruments used for recording attitudes do affect the attitude, they become subjects of study. Examined were
1. The comparative effects on relevance judgments of rating, ranking, and ratio scales (Cuadra and Katter, 1967a; Katter, 1968; Rees *et al.*, 1967)
2. The effect of differing numbers of categories on rating scales (Cuadra and Katter, 1967a)
3. Reliability of judgments as affected by different types of scales (Rees *et al.*, 1967)
4. Interaction of scale types with other variables tested (Cuadra and Katter, 1967a; Rees *et al.*, 1967).

It may be concluded:
1. Different kinds of scales (rating, ranking, and ratio scales) may produce slightly different judgments.
2. The more categories a rating scale has, the more comfortable the judges feel in their judgment; in any case, they may be more at ease with a scale having more than two and up to some ten categories.
3. It is not clear what type of scales is most reliable for use in recording relevance judgments. Some form of the ratio scale appears to have some advantage over other types of scales.
4. On the scales tested, judges with a high level of subject expertise tended to agree with themselves over a short period of time (e.g., a month).
5. It was found that the end points of scales were used most

heavily regardless of the number of categories in the scale; i.e., documents tend to be rated very relevant or very nonrelevant.
6. Relevance judgments of a group of judges on one document are not normally distributed, but are skewed in one direction.
7. It is most significant to note that the relative relevance score of documents in a group, especially among the documents with high relevance, may be expected to be remarkably consistent even when judges with differing backgrounds make the relevance judgments. Thus, it may be more profitable to compare the relative position of documents in a set than to compare the relevance ratings assigned to individual documents.

E. People

The fundamental factor studied in all experiments reviewed was the consistency of, or agreement in, relevance judgments as affected by certain human characteristics. These characteristics usually dealt with the degree of subject or professional education. It should be noted that the human element as a variable is present to some extent in all previous conclusions presented. Investigated were
1. The ability of people to judge consistently the relevance of documents to their general interest (Resnick and Savage, 1964)
2. The comparison of users' and nonusers' (delegated) and experts' and nonexperts' relevance judgments (Barhydt, 1967; Hoffman, 1965)
3. The effect on relevance judgments of the document's intended use (Cuadra and Katter, 1967a, b)
4. The effect of academic and professional training on relevance judgments (Cuadra and Katter, 1967a; Rees *et al.*, 1967)
5. The relation between relevance judgments assigned by judges and test results from IR systems (Lesk and Salton, 1968)

On this most important variable the conclusions are as follows:
1. It may be expected that the greater the judges' subject knowledge the higher will be their agreement on relevance judgments. Subject knowledge seems to be the most important factor affecting the relevance judgment as far as human characteristics are concerned. This finding underlines the importance of considering the stock of knowledge at hand when considering relevance and people.
2. It has also been demonstrated that the level of judges' subject

knowledge varies inversely with the number of documents judged relevant; conversely, the less the subject knowledge, the more lenient are their judgments.
3. Non-subject-oriented groups (e.g., subject information retrieval specialists and librarians) tend to assign relatively high relevance ratings; they will be inclined to provide a user with all or most of the relevant material that he himself would consider relevant and in addition some or considerably more material that he would not consider relevant. However, it may be expected that the ranking of documents as to degree of relevance will be similar for persons with extensive subject background (i.e., users) and for suppliers of information (i.e., delegates) with lesser subject backgrounds.
4. Familiarity with and knowledge of subject terminology have been shown to result in higher relevance agreement.
5. It may be expected that a professional or occupational involvement with the problem giving rise to the query would increase agreement of relevance judgments among and between groups of subject specialists and suppliers of information. Increased professional involvement affects agreement among judgments, irrespective of the degree of subject knowledge.
6. The correlation in relevance agreements among people with high levels of subject expertise and the most professional involvement with the query has been found to be between .55 and .75; the correlation in relevance agreements among suppliers of information has been found to be between .45 and .60.
7. Differences in the intended use of documents may produce differences in relevance judgments, suggesting that intended use becomes part of the query. This finding relates to Schutz's (1970) "interpretational relevances" and Wilson's (1973) "situational relevance."
8. Agreement as to what is *not* relevant may be expected to be greater than agreement as to what is relevant; judging relevance is not the same as judging nonrelevance.
9. Tests of retrieval system performance, given of course that they are well designed and controlled, may produce reliable comparative results within test experiments, regardless of relative instability of relevance judgments (instability within the range elaborated under item 6).

One of the major conclusions that can be drawn from experiments is that relevance judgments are not at all associated with a random distribution. Although it may appear that relevance judgment is a very subjective human process, it does have associated with it some remarkable regularity patterns.

REFERENCES

Anderson, A. R., and Belnap, N. D., Jr. (1962). The pure calculus of entailment. *Journal of Symbolic Logic* **27**, 19–52.

Barhydt, G. C. (1967). The effectiveness of non-user relevance assessments. *Journal of Documentation* **23**, 146–149, 251.

Bell, D. (1973). "The Coming of Post-Industrial Society—A Venture in Social Forecasting." Basic Books, New York.

Bradford, S. C. (1948). The documentary chaos. *In* Bradford, S. C. "Documentation," pp. 106–121. C. Lockwood & Son, London.

Brookes, B. C. (1973). Numerical methods of bibliographic analysis. *Library Trends* **22**, 18–43.

Bush, V. (1945). As we may think. *Atlantic Monthly* **176**, 101–108.

Carnap, R. (1950). "Logical Foundations of Probability." University of Chicago Press, Chicago, Illinois.

Cleverdon, C. W. (1960). ASLIB Cranfield Research Project on the comparative efficiency of indexing systems. *ASLIB Proceedings* **12**, 421–431.

Cooper, W. S. (1971). A definition of relevance for information retrieval. *Information Storage and Retrieval* **7**, 19–37.

Cooper, W. S. (1973). On selecting a measure of retrieval effectiveness. Part 1. *American Society for Information Science Journal* **24**, 87–100.

Cuadra, C. A. (1964). "On the Utility of the Relevance Concept." Systems Development Corporation, Santa Monica, California. (Technical Report SP 1595.)

Cuadra, C. A., and Katter, R. V. (1967a). "Experimental Studies of Relevance Judgements," 3 vols. Systems Development Corporation, Santa Monica, California. (TM-3520/001, 002, 003/00.)

Cuadra, C. A., and Katter, R. V. (1967b). Opening the black box of "relevance." *Journal of Documentation* **23**, 291–303.

Doyle, L. B. (1963). Is relevance an adequate criterion for retrieval system evaluation? *American Documentation Institute Proceedings, Oct. 6–17, 1963*, Part 2, pp. 199–200.

Fairthorne, R. A. (1969). Empirical hyperbolic distributions (Bradford-Zipf-Mandelbrot) for bibliometric description and prediction. *Journal of Documentation* **25**, 319–343.

Foskett, D. J. (1972). A note on the concept of "relevance." *Information Storage and Retrieval* **8**, 77–78.

Gifford, C., and Baumanis, G. J. (1969). On understanding user choices: textual correlates of relevance judgements. *American Documentation* **20**, 21–26.

Goffman, W. (1964). On relevance as a measure. *Information Storage and Retrieval* **2**, 201–203.

Goffman, W. (1970). A general theory of communication. *In* Saracevic, T. "Introduction to Information Science," pp. 726–747. R. R. Bowker, New York.

Goffman, W., and Newill, V. A. (1966). Methodology for test and evaluation of information retrieval systems. *Information Storage and Retrieval* **3**, 19–25.

Goffman, W., and Newill, V. A. (1967). Communication and epidemic processes. *Royal Society Proceedings,* A,**298**, 316–334.

Harmon, G. (1973). "Human Memory and Knowledge: A Systems Approach." Greenwood, Westport, Connecticut.

Hillman, D. J. (1964). The notion of relevance (I). *American Documentation* **15**, 26–34.

Hoffman, J. M. (1965). "Experimental Design for Measuring the Intra- and Inter-Group Consistency of Human Judgment of Relevance." Master's thesis, Georgia Institute of Technology.

Katter, R. V. (1968). The influence of scale form on relevance judgment. *Information Storage and Retrieval* **4**, 1–11.

Kemp, D. A. (1974). Relevance, pertinence and information system development. *Information Storage and Retrieval* **10**, 37–47.

Kent, A., Berry, M., Leuhrs, F. U., and Perry, J. W. (1955). Machine literature searching. VIII. Operational criteria for designing information retrieval systems. *American Documentation* **6**, 93–101.

Kochen, M. (1974). "Principles of Information Retrieval." Melville, Los Angeles, California.

Kozachkov, L. S. (1969). Relevance in informatics and scientology. (In Russian.) *Nauchno-Teknicheskaya Informatsiya, Ser. 2* No. 8, 3–11.

Lesk, M. E., and Salton, G. (1968). Relevance assessments and retrieval system evaluation. *Information Storage and Retrieval* **4**, 343–359.

Line, M. B., and Sandison, A. (1974). "Obsolescence" and changes in the use of literature with time. *Journal of Documentation* **30**, 283–350.

Lotka, A. J. (1926). The frequency distribution of scientific productivity. *Washington Academy of Sciences Journal* **16**, 317–323.

Maron, M. E., and Kuhns, J. L. (1960). On relevance, probabilistic indexing, and information retrieval. *Association for Computing Machinery Journal* **7**, 216–244.

Mesarović, M., and Pestel, E. (1974). "Mankind at the Turning Point—The Second Report to the Club of Rome." Dutton, New York.

Miller, G. A. (1956). The magical number seven, plus or minus two: some limits on our capacity for processing information. *Psychological Review* **63**, 81–97.

Mooers, C. S. (1950). Coding, information retrieval, and the rapid selector. *American Documentation* **1**, 225–229.

National Academy of Sciences (1959). "Proceedings of the International

Conference on Scientific Information," 2 vols. National Academy of Sciences, National Research Council, Washington, D. C.
National Science Foundation (1964). "Summary of Study Conference on Evaluation of Document Searching Systems and Procedures." National Science Foundation, Washington, D. C.
O'Connor, J. (1967). Relevance disagreements and unclear request forms. *American Documentation* 18, 165–177.
O'Connor, J. (1968). Some questions concerning "information need." *American Documentation* 19, 200–203.
O'Connor, J. (1969). Some independent agreements and resolved disagreements about answer-providing documents. *American Documentation* 20, 311–319.
Perry, J. W. (1951). Superimposed punching of numerical codes on hand-sorted punch cards. *American Documentation* 2, 205–212.
Price, D. J. de S. (1963). "Little Science, Big Science." Columbia University Press, New York.
Price, D. J. de S. (1965). Networks of scientific papers. *Science* 149, 510–515.
Rath, G. J., Resnick, A., and Savage, T. R. (1961). Comparisons of four types of lexical indicators of content. *American Documentation* 12, 126–130.
Rees, A. M., and Saracevic, T. (1963). Conceptual analysis of questions in information retrieval systems. *American Documentation Institute Proceedings, Oct. 6–11, 1963*, Part 2, pp. 175–177.
Rees, A. M., and Saracevic, T. (1966). The measurability of relevance. *American Documentation Institute Proceedings* 3, 225–234.
Rees, A. M., Schultz, D. G., Baumanis, G., Marcus, S., Rothenberg, L., Saracevic, T., Stern, M., and Zull, C. (1967). "A Field Experimental Approach to the Study of Relevance Assessments in Relation to Document Searching," 2 vols. Case Western Reserve University, Center for Documentation and Communication Research, School of Library Science, Cleveland, Ohio.
Resnick, A. (1961). Relative effectiveness of document titles and abstracts for determining relevance of documents. *Science* 134, 1004–1006.
Resnick, A., and Savage, T. R. (1964). The consistency of human judgments of relevance. *American Documentation* 15, 93–95.
Saracevic, T. (1969). Comparative effects of titles, abstracts and full texts on relevance judgments. *American Society for Information Science Proceedings* 6, 293–299.
Saracevic, T. (1970a). "Introduction to Information Science." R. R. Bowker, New York.
Saracevic, T. (1970b). Ten years of relevance experimentation: a summary and synthesis of conclusions. *American Society for Information Science Proceedings* 7, 33–36.
Saracevic, T. (1970c). "On the Concept of Relevance in Information Science." Unpublished PhD. dissertation, Case Western Reserve University.
Schutz, A. (1970). "Reflections on the Problem of Relevance." Yale University Press, New Haven, Connecticut.
Shannon, C. E., and Weaver, W. (1949). "Mathematical Theory of Communication." University of Illinois Press, Urbana, Illinois.

Shera, J. H., and Egan, M. E. (1953). A review of the present state of librarianship and documentation. *In* Bradford, S. C. "Documentation," 2nd ed., pp. 11–45. C. Lockwood & Son, London.

Shirey, D. L., and Kurfeerst, M. (1967). Relevance predictability. II. Data reduction. *In* "Electronic Handling of Information: Testing and Evaluation" (A. Kent, ed.), pp. 187–198. Thompson, Washington, D. C.

Taube, M., and Associates (1955). Storage and retrieval of information by means of the association of ideas. *American Documentation* **6**, 1–18.

Urquhart, D. J. (1959). Use of scientific periodicals. *In* "Proceedings of the International Conference on Scientific Information," pp. 277–290. National Academy of Sciences, National Research Council, Washington, D. C.

Warren, K. S., and Goffman, W. (1972). The ecology of the medical literatures. *American Journal of the Medical Sciences* **263**, 267–273.

Weiler, G. (1962). On relevance. *Mind* **71**, 487–493.

Wiener, N. (1961). "Cybernetics: Control and Communication in the Animal and the Machine," 2nd ed. MIT Press, Cambridge, Massachusetts.

Wilson, P. (1973). Situational relevance. *Information Storage and Retrieval* **9**, 457–471.

Ziman, J. M. (1968). "Public Knowledge: An Essay Concerning The Social Dimension of Science." Cambridge University Press, London.

Ziman, J. M. (1969). Information, communication, knowledge. *Nature* **224**, 318–324.

Zipf, G. (1949). "Human Behavior and the Principle of Least Effort." Addison-Wesley, Cambridge, Massachusetts.

The Impact of Reading on Human Behavior: The Implications of Communications Research

ROGER HANEY, MICHAEL H. HARRIS, and LEONARD TIPTON

University of Kentucky

I. General Introduction	140
II. The State of the Art in Communications Research: Complexities and Vagaries	141
A. Introduction	141
B. The Scientific Method and Its Importance for Research in Communications	142
C. Research Design	145
D. Intervening Variables	148
E. Summary	150
III. Pornography and Deviant Sexual Behavior	151
A. Introduction, Legal History, and Implications	151
B. The Effects of Pornography	155
C. Summary	164
IV. Violence	165
A. Introduction	165
B. Definition	166
C. Availability	168

		D. Effects	169
		E. Summary	176
	V.	Reading, Attitude Formation and Change, and Prejudice	176
		A. Introduction	176
		B. Principal Research Traditions	177
		C. Reading and Racism	182
		D. Sexism and Reading	188
		E. Summary	192
	VI.	Bibliotherapy: Reading in a Therapeutic Context	193
		A. Definition and History	193
		B. State of the Art in Bibliotherapy Research	194
		C. New Frontiers in Research	195
		D. Summary	197
	VII.	Implications of Communications Research for Information Professionals	199
		A. Introduction	199
		B. Children	199
		C. Adults	200
		D. Apologia	201
		References	202

I. GENERAL INTRODUCTION

The Americans' unwavering commitment to the notion that print can have a significant impact on human behavior could be demonstrated in many ways. For instance, it was in 1683 that Cotton Mather recorded in his diary that he intended to encourage an "Old Hawker" to fill the country "with devout and useful books," in an attempt to counter the pernicious impact of irreligious and profane works. In 1799, John Adams, the President of the United States, signed legislation which was designed to silence anyone who would write against the government. Ten years later he explained that he recognized that his signing of the bill violated First Amendment rights under the Constitution, but that he did so because he was convinced that such subversive writing would lead to the destruction of the Republic. More recently, hundreds of parents forced the closing of the Kanawha County, West Virginia, public schools in a controversy over the use of textbooks that the parents argued would teach their children to be irreligious, unpatriotic, and sexually promiscuous.

Such examples could be multiplied many hundreds of times, but they only tend to underline the fact that Americans generally believe in the ability of the printed word to influence—for good or evil—the way in which people behave. This intensely held belief has stimulated public sensitivity to the growing freedom of expression in America, and has caused untold problems for librarians, publishers, booksellers, teachers, journalists, and other information professionals who are involved in the dissemination of the printed word.

This general and continuing concern with the influence of reading on human behavior is reflected in the nature and extent of the research endeavor aimed at discovering "what reading does to people." This research effort, which involves hundreds, if not thousands, of scholars, is interdisciplinary in nature and includes educators, sociologists, journalists, political scientists, book publishers, historians, librarians, and many others (Harris, 1973; Steinberg, 1972). This chapter is an attempt to survey what we feel to be the most significant developments in the multifaceted research effort directed at isolating and analyzing the influence of print, since the publication of Waples' famous study *What Reading Does to People* (1940).

II. THE STATE OF THE ART IN COMMUNICATIONS RESEARCH: COMPLEXITIES AND VAGARIES

A. Introduction

The mass media became a socially significant element in human communication when science and technology combined to create machines such as the printing press (1450), the motion picture (1894), the radio (1920), and television (1941), which enabled ever larger audiences to receive the same message. These technical achievements held great promise for improving the human condition, but also stimulated growing concern for the new frightening potential for mass persuasion—a potential that was vividly demonstrated in the German propaganda efforts of World Wars I and II. It began to appear that if one could control the mass media, one could control the masses.

The obvious significance of the mass media to the communications environment of any society has encouraged a great deal of research in the area of "communications impact." However, the systematic review of communication effects is an arduous process complicated by the recent and interdisciplinary nature of the field. Schramm (1971), for example, estimates that well over half of the research conducted on communication has been completed since 1952.

A further problem is the tentative and complex nature of the findings. The demands of the scientific method require caution and care in the test of hypotheses and the evaluation of data that are often disconcerting to the laymen interested in straightforward and final answers to what they view as important questions. Scholars are constantly reminded of the imprecise nature of the research on communications impact. Facts must be interpreted in the light of constantly evolving theories. Research techniques need to be varied and compared, to ensure generalizability of findings. Models of communication need to be formulated and tested in order to facilitate the organization of existing data and heuristically suggest avenues of further investigation. Relevant intervening variables must be discovered and defined. The very question of *impact* must be systematically analyzed and divided into workable problems. Finally, the distinguishing characteristics of the print medium need to be cataloged and compared with those of other channels of communication in order to evaluate the impact of print (cf. Gordon, 1975; McGinnies, 1965; Yungman, 1969). The purpose of this section is to discuss these problems briefly as a preliminary to our attempt to assess the latest research relative to the impact of reading on behavior.

B. The Scientific Method and Its Importance for Research in Communications

Those interested in the research effort aimed at assessing the impact of reading on behavior should be aware of the increasing importance of the scientific method in the communication field generally. Although certainly not the only method by which we gain truth and knowledge, it is unique as a guard against confusing what is actually there with what a particular investigator thinks is there or what he would like to be there. It is a method of reaching agreement. But in order to ensure that research findings will cumulate, that is, in order to reach agreement on questions relative to the impact of reading, certain procedures must be followed.

1. THE SCIENTIFIC METHOD IS EMPIRICAL

All scientific research, whether undertaken by means of the astronomer's telescope, the physicist's electron microscope, or the social scientist's questionnaire, involves the process of observation. In order to establish what happens, the scholar must examine the operation of specific phenomenon under more or less closely controlled conditions. When direct observation is impossible, as is often the case in the social sciences, then one must ask people questions. In every case, moral judgments concerning what happens or personal bias relative to what should happen must be deliberately avoided.

2. THE SCIENTIFIC METHOD IS PUBLIC

This statement has several implications. For instance, it rules out much of advertising research as scientific. People are frequently convinced that because millions of dollars are spent disseminating particular advertising messages, someone is sure of the effectiveness of those messages. But this is not the case. The creative department of an ad agency often overrules the research department. An ad can be run because the creators like it rather than because there is evidence that it is effective (Bogart, 1973).

More important is the fact that the findings of ad research are not generally shared with the public. Other investigators cannot check the research to ensure that the audience was not biased in some way, or that the data were not improperly analyzed. To say that science is public is to say that any particular study must be reported in such a way that other scholars can at least attempt to *replicate* the results. Procedures must be precisely defined so that key concepts can be measured in similar fashion. Does violence, for example, refer to frantic activity as observed in a natural disaster or in a car race; to physical harm—either shown or implied—done to a person or property; or to verbal attacks? Whether television violence leads to aggression by the audience depends on one's definition of violence.

Furthermore, to say that science is public is to say that it is *authority-free*. It means little that a particular authority on bibliotherapy, for example, says that reading has proven an effective means of treating mental problems or that a member of the *Obscenity and*

Pornography Commission concludes that "one who wallows in filth is going to get dirty" (Keating, 1970, p. 622). What matters is the *evidence* an expert can present in support of such authoritative statements. The public, or at least trained information professionals, must have the means of independently validating the underlying evidence before any conclusions are considered scientifically tested and sound.

3. THE SCIENTIFIC METHOD IS SYSTEMATIC AND CUMULATIVE

All questions of significance require careful and prolonged analysis. General problems must be refined and revised with increasing precision. Before one can speak of impact with any surety, the phenomenon has to be observed in a wide variety of conditions and circumstances. Exceptions need to be discovered and evaluated in order to *test*, not prove, generalizations concerning the phenomenon. Only after a great deal of time and effort have been expended do the data of social science become definitive, and even then conclusions remain tentative.

4. THE SCIENTIFIC METHOD IS THEORETICAL

Science is theoretical for two reasons. First, although data are collected and propositions are tested in specific investigations, the scientist is primarily interested in *generalizing* the results of a particular study to all those situations which exist under similar conditions. The scientist assumes there are lawlike relationships between phenomena, that findings hold for similar circumstances and populations. But such an assumption is subject to error. Processes of human behavior are subject to change. Particular findings are subject to revision. Unobserved variables may intervene in observed relationships. Thus the scientist is generally quite conservative in his stated conclusions, often hedging against future exception and present misinterpretation.

The second reason why science is theoretical is that the scientist is interested in *explanation* and *prediction*, not simply description. Facts in themselves are of little value. They simply describe what happened in a particular situation. They do not provide explanations for why something happened or what is likely to happen in the future. Theory provides a frame of reference around which to organize and evaluate facts. For this reason, any discussion of the effects of print must deal with the theories involved as well as with specific research findings.

C. Research Design

While all scientists share a concern for the characteristics of the scientific method, different disciplines have different techniques for gathering the empirical data central to their specific research problem. In the social sciences, data collection can take various forms in the context of an experiment, a survey, a case study, or content analysis (Berelson and Steiner, 1964; Bowers, 1970; Emmert and Brooks, 1970; Kaplan, 1964; Kerlinger, 1965). Each type of research design has advantages and disadvantages, and findings from each need to be compared to ensure confidence in the results. Much of the confusion and uncertainty surrounding the study of the influence of print is an outgrowth of conflicting findings produced by variations in research designs, or a lack of data relating to the influence of reading under certain environmental conditions.

1. THE EXPERIMENT

The experiment has the principal advantage of *control* and thereby is most useful for investigating the causal relationship of one variable (the independent variable) to another (the dependent variable). In its classic form groups are "randomly assigned" or "matched" on relevant variables to the "experimental" or "control" condition. In the study of the impact of print, the experimental group receives the particular message or book under consideration and the control group does not. Any changes between the two groups (such as increase in learning or aggressive behavior) can now be said to be due to the manipulated variable (the message or book).

Experimental design is advantageous for its ability to control the order in which particular variables occur, thereby making causal statements more viable. For A to cause B in a strict sense (for reading pornography to cause sex crimes, for example) two conditions must be met. A must be *necessary* for the occurrence of B. That is to say, B will not occur unless A has already occurred. If someone who has never read pornography commits a sex crime, then pornography cannot be said to be the cause of that particular sex crime, or of sex crime *in general*. It may be related, it may be a "precipitating factor," but it is not the cause.

The second condition is whether A is *sufficient* to cause B. In this case, whenever A occurs, then B occurs. A may thus be *one* of the "causes" of B, but it is not necessarily the only one. If A occurs, but B does not, then A is not the cause of B. If some people read pornography but do not commit sex crimes, then reading pornography is not the cause of sex crimes. It might be related, it might be a precipitating factor, it might have an effect, but it is not the cause. Other factors, called intervening variables, need to be considered. Specific possibilities for causal relationships are most easily controlled and manipulated in the laboratory setting.

The disadvantages of experimental research are twofold. First, results of experiments cannot be safely generalized to real life because of the possibility of intervening variables affecting the relationship found in the laboratory and because relationships can change over time. Individuals can change their attitudes as the result of a particular message, but return to their original attitude in a few weeks, or possibly increase their attitude change (e.g., Hovland *et al.*, 1953). It is very difficult to involve human subjects in experiments over time and still maintain control. People can be studied over time, but they cannot be easily controlled over time.

Second, direct observation of behavior, while used extensively in the laboratory study of the impact of violence for instance, is often impossible in other areas of interest. Behavior that is essentially private, such as sexual behavior, or taboo, such as deviant behavior, or which involves internal processes, such as changes in attitudes, values, or other mental states, cannot be easily observed. In these cases the investigator frequently turns to verbal or written reports. Subjects, now called respondents, are asked to respond to questions posed by the investigator.

2. THE SURVEY

A means of studying people over time, which does not have the same advantage of control but does have the advantage of generalizability, is the *survey*. A survey involves *sampling* some "representative" segment of the population of interest (children, voters, prisoners, etc.) and asking them questions about the phenomenon. The difficulties here are in: (1) ensuring representativeness (not everyone asked will participate, especially over time); (2) people may become "sensitive" to the phenomenon because they are being asked questions about it, especially over time, and thus act differently than they ordinarily would; and (3) the loss of control in what might be determinates of the phenomenon.

Nevertheless, survey research has a definite place in social science and needs to be utilized far more often than it has been in the areas with which we are presently concerned. Much of the research reported here is of the experimental variety, making generalizations difficult. As Hovland (1959) pointed out when comparing results from experiments versus surveys: in the laboratory one can ensure complete exposure to a message, while this is not possible in natural settings; particular messages are studied in the laboratory, while surveys can more easily involve books or entire communication programs; and the influence of group memberships, interpersonal communication, and other intervening variables can show up in natural situations simply because they have not been controlled through randomization.

A major difficulty with the survey design is that even though it is very useful for measuring change over time, the order in which variables occur is not easily measured. Although there are procedures for doing so (cf. cross-lagged analysis; Pelz and Andrews, 1964), most survey research must simply conclude that there is a *relationship* (specifically, a correlation) between A and B. Whether A causes B, or B causes A, or some other variables cause both are moot points. If sex deviants read more pornography, and that is all that is known, it is equally possible that committing sex crimes "causes" an increase in reading pornography, or that reading pornography "causes" one to commit sex crimes, or that something else, e.g., childhood development, "causes" both. A great deal of additional information is needed before one can reasonably choose between these alternatives.

3. THE CASE STUDY

Case studies are a third design used to collect data and are important whenever one wants in-depth information about a particular individual (a sex deviant, a violent psychotic, a child with a learning problem). The survey studies many people on a few characteristics; the case study measures one individual on many characteristics. Thus the two can go hand in hand nicely. Some of the research reported here involves the use of the case study, but since only one person is involved at a time, generalizations made from this source of data are extremely tenuous. The greatest use of the case study is to gain insight into the relationship between reading and behavior as evidenced in one intensely studied example as a means of generating hypotheses or theories that may be tested on a broader and more generalizable scale.

4. CONTENT ANALYSIS

Another technique frequently used in communication research is content analysis. It differs from the other techniques in that the phenomenon being observed is generally a message rather than people. In order to be scientific and not merely impressionistic, it is necessary to specify precisely the unit of analysis and the content categories. The unit of analysis may be a word, a sentence, a paragraph, an article, a picture, a book. The content categories will depend upon the particular problem under investigation. These, however, must be defined in such a way that results, if not conclusions, can be replicated or compared with other message samples.

Content analysis can be very useful in determining the scope or availability of particular information or presentations. However, content analysis in and of itself can say nothing about the effects of messages on an audience. Researchers do make statements about effects based upon content analysis alone, but such statements are highly speculative at best. For more rigorous conclusions, content analysis must be used in connection with other research techniques.

D. Intervening Variables

Much attention has been given to variables "intervening" in the relationships found in various research settings. As stated earlier, the scientist is interested in generalizing the results of his particular investigation to all those situations which have similar conditions. One of the most obvious aspects of communication behavior is that it is very complex. An early model of communication, referred to as the "bullet theory" (Schramm, 1971, p. 8) or the "hypodermic needle model" (see Berelson *et al.*, 1954, p. 234) assumed that messages in the mass media had a *direct* and *pervasive* effect on their mass audiences. Subsequent research has shown the general fallaciousness of this assumption (Katz, 1957; Katz and Lazarsfeld, 1955; Klapper, 1960; Troldahl and Van Dam, 1965). Audiences now appear to be *active* participants in the total communication process, influencing, as well as being influenced by, the mass media. Several factors can affect this "active" audience and they deserve our attention here.

First of all, family and peer relationships can make a difference. Parents and friends not only influence whether one reads and what one reads (Chaffee *et al.*, 1971; Hansen, 1967), but also influence one's interpretations of what is read. *Psychological variables* also make a difference. Some people are "predisposed" to read and react in ways that others are not. Some people are more "authority-oriented" than others and therefore may read and react differently, depending on the source of the message or the presence of the authority.

The *message* itself makes a difference. One reason why books are so difficult to study is that books, even of the lowest quality, are exceedingly complex as messages. One sex-oriented message might be stimulating but several might be satiating. One violence-oriented message might be provoking but the context possible in books might provide a "justification" for the described aggression which, in turn, could *increase* the proclivity for aggression on the part of the reader. This complexity explains the great amount of research on particular *types* of messages, especially in the areas of attitude change and source credibility, and the concomitant lack of research on the effects of reading per se.

Not only are books complex, but the sheer number of new titles each year and the great diversity of availability from community to community further complicate the issue (Lacy, 1965). The potential reader has many sources of information to choose from, leading, in part, to a future shock of bombarded senses (Toffler, 1970). What *is selected*, as well as the effects of that selection, represents a major research question. Some researchers find that selection is on the basis of "utility" (Sears and Freedman, 1967). If the information is useful to the receiver in some way, then the receiver will select it. Another major theorist (Berlyne, 1960) argues that messages are selected on the basis of "novelty." People select material because it is new and can conceivably broaden their horizons. These people may not show the same effects of that usage as those psychologically predisposed to select particular message content. Other theorists argue, with supportive evidence, that people "selectively perceive" message content in a manner consistent with their prior attitudes and beliefs, thus "reinforcing" their predispositions rather than changing them (e.g., Cooper, and Jahoda, 1947; Klapper, 1960).

In addition to the complex problems caused by the nature of the message and the audience, the *medium* or *channel* in which the message is carried can also make a difference. Research on the effects of mass media has shown the importance of *interpersonal communication*, and it is now felt that there is at least a "two-step flow" of influence rather than the direct effect originally supposed (Katz, 1957). But what difference does the channel make? Are there differences between print and television, for example, that affect the flow of influence? Unfortunately, Innis and McLuhan notwithstanding (Carey, 1967), there is simply not sufficient evidence to answer these questions.

Finally, demographics can make a difference (Kline, 1971; Samuelson *et al.*, 1963). Research has shown that women, for example, are often more persuadable than men (Janis and Field, 1959; McGuire, 1969). More important for the concerns of this review is the fact that children may be more susceptible to the influence of the media than are adults (Bandura *et al.*, 1963a,b; Flanders, 1968; Peterson and Thurston, 1933; Siegel, 1958). This may be because normative cultural values are not yet instilled in young children (Zajonc, 1954); the media can provide information on previously unstructured aspects of the world, hence the particular vulnerability of young children (Bandura, 1969; Klapper, 1960). Education and social economic status are other factors that can make a difference.

E. Summary

In summary, it can be safely said that a great deal of research has been completed on the relation between communication and behavior and that research is becoming increasingly sophisticated but remains imprecise and tentative. The various means of gathering information on the impact of communications on behavior—experiment, survey, case study, and content analysis—all have advantages and weaknesses, and while the various methods have contributed much to our understanding of the impact of communications on behavior, readers must remain cautious in the use of findings based on this work.

III. PORNOGRAPHY AND DEVIANT SEXUAL BEHAVIOR

A. Introduction, Legal History, and Implications

The first step in determining the effects of a message variable on an audience is to define the variable adequately. In the area of pornography, this has been most difficult—perhaps because judges have been more concerned than scientists. Pornography is a legal, not a scientific, term. There is no scientific literature that allows one to *operationally* construct a message which is regarded as pornographic. Inclusion of sexually oriented material is not sufficient because the term pornography is usually taken to mean more than this—exactly what still being unclear, both legally and scientifically. Because it is essentially a legal term, however, that is where our analysis must begin (for a history, see Obeler, 1974).

1. HICKLIN RULE

The term "pornographic" is used to describe material which many people would regard as sex-oriented, particularly material which depicts nudity, homosexuality, and similar topics and which is candid with respect to sex items. The term is generally regarded as a subset of *obscenity*, the latter including such things as "scatological literature" and referring to the possibility or actuality of legal prohibition (Gerber, 1965). It is this (legal) judgment which makes pornography so difficult, if not impossible, to define operationally.

In 1633, the British Parliament passed the first act of censorship, including seditious and heretical materials, but it was the "Hicklin rule" [*Regina* vs. *Hicklin*, L.R. 3, Q.B. 360 (1868)] that served as the basis for early American law on obscenity. In it, Judge Cockburn established the test "whether the tendency of the matter charged as obscenity is to deprave and corrupt those whose minds are open to such immoral influences, and into whose hands a publication of this sort may fall." This ruling established the "most susceptible persons" test for obscenity and the troublesome notion that a work was obscene if "impure and libidinous" *thoughts* were suggested. There was no requirement, and there is none to this day, that antisocial *actions* must be caused by reading such material. American law eventually added the "partly obscene" test to the Hicklin rule allowing an entire work to be judged on the basis of passages pulled out of context (Lockhart and McClure, 1954, p. 343, No. 10).

2. COMSTOCK ACT

In 1873, largely through the efforts of Anthony Comstock, the Postal Reorganization and Codification Act was passed by Congress (Paul and Schwartz, 1961). What came to be known as the Comstock Act made it a felony for any person knowingly to deposit in the mail any obscene, lewd, or lascivious book, pamphlet, picture, paper, writing, print, or other publication of an indecent character. Comstock further used his influence to gain the post as Secretary of the New York Society for the Suppression of Vice. In that position he managed to seize some 100,000 books, 200,000 pictures and photographs, and more than 60,000 "rubber articles" in a single year. He also contrived, as a special agent for the United States Post Office, to obtain for himself a portion of the fines collected on successful prosecutions. The fine could amount to $5,000 for the first offense and $10,000 for a second offense.

Over the years, enforcement of the Comstock Act (18 United States Code 1461) has been inconsistent. Often the Post Office Department would declare a book nonmailable rather than bring a publisher or seller to court. In 1943, however, the Department attempted to withdraw second-class mailing privileges from *Esquire* because of its "smoking-car" humor. The Supreme Court ruled that the Post Office had no right to withdraw what in effect is a subsidy to the press [*Hannegan* vs. *Esquire*, 327 U.S. 146, 148–149, 66 S. Ct. 456, 457–458 (1946)]. Since then the Department has seldom attempted to revoke mailing privileges as a means of keeping materials out of the mails.

3. PANDERING

Two cases of importance at this time involved Ralph Ginzburg, the publisher of *Eros*, and Sam Ginsberg, the owner of a luncheonette which sold "girlie" magazines. In the *Ginzburg* case [383 U.S. 463, 465–466, 86 S. Ct. 942, 944–945 (1966)], it was ruled that materials could be regarded as obscene on the basis of their advertisement "to appeal to the erotic interest of their customers." The *Ginsberg* case [*Ginsberg* vs. *New York*, 390 U.S. 629, 634, 88 S. Ct. 1274, 1277 (1968)], led to the "variable obscenity" criterion which states that material which might not be obscene for one audience (e.g., adults) might well be obscene for another (e.g., children).

4. ULYSSES

In 1933, James Joyce's *Ulysses* was brought to trial after Bennett Cerf, publisher of Random House, had arranged to have it brought into the country [*United States* vs. *One Book Called "Ulysses,"* 5 F. Supp. 182 (S.D.N.Y. 1933)]. This case, although not regarded as a precedent, did establish two important principles relative to the question of obscenity: (1) it was not whether the material would arouse the sex interests of *any* person (or child), but whether it would arouse the sex instincts of a knowledgeable person; and (2) that passages cannot be taken out of context. The book must be judged as a unit.

5. ROTH–ALBERTS

The Supreme Court finally dealt directly with the constitutionality of obscenity laws in its simultaneous review of the *Samuel Roth* and *David S. Alberts* cases [*United States* vs. *Roth*, 237 F. 2d 796 (1956); *People of California* vs. *Alberts*, 138 Cal. App. 2d Supp. 909, 911 (1956)]. Roth was convicted on a charge of violation of the federal mail statute against the mailing of obscene literature. Alberts was convicted on a state law against keeping, for sale, lewd material. All previous references of the constitutionality of obscenity by the Supreme Court had been made during discussion of other issues. Such offhand remarks are not considered binding precedent and are called "dicta." Thus the *Roth–Alberts* review was considered an opportunity to clarify what was meant by obscenity and to establish precedent.

The case is a complex one, containing a majority opinion (Justice Brennan), a concurring opinion (Chief Justice Warren) in which it was argued that men, and not books, should be judged, a mixed opinion (Justice Harlan) in which it was argued that states, but not Congress, have the right to protect sexual morality, and dissenting opinions (Justices Black and Douglas) in which it was argued that obscenity censorship is unconstitutional unless it could be demonstrated that the work affects actions under the control of the government (i.e., sex crimes rather than thoughts).

Two important points were established by the majority opinion. First, "this court has always assumed that obscenity is not protected by the freedoms of speech and press" [354 U.S. 476, 77S. Ct. 1304, 1307 (1957)]. Obscenity laws were ruled constitutional. Second, a definition of obscenity was provided:

> Obscene material is material which deals with sex in a manner appealing to prurient interest, and the test of obscenity is whether to the average person, applying contemporary community standards, the dominant theme of the material appeals to prurient interest [354 U.S. 476, 77 S. Ct. 1304, 1311 (1957)].

The key implications of this definition are that it is not whether the work contains references to sex, but what interests of the reader are appealed to (emphasis being on effects on thought, not behavior), the reader is not the child but the average person, standards are set by the community, and the work in its entirety rather than isolated passages must be judged.

6. MILLER

The *Miller* case was one of five handed down simultaneously by the Supreme Court in 1973 [*Miller* vs. *California*, 413 U.S. 15, 93 S. Ct. 2607]. In this case, the court held that states can regulate material without "redeeming social value" and recognized contemporary local "community" standards, rather than national criteria, as the test for obscenity. In addition, they offered several guidelines for the states in the consideration of obscenity. Examples of what could be considered obscene include "representations or descriptions of ultimate sexual acts, normal or perverted, actual or simulated," and "representations or descriptions of masturbation, excretory functions, and lewd exhibition of the genitals."

7. IMPLICATIONS

The first question one is likely to have when considering the effects of pornography is whether or not pornography leads to, or is correlated with, the commission of sex crimes. A second question of perhaps greater significance is whether or not children are affected in either their attitude toward sex or their future sexual behavior through the perusal of pornography. Similar questions can be raised concerning adults. The context (verbal and situational) in which the material is embedded is also a question of concern (as it is in the violence area).

The Supreme Court has made it clear that *thoughts*, not *behaviors*, are the principal concern *legally*. The determination of such effects is, obviously, most difficult. The Court's position on children is less clear. Generally the effects on "knowledgeable persons" are to be considered, but a "variable obscenity" notion has also been recognized. The importance of the "total message," as well as the context in which material is made available (sold or advertised), has been recognized by the court, but the importance of "predispositional factors" and the situation involved in decoding such messages have not been legally recognized. Finally, the Court has made it clear that (local) "community standards" decide what material is pornographic but has left it unclear how to determine such standards. At any rate, since pornography is essentially a legal concept, it seemed most appropriate to discuss what is known about effects within this legal framework.

B. The Effects of Pornography

In 1967 Congress declared that obscenity and pornography were matters of national concern and called for a thorough study of the nature and extent of the problem. This led to the Commission on Obscenity and Pornography Report (1970) and the subsequent publication of several reports of research supported by that Commission (Commission on Obscenity and Pornography, 1971; Goldstein and Kant, 1973; Wilson and Goldstein, 1973). The purpose of the Commission was to: (1) analyze extant obscenity laws; (2) ascertain the volume of traffic in pornography; (3) study the effects of obscenity and pornography on the public, and the relationship to crime; and (4) recommend appropriate action.

The Commission recommendations are as follows (Commission on Obscenity and Pornography, 1970, pp. 53–72):
1. That a massive sex education program be launched
2. That open discussion on the issues involved be encouraged

3. That additional factual information be obtained
4. That citizens organize to aid in implementation of the above recommendations.

In addition, the Commission recommended that all existing federal legislation which prohibits or interferes with consensual distribution of "obscene" materials to adults [18 U.S.C., Section 1461, 1462, 1464, and 1465; 19 U.S.C. Section 1305; and 39 U.S.C. Section 3006] be repealed for the following (summarized) reasons:

1. Extensive empirical investigation provides no evidence of harm to the society due to exposure to explicit sexual materials.
2. Such materials are sought by substantial numbers of adults as a source of entertainment and information.
3. Attempts to legislate in this area have not been successful.
4. Public opinion is not supportive of such legislation.
5. The lack of consensus on censorship makes enforcement difficult.
6. Censorship laws generally deal with speech and communication, important rights to the individual.
7. Protecting children is not a justifiable reason for denying adults.
8. The availability of other (nonsexual) materials would not be adversely affected.
9. There is no evidence that exposure to explicit sexual materials has a deleterious effect on individuals or the society.

The Commission did recommend enactment of state and local legislation prohibiting display and unsolicited mailing of sexually explicit materials. The Commission also concluded that because of insufficient evidence demonstrating that pornographic materials are *not* harmful to children, state legislation be enacted to prohibit the commercial distribution or display for sale of such materials to minors.

1. COMMUNITY STANDARDS

Several studies have been done in order to determine community standards concerning pornography. In general they have found that there is no single standard, no uniform criterion, utilized by all communities. In a national survey involving 2,500 adults, Wilson and Abelson (1973) report that 84 percent of the men and 69 percent of the women had encountered material likely to be labeled pornographic by age twenty-one. The median age of first exposure was seventeen years for the men, twenty for the women. The material was usually pictorial for men rather than printed (e.g., 66 percent of the males had seen pictures of intercourse, 60 percent read passages concerning intercourse), but the reverse was true for women. Age, education, and income are related to exposure, as is consumption of books, being politically "liberal," and not attending religious services in the preceding month. Exposure to pornography was also found to be related to early sexual experience and frequency of intercourse, but was not related to satisfaction with one's sex life.

The studies found no consensus relative to pornography. Attitudes varied with availability of pornography and individual characteristics. Although a majority of respondents would allow some materials to be available, a sizable minority (30 percent) would not. Opinion on this point is most dependent upon whether the material is available to adults only but is also related to content (53 percent would allow textual or pictorial depictions of intercourse but only 35–40 percent would allow oral–genital depictions). There was little overall difference in acceptability in terms of the mode (print vs. film) of depiction.

A wide variety of beliefs concerning the effects of pornography are held: more than 65 percent felt it excited people sexually, 50 percent felt it led people to commit sex crimes (and would improve the sex relations of some couples). Slightly over 25 percent felt it can give relief to people who have sexual problems.

Having a positive attitude toward the availability of pornography was found to be correlated with age, education, income, and liberal political views. Wallace (1973) found that more than 80 percent of a student and professional Detroit sample felt that pornographic material should be available to those who want it, while only 35 percent of a church sample felt so.

In a national sample of district attorneys, variable attitudes were again found (Wilson, 1973). The lawmen were most concerned in large urban areas where availability seems to be on the increase. Difficulties of actual enforcement of pornography laws were felt to be the result of a generally apathetic public, a feeling supported by research (Abelson *et al.*, 1971). The district attorneys also felt that distribution of pornography to minors and to adults through the mails was relatively rare.

In a study of attitudes and reactions of college students (White and

Barnett, 1971), it was found that exposure to some form of pornography was common and likely to occur at an early age. The students had little agreement as to what constitutes pornography, but were agreed that it had little appreciable effect (as many found it humorous as found it arousing). Interestingly, they generally felt that depictions of sexual behavior are less pornographic when written than when pictorial.

In a similar study, Roach and Kreisberg (1971) found that 68 percent had encountered pornography in high school and 30 percent in grade school. The students expressed little concern over possible effect, but felt that it should be restricted by age. Females were more likely to feel embarrassment or disgust (52 percent) than males (19 percent).

The typical consumer of erotica (in movie theaters, bookstores, and arcades) was studied, using observation and self-administered questionnaires in San Francisco, and was found to be a white, middle-aged, married, well-educated, high income male who reported an active and varied sex life (50 percent with one partner) and who felt that involvement with explicit sexual material increased his social and sexual interaction (Nawy, 1973).

2. DEMOGRAPHICS

a. Sex. Males are more likely to be aroused by explicit depictions of sexual activity (Kinsey *et al.*, 1953; Loiselle and Mollenauer, 1965) while *fantasy* is more important for female arousal. Mosher (1971) found equal arousal in males and females in response to film but males were more aroused than females were by depiction of oral–genital sex. Females were more likely to regard activities in film as pornographic, disgusting, and offensive.

b. Education. Kinsey *et al.* (1948) found that the use of literature and pictures for stimulus during masturbation was *not* common and tended to occur only with better educated individuals. It was also found that prisoners interviewed were unlikely to be aroused by anything short of actual contact with a sexual partner.

c. Sex Roles. Miller and Swanson (1960) found that males who are insecure in their masculinity are more likely to be disturbed by exposure to a heterosexual erotic stimulus. Zamansky (1956) found that homosexual subjects spent a longer time viewing pictures of (nonnude) men, in preference to pictures of women, than did heterosexual subjects, implying that feelings of discomfort aroused are actively avoided. Goldberg and Milstein (1965) found further support among women uncertain of their sexual identity for the contention that threatening (heterosexual) stimuli are avoided. Mosher and Greenberg (1969) found that subjects with high "sex guilt" were more likely to experience an increase in sex guilt after reading an erotic literary passage. Mosher (1971) found that while people with high sex guilt are likely to be aroused by erotic material, they generally avoid it and are more likely to be offended by it after exposure. It is interesting, however, that married males with high general sex guilt reported more stimulation and less guilt from exposure to erotica than did low sex guilt married males. They also reported less sexual satisfaction in their marriage and greater masturbation, leading Mosher to hypothesize that masturbation and pornography can provide an outlet for high guilt males who have poor sexual relations with their wives.

  d. Children. Little has been done with children, possibly because it is illegal to study them in this context. Gilligan *et al.* (1971) tested the level of moral reasoning (Kohlberg, 1969) used by high school juniors to evaluate various dilemmas. They found that the level of reasoning utilized was generally lower for lower I.Q. and social class and for dilemmas that involved sexual problems. This finding indicates that adolescents have greater difficulty reasoning about sexual matters, but several alternative explanations are possible. It could be due to a general cultural problem rather than maturity or to affective considerations in an area of immediate concern and development. Further research is needed on these questions and the relationship that exposure to pornography has on reasoning ability concerning sexual matters.

  Another important question concerns the relationship between pornography and juvenile delinquency. Police officers, juvenile court judges, and psychiatrists are often convinced that there is a direct causal relationship between the use of pornography and juvenile crime, but such evidence is anecdotal and not authority-free. To gain a better indication, Thornberry and Silverman (1971) selected 436 case records of the neuropsychiatric division of a large urban municipal court. They found absolutely no mention of pornography in any of these records (8 percent involving sex-related offenses). Although the relationship to pornography was not systematically investigated in the compiling of the records, it is clear that it was not a salient issue.

In a study further investigating the Kinsey finding that female sexual arousal is dependent upon whether erotic material elicits feelings of emotional involvement and romantic love, Schiller (1971) compared findings from the Webster School for pregnant junior and senior high school girls (ages 13–18) to findings from a girls' junior college. She found little evidence of hard-core pornography reading in either group, although the college girls had read such works as *Candy, The Harrad Experiment, Fanny Hill,* and *Lady Chatterley's Lover.* Both groups read "romantic" magazines and gave some evidence of being sexually aroused by these. The younger girls, especially, were exposed to a great deal of music—primarily rock and roll—which they found erotically stimulating. The sexual arousal of the adolescent female seems to be strongly tied to the awakening of feelings associated with romance and love.

3. THE STIMULUS

Erotic stimuli include a plethora of material in written, filmed, or live form, ranging from various sexual activities to depictions of partial nudity. In an early study of females (Kinsey *et al.*, 1953), it was found that only 20 percent were aroused by either pictures of nudity or reading erotic stories. Sixty percent, however, reported being aroused by "romantic" stories. A similar percentage of males (Kinsey *et al.*, 1948) reported arousal by printed material.

In one of the few studies involving adolescents, Ramsey (1943) found that eleven- to fourteen-year-olds ranked conversations about sex as most arousing, followed by female nudity and obscene pictures as stimuli to arousal. Goldstein and Kant (1973, p. 15) surmise that direct representations of sexual activity become arousing as sexual experience increases.

In a more recent study of male graduate students (Levitt and Hinesley, 1967), various scenes were ranked in terms of arousal properties. Heterosexual coitus was ranked at the top, partly clad female in the middle, and nude male at the bottom. Unfortunately, printed material was not used and it is not known whether or not a similar ranking would result. The importance of "fantasy" in arousal has been found by Goldstein and Kant (1973), but whether printed material can serve this purpose as well as (or better than) pictorial has not been studied.

4. CONTEXT

The two distinguishing features of printed pornography would seem to be its reliance on imagination and its ability to provide a context. The Supreme Court decisions have emphasized the notion of "redeeming social value." The effect this has on the arousing erotic passage itself is not known. Nor is it known what effect allusion to a total sexual situation has on arousal. But some studies do suggest that reactions to erotica depend on the social context of exposure.

Clark (1952) found that subjects asked to create short stories based on ambiguous TAT (Thematic Apperception Test) cards, after they had viewed nude pictures, produced more sexual content in the stories when in a fraternity beer party situation than they did in the classroom. Furthermore, there were fewer sexual allusions in the classroom situation, following exposure to nudity, than there were when subjects were preexposed to nonsexual pictures. Apparently the classroom inhibited the verbalization of sexual fantasies. Mussen and Scodel (1955) found that there were fewer sexual stories when the experimenter in the classroom situation was older and more formal than when he was a more informal, relaxed graduate student.

Mosher and Greenberg (1969) presented an erotic passage from Calder Willingham's *Eternal Fire* and a scientific passage to college females. They found that females experienced arousal as a consequence of reading the erotic passage. They also found that the presence of even a young, nonthreatening female experimenter increased anxiety and inhibited arousal. They further suggested that arousal is greater in response to romantic or tender passages than to erotica because the latter produce concomitant anxiety which inhibits arousal.

In an interesting application of technique, Galbraith and Mosher (1968) had males distinguished in terms of high and low sex guilt fill out an association test to double-entendre words. They found that sex guilt inhibited sex-oriented responses, even after viewing nude pictures. They found that the experimenter's expression of a permissive attitude toward the nude pictures increased sex-oriented responses only among the low-guilt subjects. They concluded that internalized variables affect responses to erotic stimuli.

In two other studies using erotic stimuli in printed form, it was found that males react with increased skin conductance to erotic passages (Wenger *et al.*, 1968) as do females (Jordan and Butler, 1967). The latter study found that females scoring high on a measure of hysteria had greater response to erotic passages than those scoring low. The implications of this, however, are unclear.

5. AROUSAL

The bulk of the literature concerned with pornography has been concerned with *arousal* (Cairns *et al.*, 1971; Mann, 1971; Zuckerman, 1971). While this may or may not be the operationalism of "thoughts" that the Supreme Court had in mind, the evidence strongly supports the contention that people are aroused by pornography. Arousal is generally indexed through self-reports, but several additional techniques have become prominent, including: pupillary response (Hess and Polt, 1960; Peavler and McLaughlin, 1967), penile plethysmography (Freund, 1957, 1967; McConaghy, 1967), galvanic skin response (Loiselle and Mollenauer, 1965), and the direct measure of arousal (Masters, 1967; Masters and Johnson, 1966).

Each of these techniques has its share of difficulties, including the pervasive problem that arousal is a general physiological reaction including anxiety, guilt, and fear. Nevertheless, together they indicate that both males and females experience arousal when presented with visual or symbolic erotic stimuli. Positive, negative, or ambivalent reactions may occur, depending on the sex and personality of the subject, nature of the stimulus, and the context in which it is presented. The question concerning more long-lasting effects remains unanswered.

Several studies have found reports of slightly increased sexual activity in the 24-hour period following exposure to erotic film (Schmidt and Sigusch, 1970; Schmidt *et al.*, 1969; Sigusch *et al.*, 1970). This supports neither a catharsis hypothesis (where decreases in sexual activity would be expected), nor an instigational hypothesis (where a high proportion of subjects seeking sexual relief would be expected).

In a 12-week longitudinal survey of some 85 voluntary married couples, Mann *et al.* (1973) assessed behavioral and attitudinal consequences of viewing erotic films. They found that couples who viewed erotic films reported significantly more sexual activity on viewing nights and became more tolerant of legal exhibition of such films. No stable changes in sex behavior appeared, and filling out the questionnaire seemed to have more effect on activity than viewing films. No indication of harmful social effects was found.

In an attempt to determine if pornography is "addicting" or if it brings about significant behavioral or attitudinal changes, Howard *et al.* (1973) made pornographic material (movies, photos, novels) available to experimental subjects 90 minutes per day over a 4-week period. They found initial arousal and increase in sexual thoughts but a decrease in interest and arousal with continued exposure. No detrimental changes in behavior or attitudes were found after extensive exposure to pornography.

6. SEX OFFENDERS

One of the traditional fears regarding the effect of pornography is whether it leads to, or is indirectly related to, the commission of sex-oriented crimes. A summary of past research (Kupperstein, 1971), examination of court records (Thornberry and Silverman, 1971), as well as recent research, indicate no direct relationship between exposure to pornography and the commission of sexual offenses. There is evidence of indirect relationships in some cases, however.

A unique opportunity for testing hypotheses concerning the relationship between pornography and sex offenses in a natural situation presented itself with the Danish liberalization of laws concerning pornography. The availability of pornography during recent years has been high in Denmark, further making study of its effect a critical test (Ben-Veniste, 1971). There has been no increase; in fact, there has been a dramatic decrease (from a stable 85 cases of sexual offenses per 100,000 inhabitants to an average of 50 cases (Kutchinsky, 1973). In a careful analysis of alternative explanations (changes in registration procedures, changes in tendencies to report crimes, changes in police tendencies to file complaints), Kutchinsky concluded that in at least one type of offense (child molestation) the decrease represents a real reduction (200 to 87). Child molesters were found to prefer normal heterosexual relationships and children were regarded as poor, but acceptable, substitutes for their unobtainable preferences (findings supported by Gebhard et al., 1965). Kutchinsky further concluded that potential offenders obtained sexual satisfaction through the increased use (and availability) of pornography, probably combined with masturbation.

Davis and Braucht (1973) found a relationship between exposure to pornography and poor character scores, but conclude the relationship is not causal in that first exposure tended to be at age seventeen or later. They also found a relationship between sexual deviance (including such things as voyeurism) and pornography but could not determine causality (panel studies being minimally required). Furthermore, Goldstein and Kant (1973) found that adolescent exposure to erotica was significantly *less* for all nonheterosexual and offender groups than for a community control group. Homosexuals did have greater exposure (preferring nonheterosexual material during adulthood), but the control group had greater exposure during adolescence than did sexual deviants, convicted sex offenders, or heavy adult users of pornography.

In an earlier large-scale interview-study, involving 1,500 institutionalized sex offenders, 888 institutionalized nonsex offenders, and 477 noninstitutionalized controls, it was found that 28 percent of the sex criminals reported strong arousal from viewing pictures of sexual material (Gebhard et al., 1965). But so did 34 percent of the noninstitutionalized controls and 36 percent of the nonsex offenders. Furthermore, 43 percent of the sex offenders reported little arousal, compared to 33 percent of the controls and 38 percent of the nonsex offenders. Nor does possession of pornography differentiate these groups (one-third of the control group and one-half of the nonsex offenders reported having owned it, with sex offenders somewhere in between these percentages). Certain differences among these groups did appear, however. Child molesters and controls reported the highest arousal to erotica, while rapists and homosexuals reported the least arousal to heterosexual stimuli.

C. Summary

Little theoretical explanation has been offered in the research on pornography. One exception to this general shortcoming of the area is the commodity theory proposed by Brock (1971). He suggests that materials are more desirable and more effective to the extent that they are basically unavailable. Little direct support of this has been

offered, but the implication is that censorship laws may have done more harm than good.
1. Erotic stimuli are arousing. The effect is dependent upon the nature of the stimulus and the social context in which it is provided.
2. Effects of, and preferences for, erotica vary among individuals. Anxiety may increase. Females respond more strongly to literary than to visual stimuli, and their responses frequently include negative reactions. Demographics (age, education, income) and personality characteristics (sexual deviances—homosexuality, sex guilt) intervene.
3. There seem to be no direct harmful consequences to society. Early development (moral reasoning, sex identification) intervenes. Rape may be better conceptualized as an offense of violence rather than of sex (given the rapist's tendency to experience little arousal from heterosexual stimuli).

The evidence regarding the effects of pornography suggests that the librarian's long-standing fear of making works dealing with sex in an explicit manner generally available to the public is unfounded (on librarians and censorship, see Busha, 1972; Fiske, 1959; Pope, 1974). Such material is arousing, but for females romantically oriented stories seem to be more so. Although there is an indirect relationship, sometimes negative, between pornography and certain forms of deviancy, there is no indication that this involves the print material found in libraries. When print is cited, and it seldom is in comparison to pictorial material, it is of the sort of erotica found in bookstores. The relationship found in regard to character, reasoning ability, some forms of deviancy and pornography suggests the need for a *positive promotion* of sex education materials, rather than a *negative prohibition* of erotica, *especially at a relatively early age*. This would correspond to the recommendation of the Commission on Obscenity and Pornography cited earlier.

IV. VIOLENCE

A. Introduction

Anyone characterizing modern society in the United States would be compelled at some point to comment upon its violent nature. The

Black liberation movement, student involvement in the Vietnam protest, crime in our cities, all contribute to the strong feeling that this time is more violent than most. Our concern here is not with whether this portrayal is correct, but whether the media contribute to the amount of violence that *does* take place. To investigate this issue, the National Commission on the Causes and Prevention of Violence was created by President Johnson in 1968, and much of the research reported here was summarized by that Commission (Baker and Ball, 1969).

While the Commission was interested in all media, most studies of mass media and violence concern television. Television is the day's dominant medium. It is pervasive and heavily used. News programs have certainly increased awareness of the incidence of violence. Prime-time entertainment programs are noted for the dependence on violent content. There is also evidence that television has largely displaced other media in the portrayal of violence. Schramm *et al.* (1961) reported evidence suggesting television reduced the use of detective and mystery magazines and comic books. All of these remain, but their audience does not match television's. There is also evidence that those who do read such materials are more likely to watch violent content on television.

For these reasons the bulk of the research on violence has centered on television, although the theory discussed in this section is not medium-specific. Whether or not findings based on television or film violence are generalizable to print violence is simply not known. Too little research has been done on the latter to be conclusive in this regard.

B. Definition

Violence has been defined as "the overt expression of force intended to hurt or kill" (Baker and Ball, 1969, p. 314). Although such a definition is useful, it is somewhat misleading. First of all, because of its emphasis on intent, it does not cover acts that would be described as violent because of their activity. Storms are violent but not generally thought of as having intent to harm. The definition does not allow analysis of acts that do have intent to harm. Is yelling at someone more or less violent than stabbing them? One would think it is less violent, but children may be more frightened by it. Is stabbing someone more or less violent than blasting them with a shotgun? Here the harm may be the same, but the activity, and therefore the response elicited, may be different.

Second, the definition does not make it clear that violence is generally taken to be a message content variable. The response to that content, if it includes "intent to harm," is termed *aggression*. Most psychologists studying the phenomenon of aggression tend to regard it as a response to some frustrating act, the classic formulation being provided by Dollard *et al.* (1939). They argued that a "frustration" is "an interference with the occurrence of an instigated goal-response at its proper time in the behavior sequence" (p. 7). This can occur in a variety of ways including: (1) physical barriers; (2) delays between the initiation and completion of the response sequence; (3) omission or reduction of a customary reward; and (4) the eliciting of a response tendency that is incompatible with the ongoing one.

"Aggression" was defined as a "sequence of behavior, the goal-response to which is the injury of the person toward whom it is directed." The behavior need not be overt and may be direct or indirect. To avoid the teleological problems that result if "intent to harm" is the implication of such a definition, Buss (1961) emphasized the reinforcing aspect of aggressive behavior, either in the form of the stimulation provided by the victim suffering injury or being in pain, or from extrinsic rewards, such as money gained from a mugging. Buss defines physical aggression in terms of its consequences: either (1) pain or injury or (2) the overcoming of a barrier or the source of noxious stimuli. Verbal aggression is similarly defined as a "vocal response that delivers noxious stimuli to another organism" (p. 6). Noxious stimuli in this case are such things as rejection and threat, rather than pain or injury.

Berkowitz, in his formulation (1962), avoids an emphasis on intent by arguing that aggression, following a frustrating experience, may not so much be "pushed out" by strong emotions as "pulled out" by appropriate cues in the environment. Much of Berkowitz's research has been concerned with determining the nature and efficacy of the "appropriate cues."

The Berkowitz paradigm utilized in studying the effect of violence is one which varies the presence of violence in two messages presented to subjects, most often in a laboratory situation involving college students. The subjects, having been generally frustrated in some manner, usually in an insult technique, are then presented with the message; and then some subsequent measure of aggression is made, often in terms of a questionnaire tapping aggressive attitudes or in a measurement of some form of actual aggressive behavior (administering shocks, hitting a bobo doll).

C. Availability

The first question that arises concerning the effect of media violence is the extent to which that content is available.

The amount and nature of violent content on television was analyzed for the Commission by George Gerbner (1969). He found that some violence occurred in eight out of every ten prime-time and Saturday morning television programs. Violent episodes were an integral part of the programs in which they occurred, and the average number of violent acts was eleven per program (higher for cartoons). While this analysis was done in 1967, and some concern has been evidenced by the networks since then, it can be safely concluded that violence remains a significant aspect of television content.

The extent of violence in the print media was analyzed for the Commission by Jack Haskins (1969). His evidence was organized around the media involved: newspapers, magazines, paperbacks, hardcover books, and comic books. Violence, as a percent of total news, was found to range from 2 to 34 percent (Otto, 1963). Otto also found 10 percent of the paperback titles on newstands in one city concerned violence-sadism. Blum (1959) found 14 to 19 percent of the subject matter of paperbacks dealt with westerns or mysteries respectively, compared to 1 to 1.5 percent for hardcovers. Barcus (1961) found that 16 percent of Sunday comic strips had a crime-detective theme.

In terms of evidence regarding exposure to such content, there is support for the notion that violent content is interesting to the public. Swanson (1955) summarized 130 newspaper readership studies and found that comparative readership of violent–nonviolent news items was 27 percent–19 percent. Men were somewhat more interested than women. The American Newspaper Publishers Association (1967), in a national survey of interest in a wide variety of topics, found that "high violence" stories ranked 52 (on a scale from 1 = highest to 120 = lowest) in interest, stories with "some violence" ranked 50, and "nonviolent" stories ranked 37. Stories dealing with violent, "impersonal remote" death, however, ranked 27 in terms of interest. Regarding comic books, crime and violence themes have been found to be highly interesting to boys, but not to girls (Butterworth and Thompson, 1951). Violent comic books seem to be equally interesting to "normal" and delinquent-aggressive boys, especially when personality characteristics are held constant (Hoult, 1949; Karp, 1954).

There is evidence, then, that violence is a major component of print media content, although the sheer volume makes estimation in this category difficult. Second, violent content seems to be interesting to audiences. There is also evidence that certain subsegments of the population are especially interested in violent content. Israel *et al.* (1971) found that 12 percent of the men and 11 percent of the women watched 8½ hours of "most violent" programs during a 2-week period, constituting one-third of the audience of these programs. Studies done under the sponsorship of the Surgeon General's scientific "Advisory Committee for Television and Social Behavior" have found that those most likely to watch violent fare on television are less educated, poor, and more likely to have personal experience with aggressive behavior (Comstock and Rubinstein, 1971, Vol. 3).

In a summary of the "approvers" of high-level (beating, knifing, shooting) and low-level (spanking, slapping face) violence, Baker and Ball (1969, pp. 351-354) reported that the use of violence is never unconditionally approved by a majority of adults or teenagers (more than 75 percent could imagine situations in which they would approve of a policeman shooting an adult male citizen). The most common groups of high approvers of low-level violence are (1) males, (2) eighteen to thirty-five years of age, (3) residing in cities, and (4) without a college education. Among teenagers living in metropolitan areas, a greater proportion of Blacks than non-Blacks were found to approve of low-level violence. These demographic characteristics also tend to describe the people most likely to be high approvers of a high level of violence.

D. Effects

The research concerned with violent media content can be divided into three areas: (1) studies showing an increase in aggressive behavior following exposure to violent content; (2) studies showing a decrease in aggressive behavior following exposure to violent content (catharsis); and (3) studies dealing specifically with children, either in terms of aggressive behavior or in terms of effects on "values." Most, but not all, of the research was done in a laboratory setting utilizing some form of film as the medium of violent content. As a result, generalizations to real life situations and to the effects of print must remain tentative.

1. AGGRESSION

Some of the most interesting research showing an increase in aggression, following exposure to violence, has been done by Leonard Berkowitz at the University of Wisconsin. In the typical Berkowitz experiment, subjects are first separated into two groups: insult and noninsult. This insult factor serves as the frustration manipulation. The emotional state resulting from the frustration is termed "anger" and this is said to create a proclivity for an aggressive act. Subjects then view either a violent (often a scene from a boxing movie, *The Champion,* in which one of the fighters, Kirk Douglas, is severely beaten) or a nonviolent film (a foot race). The efficacy of various cues relating the film to the frustration act or reducing inhibitions is then tested. The dependent variable is some measure of aggression and most often consists of the number of shocks the subject believes he is administering to the frustrating agent through the use of an aggression machine. This research tends to show that: (1) aggression can occur when subjects have not been angered, but is more likely when they have been angered; (2) aggression is more likely when the depictions of violence are "justified" rather than "nonjustified"; and (3) certain cues in the violent content can relate that content to the aggressive situation or disinhibit tendencies to aggress.

Walters and associates (Walters and Thomas, 1963; Walters *et al.*, 1962) found that the observation of violence increases the viewer's subsequent aggressiveness in the absence of any prior frustration or "aggression arousal treatment." A number of studies, however, have found that when subjects have been insulted and then exposed to film violence, they display more aggression than do subjects who have not been attacked (Berkowitz, 1965; Berkowitz and Rawlings,

1963; Berkowitz *et al.*, 1963; Geen, 1968, Geen and Berkowitz, 1966, 1967). These studies support the conclusion that insult or frustration produces a general state of arousal which increases the likelihood of aggression upon viewing violence (Berkowitz, 1968). In an interesting study by Tannenbaum (1971), it was also found that humor can increase arousal, which in turn can increase subsequent aggression to observed violence. The implications of this finding become more serious when the arousing characteristics of erotic stimuli are remembered.

Many of these same studies have also found that aggressive responses were more likely when the violence presented was portrayed as justified (the victim is portrayed as well deserving of the violent treatment) rather than unjustified (the victim is an admirable character suffering from unfortunate circumstances). A study by Hoyt (1967) investigated the consequences of justification more extensively. In one condition, justification was based on a revenge motive where the victor in the film was portrayed as avenging an unfair beating that was previously received. In the second condition, justification was based on a "self-defense" motive where the victor was portrayed as being in a "kill or be killed" situation. In the third condition, both motives were presented, and in a final condition no justification was offered.

Least aggression, in terms of the number and duration of shocks administered, was found in the no justification condition. Most aggression was found in the condition where vengeance was provided as the motive, a situation very similar to the circumstances of the subjects since they had been unfairly abused by a confederate of the experimenter in the frustration manipulation. The significance of providing justification as a means of disinhibiting tendencies to aggress is that media portrayals of violence often depict the hero's use of violence as a means of punishing the "bad guys." Depictions of "crime does not pay" may create the very conditions most conducive to eliciting aggressive responses among the audience.

Cues provided in the violent content may also facilitate aggressive responses. Berkowitz (1965) has argued that aggressive tendencies may not become overt behaviors unless appropriate aggression-evoking cues are present in the environment that have some association with the observed violence. In this study, the confederate who initially insulted the subjects was introduced as either a college boxer or a speech major. After viewing the boxing film, when subjects were given the opportunity to administer shocks to the confederate, they did so to a greater extent when the confederate had been introduced as a boxing major. Berkowitz and Geen (1966) found similar results when the confederate was introduced as having the same *name* as the victor in the boxing film. Further research along this line found that most aggression took place when the confederate had the same name as the boxing victim rather than the boxing victor (Geen and Berkowitz, 1966). An additional study found similar results even when the name-mediated association took place *after* the showing of the film (Berkowitz and Geen, 1967).

2. CATHARSIS

The concept of catharsis can be traced to the early analysis of drama where it was argued, principally by Aristotle, that viewing tragedy serves to discharge one's emotions. Breuer and Freud (1957) introduced the term in their study of hysteria to refer to the tension-reducing consequences of emotional expression. Symptoms of hysteria would disappear if, under hypnosis (and later in free association technique), the patient recovered the traumatic memory of a past difficulty and described the disturbing event in detail.

There are two basic formulations of the catharsis hypothesis. The first argues that reading violent material can vicariously serve to reduce the instigated drive for aggression in the receiver. The Berkowitz research tests (and refutes) this form of the hypothesis.

The second formulation argues that the expression of aggression can serve to mitigate the drive for further aggression. This expression of aggression can take place either in linguistic (Breuer and Freud, 1957) or in physical (Dollard *et al.*, 1939) form and supposedly may be direct or indirect (Buss, 1961). It is important to note that Berkowitz has not generally tested for aggression after the expression of aggression. In one study that did have a postaggression measure, however, it was found that angered subjects who gave the most shocks later expressed significantly more favorable judgments of the frustrator's fairness (Berkowitz and Holmes, 1960). This finding supported the earlier research of Pepitone and Reichling (1955).

Much of the research purporting to support the catharsis notion was tested for it in the second sense of the formulation. Thibaut and Coules (1952, p. 773) found that "the thwarting of communication back to the instigator immediately after instigation increases the level of hostility." Rosenbaum and de Charms (1960) found that college men who were low in self-esteem expressed less resentment toward a peer-frustrator after they heard someone else attack him, especially when they themselves had been given the opportunity to communicate back to the instigator. These studies indicate that a reduction in aggressive tendencies can occur if communication toward the source of the original frustration can take place or if some punishment toward that source is witnessed.

This later finding leads to the possibility that while observation of an aggressive attack (violent content) may not reduce aggressive tendencies, catharsis may result if the *results* of an aggressive attack (the suffering of the victim) is emphasized. In a study by Bramel *et al.* (1968), it was found that subjects' aggressiveness was reduced by observing the insulting experimenter suffer. In a study by Haney (1971), however, which employed written rather than film messages, subjects were asked either to read a message attacking the source of frustration or attacking another person, or to write such messages. In general the results support an increased aggression hypothesis rather than a catharsis hypothesis.

Three additional studies have found support for a catharsis hypothesis (Feshbach, 1955, 1961; Feshbach and Singer, 1971). Berkowitz and Rawlings (1963), however, argued that Feshbach's subjects may have been inhibited. (They were told that evaluations of the frustrator would be reviewed by that person's departmental chairman.) Hartmann (1969) also found contradictory results. In that study, adolescent delinquents who saw either of two versions of a fight scene were more aggressive (as measured by intensity and duration of administered shocks) than were those who did not observe the scene. On the other hand, Feshbach employed evaluative questionnaires whereas the increased aggression studies employed administration of shocks (the wires are not actually attached to the frustrator). It may be that the latter condition makes it easier to aggress, simply because there is an expectation and situation established to aggress. This would not account for differential amounts of aggression resulting from the type of message content viewed, however.

Feshbach and Singer (1971) conducted a 6-week longitudinal study of preparatory school boys in California and New York. Boys were randomly assigned to watch either aggressive or nonaggressive television programs during evening and weekend hours. Personality tests and attitude scales were given at the beginning and end of the 6 weeks. Daily behavior forms were also completed for each boy. No evidence was provided by this study to support the hypothesis that viewing violent content increases aggressive behaviors or attitudes. The study did find that exposure to violent content serves to control or reduce aggressive behavior in preadolescent boys with aggressive tendencies and low socioeconomic backgrounds.

In summary, the research has generally found an increase in aggression when subjects have been frustrated in some manner and have viewed a violent message. This tendency is enhanced when there are cues relating the aggressive situation to the violent content and when the violence has been presented as justified. Some research has found little increase or a decrease in aggressive responses upon viewing violent content, but the reasons for this, whether aggressive responses were inhibited, for example, are still unclear. On the other hand, generalizations from the laboratory without additional support from field studies must remain tentative. Generalizations to the print media must likewise remain tentative.

3. CHILDREN

A considerable body of research has revealed that violent content may affect audiences in a number of ways: (1) it may reduce inhibitions against behaving in an aggressive manner; (2) attitudes and values may be affected; (3) novel responses and forms of aggression may be learned; and (4) it may stimulate or instigate aggressive behaviors that have already been learned. This section will focus on the effects of violent content on children.

a. Attitudes and Values. It is conceivable that heavy doses of violent content can lead to a greater acceptance of aggressive behaviors. Although a direct test of this possibility is most difficult, there is a great deal of evidence (considered throughout this chapter) that exposure to media content is related to various attitudes and values held by audience members and that such attitudes and values can be affected by such exposure.

Bandura and Menlove (1968) for example, found that children in a nursery school who were afraid of dogs became less so after viewing another child making progressively bolder advances toward a dog. Schramm et al. (1961), in a study of high-and-low users of print and television among tenth graders, found that those high in exposure to print (and low in exposure to television) were more "reality-oriented" and more likely to favor deferred gratifications. The importance of print, as in the pornography area, may be in terms of teaching such attitudes and values rather than in terms of teaching aggressive (or sexual) behaviors per se. Lovibond (1967) found that eighth-grade boys in Australia were more likely to have positive attitudes toward force and violence when there was high exposure to comic books, cinema, and television.

b. Response Acquisition. There is evidence that children can learn aggressive behaviors from violent content. It should be remembered, however, that the research carried out in this area is conducted in a somewhat unusual set of circumstances. Children are frustrated just prior to exposure. They are tested for *aggression* in a situation highly similar to the one in which they see a model perform. Furthermore, they are tested right after exposure.

An extensive program of research, conducted by Albert Bandura and associates at Stanford, has found that children will imitate aggressive responses observed in adults, live or filmed, or in cartoons (Bandura, 1965; Bandura and Huston, 1961; Bandura et al., 1961, 1963a,b; Lovass, 1961; Mussen and Rutherford, 1961). Most often the observed behavior is aggressive play exhibited toward a bobo doll. Other studies have found that observed violent behaviors can be retained up to 8 months (Hicks, 1965, 1968) and that frustrated children are more likely to retain violent material (Maccoby et al., 1955, 1956).

c. Intervening Variables. Several factors affect the acquisition of aggressive behaviors. Much of the research described in the preceding has indicated that children who have been frustrated are more likely to aggress after viewing violent content. The *similarity* of the depiction of violence to the aggressive situations also makes a difference (Lovass, 1961; Meyerson, 1966; Siegel, 1956). The *social context* of the viewing situation also affects likelihood of aggressive responses. Permissive attitudes expressed by the experimenter can increase aggression (Hicks, 1968), while verbal prohibitions can inhibit aggression (De Rath, 1963). *Reinforcement* of either the model in the film or the subject also makes a difference. When models are reinforced for their violent behavior, there is more subsequent aggression than when they are punished (Bandura and Walters, 1963). Providing incentives (food and trinkets) to the subjects increases aggressive responses (Bandura, 1965) and retention of violent behaviors (Hicks, 1965).

E. Summary

A great deal of evidence has accumulated which indicates that children and adults respond aggressively after exposure to violent media content. This response is greater when subjects have been frustrated, are in a permissive situation where aggression can be easily exhibited, have cues provided in the violent content relevant to the aggressive situation, had observed the victor reinforced for his behavior, or have had the violent behavior portrayed as justified. Since the great majority of this research utilized the film medium, generalizations to print are extremely hazardous. The effects of reading materials depicting violence are simply not known. Books which portray violence in the manner previously described may have similar effects. Before a statement like this can be considered definitive, however, a great deal of research in this medium needs to be done.

V. READING, ATTITUDE FORMATION AND CHANGE, AND PREJUDICE

A. Introduction

The preceding sections have been principally concerned with behavior: sexual and aggressive. This section concerns attitudes, especially those relating to prejudice.

Curiously, the research literature in this area clearly suggests that attitudes do *not* predict behavioral acts of discrimination (Ehrlich, 1973; Hartmann and Husband, 1974). Many prejudiced people do not practice discrimination; many nonprejudiced people do. Nevertheless, librarians, journalists, educators, and others who serve as information gatekeepers in our society are constantly pressured by various groups demanding suppression of material that presents views counter to conventional or normative attitudes, beliefs, and values.

The gatekeepers' responses to such demands for censorship frequently lead to dilemmas and paradoxes. One philosophical response has come in the libertarian notion that no view should be suppressed. Those who are of a more empirical bent might assure would-be censors that research findings indicate that reading only reinforces attitudes previously instilled by socialization agents such as the family. Yet both of these responses are disquieting to information professionals who like to think that their decisions effect desirable social change and to a concerned public convinced of the "power of print" to change attitudes.

The questions and problems involved in attitude formation and change have been subjected to intensive analysis by social scientists. The focus of their work, of course, varies with the particular discipline of the investigator. Whatever the field, most scholars would agree that voluntary reading plays a relatively minor role unidimensionally in the process. It is thus easy to discount the importance of the print media as a force in shaping or altering people's stereotypes. Yet, there is no doubt that people's attitudes *do* change; that some people have undergone radical conversions as a result of reading. Even if that were never the case, information gatekeepers must be alert to ways in which the printed word supports and reinforces a culture's prejudices. A balanced perspective somewhere between the "no effect" and the "hypodermic effect" theories is needed. Communication research promises to provide this perspective.

B. Principal Research Traditions

The area of communication theory and research most relevant to the issues of this section is that which comes under the rubric of "persuasion." Much of what we know of this area is derived from research on persuasive oratory. Since this research does not involve written messages, it is not directly relevant to our concerns here. However, there remains a substantial amount of work which does bear on our interests. Three research traditions seem particularly relevant:

1. The work of Carl Hovland and the Yale Communication and Attitude Change Projects
2. The "inoculation theory" formulated by William McGuire
3. Cognitive consistency theories—especially the cognitive dissonance theory developed by Leon Festinger.

1. HOVLAND'S RESEARCH

Carl Hovland must be considered one of the most influential of the "founding fathers" of communication research in the United States (Schramm, 1963). Hovland was a psychologist who developed an interest in the communication process while serving as an army research consultant during World War II. His major work involved identifying the kinds of arguments most effective for use in military training and orientation programs. He continued this research at Yale, producing a series of books that combined to form a basic component of communication research in America (Hovland, 1957; Hovland et al., 1949, 1953).

a. Source Variables. One of Hovland's principal contributions was his recognition that the "source," as well as the "message," was an important communication variable. One portion of his work dealt with the effects of source credibility, or source expertise, upon the effectiveness of a message. His initial studies verified the fact that sources with "high credibility" (usually defined in most studies as sources whose credentials demonstrate expertise) are most effective (Hovland and Weiss, 1951). A great deal of effort has gone into further refinements of this rather simple and intuitive notion. In the main, sources of high expertise and trustworthiness prove more persuasive, but not in a direct, linear manner (Mortensen, 1972). Attitude change is more apt to occur if sources are perceived as sharing the value system adhered to by the reader (Jones and Gerard, 1967).

It is important to note that attitude change is not the only response to a persuasive, belief-discrepant message. Sears (1969) listed three possibilities. Only one involved opinion change. The other two involved changing attitudes about the *source* rather than the *topic,* or distorting the source's position. Opinion change is most apt to occur when the reader has a "weak" opinion about the topic *and* a favorable perception of the source. Distortion seems most likely when feelings about both topic and source are strong.

One finding, emerging from Hovland's initial work, was a concept that could prove very important to librarians. He labeled it the "sleeper effect." Hovland found that the impact of source credibility tended to be short-lived: the arguments of the expert have a high initial impact that dissipates over time. In the case of the nonexpert, Hovland suggested that people will *remember* the arguments and *forget* the source. However, a cautionary note should be sounded. It is important to remember that these were laboratory findings: the messages and arguments used were identical, a source—message connection not apt to be found in nonexperimental material. Furthermore, recent studies have questioned the viability of the entire concept (Capon and Hulbert, 1973; Gillig and Greenwald, 1974).

b. Message Variables. Much of Hovland's work concerned the effects of different message strategies on different types of individuals. To summarize a very broad and multifaceted area, Hovland demonstrated that messages presenting only one side of an argument were more effective with less educated people, whereas messages that at least mentioned arguments on the other side were more effective with better educated people. That effect will be moderated by such things as the strength of initial attitudes, the novelty of the arguments, and the awareness on the part of readers or listeners that another side to the controversy does indeed exist.

Another of Hovland's works, *The Order of Presentation in Persuasion* (Hovland, 1957), attacked the problem of whether arguments presented first (primary) or last (recency) are more effective. This area of research has proven to be very contradictory and inconclusive. Rosnow and Robinson (1967) have summarized developments in this area and note that recent work yields no "laws," but rather an "assortment of miscellaneous variables."

A third message area of considerable interest concerns the effects of "fear-arousing appeals" in messages. Initial research indicated that moderate fear-arousing appeals are more influential than high fear-arousing signals (Janis and Feshbach, 1953; Janis and Terwilliger, 1962). The latter seem to stimulate such intense reactions that the response seems to be: "I can't do much about it anyway, so why try." Subsequent research has identified a variety of intervening variables and conditions that qualify that general conclusion (Mortenson, 1972).

2. INOCULATION THEORY

In one of his last works, Hovland (1959) made passing reference to a concept that since has assumed great importance in persuasion research. This is the concept of "forewarning" an audience that a propaganda-style message is coming up. Limited evidence supports the intuitive conclusion that such an initial statement does tend to make a propaganda message less persuasive.

This point should raise some ethical or policy considerations in the minds of librarians. The idea of "good" persuasion (i.e., education) versus "bad" persuasion (i.e., propaganda) is deeply rooted in value considerations. Such issues in regard to persuasion have been discussed by McGuire (1964) and more extensively by Zimbardo (1972). The effect of forewarning, however, might suggest that librarians (and other gatekeepers) should reconsider some form of labeling of books that attempts to persuade readers to accept a particular point of view. Newspapers, for instance, frequently use such labels on editorials or other deliberately polemic pieces.

Further developments of the forewarning concept bear upon another policy consideration that librarians must often face—the temptation to screen children's literature in order to protect young minds from unpopular and controversial topics. However, anyone considering such action should be aware of an intriguing theory developed by William McGuire called the "inoculation theory" (McGuire, 1961a,b, 1962, 1973; McGuire and Papageorgis, 1961). This theory was formulated in the early 1960's, but has only recently begun to lead to new directions in persuasion research (Roberts and Maccoby, 1973).

The label derives from an analogy to medical inoculations. Just as a "small dose" of some contagious disease serves to build up the body's defenses against subsequent exposure to more powerful strains, so, the theory goes, exposing people to "weak" arguments about a given position may make them immune to stronger attacks encountered later. Not so coincidentally, most of the initial research settings used medical topics and cultural truisms as message topics: "Everybody knows that tooth brushing (or yearly chest X-rays) are good ideas," for instance. McGuire's research indicated that belief in such cultural truisms is susceptible to direct attack. He also found that providing people with supportive counterarguments to use in such situations helps resistance. Further, he indicated that exposing people first to mild arguments attacking the truism works even better as a means of building resistance.

The cornerstone of the theory is the notion of "counterarguing." Resistance to persuasion is built up by giving people practice in generating their own arguments to refute propaganda appeals. Early exposure to controversy facilitates such practice. The theory holds that cultural truisms are susceptible precisely because people have never encountered situations where their beliefs were criticized. Thus they have no counterarguing defenses.

3. COGNITIVE CONSISTENCY THEORIES

Cognitive consistency is a generic label given to a variety of different formulations and theories (Abelson *et al.*, 1968). The points of difference between them need not concern us unduly here. They all share the assumption that individuals attempt to keep their cognitions—their thoughts, beliefs, attitudes—in "balance" with one another. When individuals receive a communication indicating that two of their cognitions are inconsistent with one another, then they will try to do something to restore the balance. Various theories suggest different modes of resolution. The most obvious weakness of them all is that, with one exception, only vague and imprecise predictions are available about the modes of resolution individuals will adopt: i.e., whether or not individuals are likely to discard or alter one of the cognitions, distort the message, distort the source, etc. The sole exception is the "Congruity Theory" (Osgood and Tannenbaum, 1955), which suggests that *both* of the inconsistent cognitions will change. While the general aspects of the theory have been supported, the precise, numerical predictions have not held up very well under empirical test.

The aspect of the consistency theories most relevant to our topic— attitude change and prejudice—derives from its focus on information seeking and information processing. The theory of cognitive dissonance (Festinger, 1964), for instance, has as a key component the concept of "selective exposure to information." It suggests that individuals will seek out information that supports their views and decisions and avoid information that does not. The "seeking" hypothesis has been much easier to test than the "avoidance" prediction (Chaffee *et al.*, 1969).

The pervasiveness of tendencies toward cognitive consistency and selective exposure is a subject of some considerable debate. Despite the complex and controversial nature of work in this area, librarians would be well advised to follow developments, since the tolerance for inconsistency seems to be a fundamental part of maintaining prejudice, and the information behaviors associated with cognitive consistency have much bearing on the potential of reading to overcome prejudice.

C. Reading and Racism

1. DEFINITIONS

As noted earlier, social scientists from many different academic disciplines have attacked the problem of racial prejudice in their research. The many definitions of racism reflect the interdisciplinary nature of the work. Most of the definitions, however, involve some statement about negative or hostile "attitudes" (however that concept is defined) toward an ethnic group. There is generally a corollary statement to the effect that prejudiced people also inappropriately generalize or stereotype or categorize individuals as possessing perceived characteristics of that group.

The disciplinary differences go beyond mere academic fencing over definitions. They imply differing assumptions about the roots of the problem and thus suggest different solutions. To simplify somewhat, psychologists find racism in individuals; sociologists find it in society. Subsequently, different statements can be made about the effects of print media within the context of these two major research traditions.

Harding and his associates (1969) argued that most definitions are more or less securely attached to one of three norms. One is a rather vague "norm of human-heartedness." Another is a norm of justice, which seems to involve *acts* of discrimination more than prejudiced attitudes. The third is the norm of rationality and is most closely related to our interest in reading. As Harding (Harding *et al.*, 1969, p.

5) describes it, "this norm enjoins a persistent attempt to secure accurate information, to correct misinformation, to make appropriate differentiations and qualifications, to be logical in deduction and cautious in inference. Prejudice in the sense of deviation from the norm of rationality may occur in the form of hasty judgment or prejudgment, overgeneralization, thinking in stereotypes, refusal to modify an opinion in the face of new evidence, and refusal to admit or take account of individual differences." On the basis of this viewpoint, one must conclude that reading is apt to have little effect on reducing prejudice.

2. PREJUDICE AND INFORMATION PROCESSING

In most psychological studies, the prejudiced individual is viewed as one having a characteristically closed or rigid cognitive style. Much of the modern work stems from an interest in the concepts of "authoritarianism" or "ethnocentrism" (Adorno *et al.*, 1950) or "dogmatism" (Rokeach, 1960). This area is also characterized by controversy. However, the research to date does indicate that closed-mindedness is at least one component of prejudice. Closed-minded people appear to have such rigid belief systems that they cannot easily assimilate new or discrepant information. Thus "reading" is not likely to change any such minds.

We cannot even be sure that reading is likely to influence the attitudes of "open-minded" people. As Donohew and Palmgreen (1971a, b) have shown, "open-minded" people also show marked tendencies toward cognitive consistency. And strict application of the consistency theories would seem to make it evident that, as Zimbardo (1972) has noted, information transfer per se is probably the least effective way of changing attitudes and behaviors.

a. Selective Exposure. One of the things that makes reading such an unlikely source of attitude change is the tendency toward selective exposure mentioned earlier. Various reviews of this research have come to different conclusions about how extensive a role this process plays in communication (Atkin, 1973). But there seems to be little doubt that it does occur for some people. Thus, many prejudiced (and nonprejudiced) people will simply not read material that might, if they attended to it, indicate that they were misinformed.

b. Selective Perception. Aside from selective exposure, the research literature is replete with studies that indicate tendencies to misperceive the meaning of even "objectively obvious" messages, once attended to.

One of the most famous examples is the series of "Mr. Bigot" studies carried out by Cooper and Jahoda (1947). In these studies, racially prejudiced individuals were shown cartoons intended to lampoon bigotry. Asked to interpret the cartoons, subjects in the study replied in terms that ignored the implicit satire and consistently distorted the meaning to support their own biases. That this phenomenon is still pervasive is illustrated in a recent study of our current "Mr. Bigot"—Archie Bunker. Vidmar and Rokeach (1974) found that modern viewers use the same distortion techniques identified some twenty years ago by Cooper and Jahoda. Indeed, the authors of this study argue that "All in the Family" is reinforcing prejudice rather than diminishing bigotry.

Selective distortion also negates attempts to have highly credible sources present an antiprejudice message. Sherif's work on latitudes of acceptance and rejection demonstrates that people systematically distort a source's position by overestimating agreement with a highly valued source (Hovland, 1957; Sherif *et al.*, 1965). Recent work has introduced some limiting conditions for this general effect (Burgoon and Miller, 1974; Granberg and Steele, 1974; Sears, 1969).

The consistency theories also take into account those instances where people will simply refuse to believe a communication. Osgood and Tannenbaum (1955), for instance, found an "incredulity" effect in their studies. If a favorable source were linked with an unfavorable topic, many people would simply refuse to believe the source actually said or wrote or otherwise endorsed a position with which they strongly disagreed.

As might be expected, racial prejudice influences judgments of source credibility. Rokeach and Mezei (1966) reported that shared beliefs may mitigate initial judgments of sources based on race alone. On the other hand, Aronson and Golden (1962) found racially prejudiced sixth graders discounting the views of a Black person about the importance of studying arithmetic, even when the person was presented as an M.I.T. engineering graduate. Aronson and Golden labeled this reaction as irrational. Jones and Gerard (1967) argued that it may have been due to a perceived lack of shared beliefs.

c. Selective Retention. Even assuming that belief-discrepant messages do get through initial defenses of selective exposure and perception, strongly held prejudices are still going to be difficult to shake through information transfer alone. There is still the tactic of "selective retention" so often documented in the research literature. People may "read" and may "learn," but they also tend to "remember" very selectively.

Taft (1954) had young Black and white male juvenile delinquents read a passage about a Black baseball player. The passage contained both positive and negative comments. The Blacks remembered more of the positive items, especially after a 3-day period. Peak and Morrison (1958) found that college students recalled new information supporting their position on desegregation much more readily than contradictory information.

While cognitive dissonance research often failed to support the selective exposure hypothesis, researchers introduced the concept of utility as an intervening variable. That is, if material has some other usefulness or relevance for people, it overrides pressures toward selective exposure. Two studies by Jones (cited in Jones and Gerard, 1967), using college students as examples, indicate that selective retention, however, is more formidable. In the first, one group of students read passages about integration and segregation. These students were better able to remember statements supporting their own positions. Another group of students were told that they were going to have to produce arguments for integration (a utility manipulation). In this case, students opposed to integration actually learned *more* of the pro-integration statements. The second study used different students but similar statements and contributed an important clarification to the general finding. The students did learn useful arguments. But they remembered the "strong" arguments that supported their own position and "weak" arguments that supported the opposing view.

3. READING AND THE REINFORCEMENT OF PREJUDICE

From the preceding section, information gatekeepers can find little support for a view that they, by themselves, can have any great impact on changing racial prejudices. But even if it is difficult to stimulate beneficial change, librarians and other gatekeepers *should* worry about whether or not they are contributing to the reinforcement of prejudice.

a. Media Content Analysis. We began this section by citing two recent works on racial prejudice: Ehrlich's *The Social Psychology of Prejudice* (1973) and Hartmann and Husband's *Racism and the Mass Media* (1974). Although the two differ considerably in focus, both agree that the mass media, including the print media, contribute to the maintenance of ethnic stereotyping. They argue that serious literature, magazines, newspapers, film, and television all serve to reinforce, through their content and presentation, whatever racial stereotypes are current in the culture. There is no empirical contention that the media cause such stereotypes. Indeed, most social scientists agree that such prejudices are generally formed in the family unit.

As we noted in the introduction, communication effects are notoriously difficult to demonstrate in short-range field studies. It should be obvious, however, that family units do not operate in social and informational isolation, and as social scientists refine their concepts and methods, empirical effects may yet be demonstrated. In the meantime, evidence gleaned from studies on attitude formation and change would suggest that information gatekeepers must be alert to the racial stereotypes their selections might be reinforcing.

Of special importance is the pervasiveness of stereotypical presentations. No one message or book may be influential, but a constant barrage may very well play an important supportive role. As Weiss (1969, p. 102) noted: "It has often been averred that a movie, a play, a television program, or a novel which portrays a member of a minority group unfavorably is likely to have an adverse effect on people's attitudes toward that group. On empirical and theoretical grounds, that is unlikely to occur with any great magnitude unless the same kind of potrayal is consistently and uniformly presented and personal, social, and attitudinal factors are neutral or sympathetic to the viewpoint presented."

Change may be occurring, but recent content-analysis studies indicate that change is slow and in many respects represents tokenism. They further indicate that, while minority groups are appearing more frequently in the media, the dominant characters are still white Anglo-Saxons. It is also easy to overestimate the degree of change unless the analysis is quantified. In their studies of Blacks in television commercials, Greenberg and Hanneman (1970) found that whites perceived an even greater increase in Black exposure than was, in actual fact, the case.

b. Children's Literature. By far most of the content analysis of racial portrayals has been concerned with children's books. The results are fairly conclusive and well known. When Blacks are presented, they are generally supportive rather than principal characters, and they still tend to exhibit "white" values and characteristics unless they are, as is most common, presented as "foreign."

The emphasis on children's literature is probably well placed. For one thing, much of the research deals with school textbooks, which the children are (in a sense) forced to read. For another, we generally feel, and the research bears this feeling out, that children's racial prejudices are not so rigid that they are impervious to change through the acquisition of new information. Of course children are not free of prejudice, and considerable research has shown "that children assimilate national and ethnic stereotypes—particularly their evaluative aspects—at a surprisingly early age" (Hartmann and Husband, 1974, p. 58). In fact these stereotypes begin to show up at nursery school age before the child has even learned to read. This does not, of course, mean that reading cannot play a part in the process. Children are read to before they learn to read for themselves. But the voluminous research does indicate that children's racial prejudices do grow more pronounced as they grow older. As Allport put it in his classic *The Nature of Prejudice* (1958, p. 282) "A bigoted personality may be well under way by the age of six, but by no means fully fashioned."

Some studies on the effects of special school courses and educational programs have reported reduction in racial prejudice. For instance, Hayes and Conklin (1953) reported that listening to and role playing Black experiences resulted in significant attitude changes for white eighth graders. However, it is impossible to separate "reading effects" from other variables in such studies. Other research would tend to indicate it is the role playing that is the most important. Nor have there been any longitudinal studies on the permanence of the change. Ehrlich (1973) contends that attitudes can be changed easily by convincing written arguments, but that maintaining that change is much more difficult. Bibliotherapeutic approaches have also been reported to be effective in changing some racial attitudes. That area will be covered in a later section of this chapter.

D. Sexism and Reading

1. ANALOGY TO RACISM

Feminists often equate sexism with racism, a contention rejected by others who argue that the seriousness of the problems is not comparable. There are, however, some important parallels between the two.

a. Theoretical Similarities. One important similarity is the central feature that "inferiority" plays in prejudice. Hartmann and Husband (1974, p. 36) noted that there may be prejudice against many ethnic or religious groups that contain elements of "ridicule, contempt, resentment, fear and even hatred." Such prejudices, however, stem from the fact that such groups are "different." Hartmann and Husband argue that the prejudice against Blacks (and to a certain extent anti-Semitism) is rooted in concepts of biological inferiority and, in addition, "serves the social function of maintaining one group in a position of subordination to another." Ethnic and religious prejudices against other groups do not share both of these features. The prejudice against women does.

Few of the numerous books on prejudice concern themselves with antifeminism. One exception is Allport (1958), who paid passing attention to male/female attitudes as an example of "in-group/out-group" relationships. Commenting on a passage by Lord Chesterfield, Allport wrote: "Such antifeminism reflects the two basic ingredients of prejudice—denigration and gross overgeneralization, ... What is instructive about this antifeminism is the fact that it implies security and contentment with one's own sex-membership. To Chesterfield the cleavage between male and female was a cleavage between accepted in-group and rejected out-group. But for many people, the war of the sexes seems totally unreal. They do not find in it a ground for prejudice" (p. 32).

b. Social Similarities. In most explications of prejudice, attitudes and discrimination against women clearly fit within the conceptual framework. Whether or not the degree of exploitation and injustice that results makes it a serious social problem seems to be more a value question than a scientific one. But another similarity can be seen in the similar tactics and social pressures and establishment responses used by the civil rights movement against racism in the 1960's and the women's movement in the 1970's. The similarity also holds when we look at the research literature on sexual prejudice. As Brown (1974) notes: "The importance of sex roles as a relevant social variable has surfaced recently due to the same sorts of pressures that moved racial differences to a high-priority position in the social sciences some years ago." One consequence of this new concern is that communication effects studies have not been applied to this area. Most of the current writing is still of the polemic nature.

2. CONTENT ANALYSIS

The bulk of the communication research in this area has focused on identifying and documenting sex discrimination through content analysis of the various media. Several of these studies are reprinted in a reader entitled *Sexism and Youth* edited by Gersoni-Stavin (1974). Women are generally portrayed as married, usually housewives, and weak and emotional. Girls are portrayed as passive, weak, and concerned with being pretty.

Susan Jacoby, in an article on efforts to change the portrayal of females in textbooks, quotes one anonymous publisher for a rather insightful observation: "Our sins in regard to Blacks were sins of omission but the sins against women are sins of commission. The Blacks just weren't in the texts. Women are there, but their image is one-sided" (Jacoby, 1973, p. 63). Larrick (1965) reported that only 6.7 percent of the children's books published between 1962 and 1964 contained one or more Blacks, and less than 1 percent treated American Negroes in modern society. Females get more attention as characters in children's books, but are still significantly underrepresented. Analyzing picture books, for instance, Weitzman *et al.* (1972) found a ratio of roughly 11 to 1 male to female appearances in pictures. They also found a 3 to 1 ratio of male to female characters in the Newberry Award books since 1922. The content analysis also indicate that especially in the treatment of adult women, female characters play insignificant roles.

a. Individualist Perspective. There is another concern that has recently been identified in addition to the role stereotypes. In his content analysis of Western children's literature, Becker (1973) noted that the books tended to stress individualistic perspectives on historical and social processes. He argues that this leads to a false conception that racial problems, for instance, can be solved only on an individualistic level.

Children do tend to view their social environments in personal and individualistic terms (Dennis, 1973). We cannot argue a causal relationship; that is, children could be learning their individualistic perspective from their books, or the authors could be reflecting the individualistic views of children, or both. Still Becker's argument should be considered in producing and selecting children's literature. Racism, sexism, and other social reforms appear to demand societal, not just individualistic, solutions.

3. ATTITUDE FORMATION AND CHANGE

Since sexual prejudice does seem to be similar to racial prejudice, the attitude change theories and findings from the previous section could apply to sexism. As in other areas of socialization, it is the family and peer groups that are most influential. The family has been shown to be more influential for girls than for boys in both the age at which the influence is first felt, and the extent to which it lasts (Brown, 1974; Floyd and South, 1972). The father—daughter relation seems to be a key factor in the development of either feminist or traditional orientations among women (Worrell and Worrell, 1974).

a. Changing Male Attitudes. Very few studies have attacked directly the effect of reading on sexist attitudes. One notable exception is Warren Farrell, who focused on this question in an experiment he conducted with 240 men. He included a summary of his experiments in a chapter in his book *The Liberated Man* (1974).

Farrell matched his subjects on socioeconomic backgrounds and attitudes and knowledge about women's liberation. Half of the subjects read seventeen articles or excerpts from feminist literature. All were then given a questionnaire on "feelings toward women and masculinity." Farrell found that the subjects who read the literature showed surprisingly more support for women's liberation than did the control groups. The strongest differences seemed to be found for men most opposed to women's liberation initially, for married men, and for men of lesser education. He attributed that last finding to the fact that most men of working-class families had been exposed only to the mass media's version of feminist literature.

Farrell's findings included a phenomenon very much akin to the "sleeper effect." His subjects would refuse to admit to changing or to learning anything from the literature. Farrell noted: "When the men read the literature, they often called it ridiculous, but a week or two later, their responses on the questionnaire were much more positive than those of the men who had not read the literature. Sometimes during the interviews the men would actually repeat phrases they had read in the literature, but would credit them to ambiguous sources."

Despite the seemingly strong results from this study, Farrell carefully pointed out that lasting attitude change, as well as behavioral change, was influenced more by the interpersonal environment of the men than by the reading material.

b. "Secondhand Reality". A recent research interest in mass communication deals with the process termed agenda setting. It is based on the assumption that what we know outside our own limited personal experience comes from the mass media. It has been noted (Weitzman *et al.*, 1972, p. 1146) that a narrow and idealized view of reality is often presented in children's books: "Perhaps these images are motivated by the same kind of impulse that makes parents lie to their children in order to 'protect' them. As a result, the child is given an idealized version of the truth, rather than having his real and pressing questions answered. Not only are the child's legitimate questions ignored, but no effort is made to create a social awareness which encompasses the wider society. Picture books actually deny the existence of the discontented, the poor, the ethnic minorities, and the urban slum dwellers."

The danger is that such views may encourage the child to develop unrealistic perceptions of his world and its experimental possibilities and limitations. Dervin and Greenberg (1972), for instance, found that urban ghetto dwellers tended to believe in the "reality" presented by television much more than did white counterparts.

c. Role Models. In addition to concerns that media may be presenting a distorted, narrow view of social reality, there are individualistic reasons for asking for a greater diversity of roles in media presentations. Although there have been no research studies that have conclusively demonstrated a causal link between reading and subsequent value learning, there are, as Brown (1974) noted, bits and pieces of evidence about its importance. Some of the modeling studies cited in the section on violence demonstrate that people do learn behaviors, and thus, probably, some attitudes, from fictional characters. Brown cites several studies that support the idea that for Blacks and women, the media potrayal is highly influential in shaping an individual's image of himself or herself.

This would suggest that a diversity of alternative lifestyles and role models should be portrayed in available media. Again to quote Allport (1958, p. 281): "The primacy of the family does not mean, of course, that school, church, and state should cease practicing or teaching the principles of democratic living. Together their influence may establish at least a secondary model for the child to follow." For many people, books may be the only source of a secondary model.

E. Summary

The theoretical formulations and empirical findings of communication research do not yield a great deal of support for the idea that reading per se influences attitude formation or change in the areas of race or sex. The social influence of family and peers and the psychological pressures of cognitive consistency make information alone a singularly ineffective tool for creating new or different beliefs about other people and our relationships with them.

However, reading apparently does have important reinforcement effects on these areas. This is not to say that the print media are necessarily limited to supporting stereotypical views of race and sex. But the content analyses of print media demonstrate that they do exactly that. As Kenneth Clark (1974) argued, it is this kind of societal and institutional reinforcement of discrimination that could be the key to attitude formation and prejudice.

Two different traditions suggest the importance of making diverse and controversial views available. There is Hovland's demonstration of the importance of presenting both sides of issues known to be controversial, extended by McGuire's findings that screening people from counter-attitudinal material makes them more readily influenced by propaganda. In addition to these arguments from the persuasion tradition, there is the more recent research dealing with "secondhand reality." In a society where much of what people know comes from media rather than from personal experience, information gatekeepers must aggressively attempt to provide a full sampling of the broader realities in our environment.

VI. BIBLIOTHERAPY: READING IN A THERAPEUTIC CONTEXT

A. Definition and History

Bibliotherapy is defined in *Webster's Third New International Dictionary* as the "use of selected reading materials as therapeutic adjuvants in medicine and psychiatry." A secondary, but legitimate, usage is cited as "guidance in the solution of personal problems through directed reading." In a very real sense, bibliotherapy represents the librarian's most deliberate attempt to influence attitudes and behavior through the use of books and other printed materials.

Long before the term "bibliotherapy" (from the Greek: *biblion*—book, + *oepatteid* = healing or treatment) was coined, individuals had emphasized the value of reading as a means of treating mental problems. In America, Thomas Bray, the Anglican Commissary to Maryland at the turn of the seventeenth century, pushed for the establishment of laymen's libraries in the colonies as one means of "rescuing those who had fallen from grace into sin," and Benjamin Rush, the noted Philadelphia physician, argued persuasively for the therapeutic value of reading (Beatty, 1962; McDaniel, 1956; Ryan, 1957; Weimerskirch, 1965).

More recently, psychologists, psychiatrists, and others concerned with the clinical care of the mentally ill have cited the value of books in the treatment of such individuals (Aring, 1968; Hynes, 1972; Leedy, 1969, 1973; Menninger, 1961). The movement gained particular impetus in the 1960's as the number of institutional librarians grew, and as librarians—especially public librarians—began to define the concept of the "readers' advisor" as a person who provides the reader with in-depth guidance based on a thorough knowledge of the available materials and the needs and interests of the client: Monroe (1971a,b) notes that bibliotherapy and sophisticated readers' advisory work are subject to the same general principles.

B. State of the Art in Bibliotherapy Research

Since advances in bibliotherapy have been the subject of frequent review, especially in the careful and informed assessments by Ruth Tews (1969, 1970; also see Association of Hospital and Institutional Libraries, 1971; Beatty, 1964; Favazza, 1966; Horne, 1975; Schwoebel, 1973), it would appear unnecessary for us to review again the very extensive literature on bibliotherapy and its applications. However, there are a number of points about the process as viewed by librarians that need discussion, and special attention will be devoted to the recent rise of what may well represent the long sought after empirical research tradition on the impact of bibliotherapy.

In an extensive review of the literature dealing with this subject, Ruth Tews notes that bibliotherapy, even among institutional librarians, has generally been "viewed with indifference, lack of understanding, doubt, and frequently open hostility" (Tews, 1970). While interest and awareness appear to be growing, there remains an embarrassing lack of substance and consistency in the literature on the subject.

What is lacking is a reliable body of empirical knowledge on the nature and effects of bibliotherapy. It is frustrating to note that after some sixty years of interest in the problem we are forced to concur that very little is known, and the work to be done, as summarized by Tews (1970), remains very great indeed:

> The pressing need for the future is analysis of bibliotherapy. The psychologic aspect of reading as a form of communication should be examined. Scientifically oriented research projects should be instituted to bring out data on the effects of reading as distinguished from the interpersonal relationships involved; the reader's projection of himself into his reading, and how this differs between the normal and the disturbed individual, ought to be investigated; the possibilities of translation of the clinical diagnosis into a prescription of specific bibliotherapeutic items should be appraised; and more studies ought to be conducted on the effects of reading on the basis of categories of patients as opposed to the traditional form of anecdotal reporting of individual cases.

Tews and most others who review bibliotherapy define its limits rather narrowly, and while they make slight concessions to the relationship between bibliotherapy and readers' advisory services, they insist on defining bibliotherapy as a "therapeutic technique involving selected reading which serves as an adjunct to psychotherapy" (Tews, 1970). Implicit in this definition is the idea that bibliotherapy is basically a technique for use in treating the mentally ill. However, much of the literature related to the remedial and therapeutic use of bibliotherapy remains in one of the following two categories: (1) exhortatory studies—the description of this approach and a plea for its wider use; or (2) case studies—the description of the use of the bibliotherapeutic approach in one or more individual applications. Unfortunately, those interested in bibliotherapy and its uses in a therapeutic setting have done little to test their theories in an experimental—empirical context. It is interesting to note that each of the recent reviews of the literature concludes with a call for the development of an experimental research tradition in bibliotherapy (cf. Horne, 1975; Tews, 1969, 1970).

Thus, as far as the institutional librarians are concerned, it must be concluded that the important theoretical statements (cf. Hannigan, 1962; Jackson, 1962; Shrodes, 1960, 1961), of the last thirty years have not been empirically tested, and as Zaccaria and Moses (1968) point out in their detailed and sophisticated review of the field, bibliotherapy remains much more an art than a science.

It would indeed be discouraging to conclude that the hundreds of articles published on aspects of bibliotherapy (Schwoebel, 1973) added up to little more than a theoretical and generally subjective endorsement of an extremely imprecise art. And, except for an important new experimental research movement directed at exploring the impact of bibliotherapy on *normal* adolescents, such would have to be the case. However, a substantial amount of new work is being done in this area and promises to provide significant insight into the impact of reading on behavior.

C. New Frontiers in Research

The essential thrust of this new research is to test the hypothesis which argues that reading selected materials can change children's attitudes toward others and/or themselves. Although this type of interest was evidenced among librarians as early as the 1940's (Jackson, 1944) it seems to have received great impetus from more recent work (Cianciolo, 1965; Moses and Zaccaria, 1969; Zaccaria and Moses, 1968). In 1968 Zaccaria and Moses published a book entitled *Facilitating Human Development Through Reading: The Use of Bibliotherapy in Teaching and Counseling,* which, while recognizing the value of bibliotherapy in treating the mentally or physically ill, focused on the concept of bibliotherapy as a technique of value to a wide variety of individuals and one which can harness "the potentially therapeutic power of literature in order to resolve personal conflict, promote psychological growth, gain self-insight, and foster more adequate mental health in students." This work carefully and provocatively reviewed the theoretical and empirical foundations of bibliotherapy and pointed out the generally overlooked experimental evidence supporting the thesis that carefully selected and utilized reading could be effective in altering student attitudes, and it called for further work in this area.

The response has been very impressive but is so recent that an assessment of "Research Related to Children's Interests and to Developmental Values of Reading" (Robinson and Weintraub, 1973) fails to recognize the new work and concludes that "research dealing with developmental values of reading is sparse."

Drawing on the earlier work of Jackson (1944) and Bryson (1953), and making use of the latest social/psychological research on children, researchers from a variety of disciplines have set out to test the general thesis: "whether measurable improvement in individual personality traits and interpersonal relations can be effected through the reading of prescribed selections from literature" (Livengood, 1961).

This research is generally experimental, in that control and experimental groups are utilized and attempts are made to identify and control variables and focus primarily on the matter of whether the reading of selected works can modify the attitudes of young people toward various racial groups in society—especially toward Blacks.

Studies by Bazalak (1973), Frankel (1972), Hayes (1969), Kozlowska (1973), Lancaster (1971), Madden (1970), Woodyard (1970), and Zucaro (1972) all test the hypothesis that bibliotherapy can change white children's attitudes toward Blacks in a favorable direction. All of the authors, while applying different experimental approaches, agreed that a measurable attitude change was present and concluded with guarded endorsements of the efficacy of bibliotherapy. Other studies of a similar nature support this guarded conclusion. Fisher (1965, 1968) attempted to change the attitudes of a group of fifth graders toward American Indians with some success, and Tauran (1967) developed an experimental approach to test "The Influences of Reading on the Attitudes of Third Graders Toward Eskimo Children," concluding "racial ideas ... can be influenced by ... reading material."

Another series of studies relate to less specific attitude change and produced findings that support, albeit somewhat weakly in some cases, the findings of studies with a more object-oriented focus. For instance, Herminghaus (1954) worked with groups of elementary school children and was somewhat successful in modifying attitudes among his subjects. Appleberry (1969), working with third graders and Lewis (1967), working with sixth graders, both concluded that reading can have a significant impact upon attitudes and recommended a careful and informed approach to the selection of literature so that attitude development and change will be desirable.

Another finding of recent studies in this area relates to the use of bibliotherapy to improve the self-image of adolescents. Kozlowska (1973) conducted an experiment on inner-city youths which demonstrated that the self-concept of the subjects was definitely enhanced. Two other studies bear out this finding: Frankel (1972) found that the reading of *The Adventures of Huckleberry Finn* had a positive impact on improving the self-image of Black subjects, while Woodyard (1970) concluded that her study demonstrated that "the self-concept or self-esteem of Negro students may be greatly enhanced by studying Black literature."

D. Summary

These findings are beginning to fit a rather persuasive pattern. Briefly they may be summarized in much the same way as Zaccaria and Moses (1968) did on the basis of far fewer findings, and Rongione (1972) did in a much less formal way.
1. There does seem to be a growing body of evidence supporting the idea that bibliotherapy is effective with normal children. And while this is occasionally contested (Kimmel, 1973), the evidence is definitely cumulating in support of the efficacy of bibliotherapy. Furthermore, advances in the theory of bibliotherapy are also being made (Ulibarri, 1970).
2. Bibliotherapy appears most effective with children of average or

better reading ability, although note the presence of other findings (Hynes, 1972; Livengood, 1961).
3. The effects of bibliotherapy are greatly enhanced by follow-up discussion and/or counseling (Madden, 1970).
4. Bibliotherapy must be constantly viewed as an adjunct to other developmental relationships rather than as an alternative or independent form of therapy.

This summary is not meant to suggest that the efficacy of bibliotherapy has been settled once and for all. Nor does it mean to suggest that the only important experimental work in bibliotherapy is being done with children (cf. Burt, 1972; McClasky, 1970; Sherrill, 1972). However, the work described here does present an impressive array of findings; and future scholars, building upon earlier studies of bibliotherapy and children and utilizing the findings of the enormous research effort directed both at the content analysis of children's literature (Bekkedal, 1973; Lukenbill, 1972; Phaedrus, 1973) and to the process of reading itself (Geyer and Kolers, 1974), can be expected to make major advances in this area over the next decade.

Such future studies will have to be more fully conversant with developments in the sociopsychology of children and will need to make careful allowance for the treatment of questions of the duration of attitude change, the influence of the bibliotherapist, and the individual differences involved.

In the latter category especially, researchers who have been laboring to overcome the narrow case-study approach to research in bibliotherapy, will need to caution themselves about a lack of attention to the individual and often unique reactions of children to reading. As Maccoby (1964) noted: "It would be a mistake to assume that the impact of the mass media would be constant, or even similar, from one child to the next. The child is not a passive entity, simply absorbing like a sponge whatever is offered to him. He is an active selector... and even during exposure, ... he deploys attention selectively, and what he remembers varies accordingly. Furthermore, what a child does take in has a different effect, depending on his pre-existing level of information, the nature of his needs, and the quality of his adjustment to his life situation."

Despite these cautionary notes, research on bibliotherapy, especially bibliotherapy and children, represents the most promising, and by far the most advanced, aspect of the interdisciplinary effort seeking some understanding of "what reading does to people."

VII. IMPLICATIONS OF COMMUNICATIONS RESEARCH FOR INFORMATION PROFESSIONALS

A. Introduction

The preceding selective review of the literature of communication relating to the question, "What does reading do to people?" reveals a number of trends that should be underscored here. Even though these trends can not be considered conclusive, and indeed some remain very tenuous, they appear well developed enough to justify our attention.

First, and perhaps intuitively obvious to every practicing librarian, is the fact that the question relating to the impact of reading on behavior must be answered in substantially different ways, depending on whether one is discussing children or adults. As a result it seems wise to conclude this chapter with a review of findings relative to the two audiences.

B. Children

1. The first, and most obvious conclusion, but one that librarians appear prone to overlook, is that a large number of socialization agents are responsible for formation of the child's attitudes and that the printed word plays only a small part in this process.
2. Furthermore, we now know that most children have formed the majority of their attitudes prior to acquiring the facility to read with any proficiency. It should be noted, however, that the child is often *read to* by his parents or others and thus librarians are justified in their concern with the nature and quality of books for preschool youngsters.
3. While it is now clear that most children have acquired their attitudes and opinions prior to acquiring literacy, it remains important to point out that they are still far more susceptible to influence by printed messages than are adults. Studies of the relationship between violence on television and aggressive be-

havior in children suggest that the influence is real and measurable, and librarians working with children would be well advised to follow the continuing research in this area with care.

4. While children seem more likely to be influenced by messages which can influence their behavior in a negative way, it is also clear that their attitudes can be altered in positive ways as well. The work summarized in Section VI of this paper points to some very encouraging conclusions relative to the diminution of prejudice by means of "bibliotherapy." However, it is also clear that other variables exert a far greater influence on attitude change (i.e., peer groups, teachers, parents, folk idols) than does the printed word.

5. At the same time it must be emphasized that the old "bullet theory" or "hypodermic needle theory" is now considered totally misleading. Laymen and librarians alike must reach at least an elemental understanding of the complexity of the communication process. It is now clear that the audience will assimilate the message in question in a great variety of ways and that the idea of a book or idea having an immediate, clear-cut, and predictable impact on a reader is generally considered naive in the extreme.

6. Finally, the information professional's long-term concern with the nature, quality, and extent of reading materials made available to children seems justified in the light of research in this matter. Although our knowledge of the ways in which reading influences behavior remains imprecise, we do know enough to be convinced of the efficacy of the print media in influencing attitudes and behavior among the young.

C. Adults

1. The first, and most immediate, conclusion to be drawn relative to the impact of print on adult behavior is that it is generally unimpressive and almost always unpredictable.
2. Studies demonstrate that adult behavior is rarely altered by the printed word and that indeed most adults read (purposefully) in order to reinforce already existing attitudes and opinions.
3. We also find that deliberate attempts to alter the prejudices of adults by means of printed (or other) messages simply lead to

rationalization to the extent that they distort the antiprejudice message so that it actually *supports* their prejudice.
4. Similarly, there appears to be no connection between the use of pornography and deviant sexual behavior.

D. Apologia

One final word must be said about the complexities involved in the process of measuring the influence of reading on behavior. The authors of this chapter are generally dissatisfied with the idea that the impact of the print media should be assessed as a separate entity, separate that is, from the other communications media. However, we finally agreed to do so since a majority of adult Americans, and indeed, a majority of the nation's librarians and publishers, insist on doing so. Throughout this chapter we have attempted to underline the interrelationships existing between the various communication media and to suggest the complexity of measuring influence or impact.

Furthermore, our focus has forced us to imply, at least in the matter of emphasis, that the "medium" has a major significance—greater, for instance, than the "message" or the "source." While we find Marshall McLuhan's work provocative, we must caution our readers that we find little support for his conclusion that the "medium is the message." Rather, research would suggest that the source, the message, and the nature of the audience still remain the most significant elements in the communications environment.

Nevertheless, it is also clear that each medium can boast certain advantages and liabilities as a communication channel. The printed word, for instance, allows examination of questions in greater depth, with greater deliberation, and over longer periods of time. Concomitantly, it requires a degree of skill in utilization which far surpasses that of the other media, and thus the audience for the printed message will always remain considerably smaller than that of the other media.

The differences in the audiences of the various media, and the obvious differences in the nature and extent of the impact of the various media, would seem to justify an intensified effort designed to measure and catalog the nature and extent of the audience for the printed word. While librarians and publishers have always demonstrated an interest in this matter, a more sophisticated and extensive effort would appear in order.

Such an effort, in parallel with the continuing research on the impact of reading on behavior, could contribute in time to a more precise definition of "what reading does to people" and provide immeasurable aid to everyone concerned with the delivery of information or entertainment via the printed word.

REFERENCES

Abelson, H., Cohen, R., Heaton, E., and Suder, C. (1971). National survey of public attitudes toward and experience with erotic materials. *In* Commission on Obscenity and Pornography, "Technical Report," Vol. 6, pp. 1–137. Government Printing Office, Washington, D. C.

Abelson, R. P., Aronson, E., McGuire, W. J., Newcomb, T. M., Rosenberg, M. J., and Tannenbaum, P. H., eds. (1968). "Theories of Cognitive Consistency." Rand McNally, Chicago, Illinois.

Adorno, T., Frenkel-Brunswick, E., Levison, D., and Sanford, R. (1950). "The Authoritarian Personality." Harper, New York.

Allport, C. W. (1958). "The Nature of Prejudice." Doubleday Anchor Books, Garden City, New York.

American Newspaper Publishers Association (1967). When people want to know, where do they go to find out? *A.N.P.A. News Research Bulletin* No. 21.

Appleberry, M. H. (1969). "A Study of the Effect of Bibliotherapy on Third-Grade Children Using a Master List of Titles from Children's Literature." Unpublished dissertation, University of Houston.

Aring, C. D. (1968). Reading is good medicine. *Archives of Internal Medicine* **122**, 537–538.

Aronson, E., and Golden, B. W. (1962). The effect of relevant and irrelevant aspects of communicator credibility on opinion change. *Journal of Personality* **30**, 135–146.

Association of Hospital and Institutional Libraries (1971). "Bibliotherapy: Methods and Materials." American Library Association, Chicago, Illinois.

Atkin, C. (1973). Instrumental utilities and information seeking. *In* "New Models for Mass Communication Research" (P. Clarke, ed.), pp. 205–242. Sage Publications, Beverly Hills, California.

Baker, R. K., and Ball, S. J. (1969). "Mass Media and Violence." Government Printing Office, Washington, D. C. (Report to the National Commission on the Causes and Prevention of Violence, Vol. 11.)

Bandura, A. (1965). Vicarious processes: a case of no-trial learning. *In* "Advances in Experimental Social Psychology" (L. Berkowitz, ed.), Vol. 2, pp. 1–55. Academic Press, New York.

Bandura, A. (1969). Social learning theory of identificatory processes. *In* "Handbook of Socialization Theory and Research" (D. A. Goslin, ed.), pp. 213–262. Rand McNally, Chicago, Illinois.

Bandura, A., and Huston, A. D. (1961). Identification as a process of incidental learning. *Journal of Abnormal and Social Psychology* **63**, 311–318.

Bandura, A., and Menlove, F. L. (1968). Factors determining vicarious extinction of avoidance behavior through symbolic modeling. *Journal of Personality and Social Psychology* **8**, 99–108.

Bandura, A., and Walters, R. H. (1963). "Social Learning and Personality Development." Holt, Rinehart and Winston, New York.

Bandura, A., Ross, D., and Ross, S. A. (1961). Transmission of aggression through imitation of aggressive models. *Journal of Abnormal and Social Psychology* **63**, 575–582.

Bandura, A., Ross, D., and Ross, S. A. (1963a). Imitation of film-mediated aggressive models. *Journal of Abnormal and Social Psychology* **66**, 3–11.

Bandura, A., Ross, D., and Ross, S. A. (1963b). Vicarious reinforcement and imitative learning. *Journal of Abnormal and Social Psychology* **67**, 601–607.

Barcus, F. E. (1961). A content analysis of trends in Sunday comics, 1900–1959. *Journalism Quarterly* **38**, 171–180.

Bazelak, L. P. (1973). "Content Analysis of Tenth-Grade Students' Responses to Black Literature, Including the Effect of Reading This Literature on Attitudes Towards Race." Unpublished dissertation, Syracuse University.

Beatty, W. K. (1962). A historical review of bibliotherapy. *Library Trends* **11**, 106–117.

Beatty, W. K., ed. (1964). Proceedings of the ALA Bibliotherapy Workshop, St. Louis, June 25–27, 1964. *AHIL Quarterly* **4**, 1–60.

Becker, J. (1973). Racism in children's and young people's literature. *Journal of Peace Research* **3**, 295–303.

Bekkedal, T. R. (1973). Content analysis of children's books. *Library Trends* **21**, 109–126.

Ben-Veniste, R. (1971). Pornography and sex crime: the Danish experience. *In* Commission on Obscenity and Pornography. "Technical Report," Vol. 7, pp. 245–261. Government Printing Office, Washington, D. C.

Berelson, B., and Steiner, G. A. (1964). Methods of inquiry. *In* "Human Behavior: An Inventory of Scientific Findings," pp. 15–35. Harcourt, Brace, and World, New York.

Berelson, B., Lazarsfeld, P. F., and McPhee, W. N. (1954). "Voting: A Study of Opinion Formation in a Presidential Campaign." University of Chicago Press, Chicago, Illinois.

Berkowitz, L. (1962). "Aggression: A Social Psychological Analysis." McGraw-Hill, New York.

Berkowitz, L. (1965). Some aspects of observed aggression. *Journal of Personality and Social Psychology* **2**, 359–369.

Berkowitz, L. (1968). The frustration-aggression hypothesis revisted. *In* "Roots of Aggression: A Re-examination of the Frustration-Aggression Hypothesis" (L. Berkowitz, ed.), pp. 29–34. Atherton Press, New York.

Berkowitz, L., and Geen, R. (1966). Film violence and the cue properties of available targets. *Journal of Personality and Social Psychology* **3**, 525–530.

Berkowitz, L., and Geen, R. (1967). The stimulus qualities of the target of

aggression: a further study. *Journal of Personality and Social Psychology* 5, 364–368.
Berkowitz, L., and Holmes, D. S. (1960). A further investigation of hostility generalization to disliked objects. *Journal of Personality* 26, 427–442.
Berkowitz, L., and Rawlings, E. (1963). Effects of film violence on inhibitions against subsequent aggression. *Journal of Abnormal and Social Psychology* 66, 405–412.
Berkowitz, L., Corwin, R., and Heironimous, M. (1963). Film violence and subsequent aggressive tendencies. *Public Opinion Quarterly* 27, 217–229.
Berlyne, D. E. (1960). "Conflict Arousal and Curiosity." McGraw-Hill, New York.
Blum, E. (1959). Paperback book publishing: a survey of content. *Journalism Quarterly* 36, 447–454.
Bogart, L. (1973). Consumer and advertising research. *In* "Handbook of Communication" (I. Pool, ed.), pp. 706–721. Rand McNally, Chicago, Illinois.
Bowers, J. W. (1970). "Designing the Communication Experiment." Random House, New York.
Bramel, D., Taub, B., and Blum, B. (1968). An observer's reaction to the suffering of his enemy. *Journal of Personality and Social Psychology* 8, 384–392.
Breuer, J., and Freud, S. (1957). "Studies on Hysteria." Basic Books, New York.
Brock, T. C. (1971). Erotic materials: a commodity theory analysis of availability and desirability. *In* Commission on Obscenity and Pornography. "Technical Report," Vol. 1, pp. 131–137. Government Printing Office, Washington, D. C.
Brown, J. D. (1974). "The Role of Communication in the Development of a Sex Role Orientation." Presented to the Theory and Methodology Division, Association for Education in Journalism, San Diego, California.
Bryson, R. J. (1953). "The Promotion of Interracial Understanding Through the Study of American Literature." Unpublished dissertation, Ohio State University.
Burgoon, M., and Miller, G. (1974). The effects of counter-attitudinal communication behavior on latitude of acceptance. *Journal of Psychology* 87, 319–323.
Burt, L. N. (1972). "Bibliotherapy: Effect of Group Reading and Discussion on Attitudes of Adult Inmates in Two Correctional Institutions." Unpublished dissertation, University of Wisconsin.
Busha, C. A. (1972). "Freedom Versus Suppression and Censorship." Libraries Unlimited, Littleton, Colorado.
Buss, A. H. (1961). "The Psychology of Aggression." Wiley, New York.
Butterworth, R. F., and Thompson, G. D. (1951). Factors related to age-grade trends and sex differences in children's preferences for comic books. *Journal of Genetic Psychology* 78, 71–96.
Cairns, R. B., Paul, J. C. N., and Wishnet, J. (1971). Psychological assumptions in sex censorship: an evaluative review of recent research, 1961–1968. *In* Commission on Obscenity and Pornography. "Technical Report," Vol. 1, pp. 5–21. Government Printing Office, Washington, D. C.

Capon, N., and Hulbert, J. (1973). The sleeper-effect—an awakening. *Public Opinion Quarterly* 37, 333–358.

Carey, J. W. (1967). Harold Adams Innis and Marshall McLuhan. *Antioch Review* 27, 5–39.

Chaffee, S. H., Stamm, K., Guerrero, J., and Tipton, L. (1969). "Experiments on Cognitive Discrepancies and Communication." Association for Education in Journalism, Lexington, Kentucky. (Journalism Monographs, No. 14.)

Chaffee, S. H., McLeod, J. M., and Atkin, C. K. (1971). Parental influences on adolescent media use. *American Behavioral Scientist* 14, 323–340.

Cianciolo, P. J. (1965). Children's literature can affect coping behavior. *Personnel and Guidance Journal* 43, 897–903.

Clark, K. (1974). "Pathos of Power." Harper and Row, New York.

Clark, R. A. (1952). The projective measurement of experimentally induced levels of sexual motivation. *Journal of Experimental Psychology* 44, 391–399.

Commission on Obscenity and Pornography (1970). "Commission on Obscenity and Pornography Report." Bantam Books, New York.

Commission on Obscenity and Pornography (1971). "Technical Report," 10 vols. Government Printing Office, Washington, D. C.

Comstock, G. A. (1971). New research on media content and control: an overview. *In* "Television and Social Behavior" (G. A. Comstock and E. A. Rubinstein, eds.), Vol. 1, pp. 1–27. Government Printing Office, Washington, D. C.

Cooper, E., and Jahoda, M. (1947). The evasion of propaganda: how prejudiced people respond to anti-prejudice propaganda. *Journal of Psychology* 23, 15–25.

Davis, K. E., and Braucht, G. N. (1973). Exposure to pornography, character, and sexual deviance: a retrospective survey. *Journal of Social Issues* 29, No. 3, 183–196.

Dennis, J., ed. (1973). "Socialization to Politics." Wiley, New York.

De Rath, G. W. (1963). "The Effects of Verbal Instructions on Imitative Aggression." Unpublished dissertation, Michigan State University.

Dervin, B., and Greenberg, B. (1972). The communication environment of the urban poor. *In* "Current Perspectives in Mass Communication Research" (F. G. Kline and P. Tichenor, eds.), pp. 195–233. Sage Publications, Beverly Hills, California.

Dollard, J., Doob, L., Miller, N., Mowrer, O., and Sears, R. (1939). "Frustration and Aggression." Yale University Press, New Haven, Connecticut.

Donohew, L., and Palmgreen, P. (1971a). A reappraisal of dissonance and the selective exposure hypothesis. *Journalism Quarterly* 48, 412–420, 437.

Donohew, L., and Palmgreen, P. (1971b). An investigation of "mechanisms" of information selection. *Journalism Quarterly* 48, 627–639, 666.

Ehrlich, H. J. (1973). "The Social Psychology of Prejudice." Wiley, New York.

Emmerich, W., Goldman, K. S., and Shore, R. E. (1970). Differentiation and development of social norms. *Journal of Personality and Social Psychology* 18, pp. 323–353.

Emmert, P., and Brooks, W. D. (1970). "Methods of Research in Communication." Houghton-Mifflin, Boston, Massachusetts.
Farrell, W. (1974). "The Liberated Man." Random House, New York.
Favazza, A. R. (1966). Bibliotherapy: a critique of the literature. *Medical Library Association Bulletin* 54, 138–141.
Feshbach, S. (1955). The drive-reducing function of fantasy behavior. *Journal of Abnormal and Social Psychology* 50, 3–11.
Feshbach, S. (1961). The stimulative versus cathartic effects of a vicarious aggressive activity. *Journal of Abnormal and Social Psychology* 63, 381–385.
Feshbach, S., and Singer, R. D. (1971). "Television and Aggression." Jossey-Bass, San Francisco, California.
Festinger, L. (1964). "Conflict, Decision and Dissonance." Stanford University Press, Stanford, California.
Fisher, F. L. (1965). "The Influences of Reading and Discussion on the Attitudes of Fifth Graders Toward American Indians." Unpublished dissertation, University of California, Berkeley.
Fisher, F. L. (1968). Influences of reading and discussion on the attitudes of fifth graders toward American Indians. *Journal of Educational Research* 62, 130–134.
Fiske, M. (1959). "Book Selection and Censorship." University of California Press, Berkeley, California.
Flanders, J. P. (1968). A review of research on imitative behavior. *Psychological Bulletin* 69, 316–337.
Floyd, H. H., and South, D. R. (1972). "Dilemma of youth: the choice of parents or peers as a frame of reference for behavior." *Journal of Marriage and the Family* 34, 627–634.
Frankel, H. L. (1972). "Effects of Reading 'The Adventures of Huckleberry Finn' on the Racial Attitudes of Selected Ninth-Grade Boys." Unpublished dissertation, Temple University.
Freund, K. (1957). Diagnostika homosexuality u muzu. *Ceskoslovenska Psychiatrie* 53, 382–394.
Freund, K. (1967). Diagnosing homo- and heterosexuality and erotic age-preference by means of a psychophysiological test. *Behaviour Research and Therapy* 5, 209–228.
Galbraith, C. G., and Mosher, D. L. (1968). Associative sexual responses in relation to sexual arousal, guilt, and external approval contingencies. *Journal of Personality and Social Psychology* 10, 142–147.
Gebhard, P. H., Gagnon, J. H., Pomeroy, W. B., and Christenson, C. V. (1965). "Sex Offenders: An Analysis of Types." Harper and Row, New York.
Geen, R. (1968). Effects of frustration, attack, and prior training in aggressiveness upon aggressive behavior. *Journal of Personality and Social Psychology* 9, 316–321.
Geen, R., and Berkowitz, L. (1966). Name-mediated aggressive cue properties. *Journal of Personality* 34, 456–465.
Geen, R., and Berkowitz, L. (1967). Some conditions facilitating the occurrence of aggression after the observation of violence. *Journal of Personality* 35, 666–667.

Gerber, A. (1965). "Sex, Pornography and Justice." Lyle Stuart, New York.
Gerbner, G. (1969). The television world of violence. In "Mass Media and Violence" (R. K. Baker and S. J. Ball, eds.), pp. 313–339. Government Printing Office, Washington, D. C.
Gersoni-Stavin, D. (1974). "Sexism and Youth." Bowker, New York.
Geyer, J. J., and Kolers, P. A. (1974). Reading as information processing. In "Advances in Librarianship" (M. J. Voigt, ed.), Vol. 4, pp. 175–237. Academic Press, New York.
Gillig, P. M., and Greenwald, A. G. (1974). Is it time to lay the sleeper effect to rest? *Journal of Personality and Social Psychology* **29**, 132–139.
Gilligan, C., Kohlberg, L., Lerner, J., and Belenky, M. (1971). Moral reasoning about sexual dilemmas: the development of an interview and scoring system. In Commission on Obscenity and Pornography. "Technical Report," Vol. 1, pp. 141–150. Government Printing Office, Washington, D. C.
Goldberg, P. A., and Milstein, J. T. (1965). Perceptual investigations of psychoanalytic theory concerning latent homosexuality in women. *Perceptual and Motor Skills* **21**, 645–646.
Goldstein, M. J., and Kant, H. S. (1973). "Pornography and Sexual Deviance." University of California Press, Berkeley, California.
Gordon, D. R. (1975). Print as a visual medium. *Library Quarterly* **45**, 34–46.
Granberg, D., and Steele, L. (1974). Procedural considerations in measuring latitudes of acceptance, rejection and non-commitment. *Social Forces* **52**, 538–542.
Greenberg, B., and Hanneman, G. (1970). Racial attitudes and the impact of TV Blacks. *Educational Broadcasting Review* **4**, No. 2, 27–34.
Haney, R. (1971). "The Role of Encoding and Decoding Aggressive Messages on Subsequent Hostility." Paper presented to the Speech Communication Convention, San Francisco, California.
Hannigan, M. C. (1962). The librarian in bibliotherapy: pharmacist or bibliotherapist. *Library Trends* **11**, 184–198.
Hansen, H. S. (1967). "The Relationship Between Home Literary Environment and Self-Commitment to Independent Reading." Unpublished dissertation, University of Wisconsin.
Harding, J., Proshansky, H., Kutner, B., and Chein, I. (1969). Prejudice and ethnic relations. In "The Handbook of Social Psychology" (G. Lindzey and E. Aronson, eds.), Vol. 5, pp. 1–76. Addison-Wesley, Reading, Massachusetts.
Harris, M. H. (1973). Historians assess the impact of print on the course of American history; the revolution of a test case. *Library Trends* **22**, 127–147.
Hartmann, D. P. (1969). Influence of symbolically modeled instrumental aggression and pain cues on aggressive behavior. *Journal of Personality and Social Psychology* **11**, 280–288.
Hartmann, D. P., and Husband, C. (1974). "Racism and the Mass Media." Rowman and Littlefield, Totowa, New Jersey.
Haskins, J. B. (1969). The effects of violence in the printed media. In "Mass Media and Violence" (R. K. Baker and S. J. Ball, eds.), Vol. 9, Appendix III, pp. 493–502. Government Printing Office, Washington, D. C.

Hayes, M. T. (1969). "An Investigation of the Impact of Reading on Attitudes of Racial Prejudice." Unpublished dissertation, Boston University, School of Education.
Hayes, M. T., and Conklin, M. (1953). Intergroup attitudes and experimental change. *Journal of Experimental Education* 22, 19–36.
Herminghaus, E. G. (1954). "The Effect of Bibliotherapy on the Attitudes and Personal and Social Adjustment of a Group of Elementary School Children." Unpublished dissertation, Washington University.
Hess, E. H., and Polt, J. M. (1960). Pupil size as related to interest value of visual stimuli. *Science* 132, 349–350.
Hicks, D. (1965). Imitation and retention of film-mediated aggressive peer and adult models. *Journal of Personality and Social Psychology* 2, 97–100.
Hicks, D. (1968). Short- and long-term retention of affectively varied modeled behavior. *Psychonomic Science* 11, 369–370.
Horne, E. M. (1975). A look at bibliotherapy. *Special Libraries* 66, 27–31.
Hoult, T. F. (1949). Comic books and juvenile delinquency. *Sociology and Social Research* 33, 279–284.
Hovland, C. I., ed. (1957). "The Order of Presentation in Persuasion." Yale University Press, New Haven, Connecticut.
Hovland, C. I. (1959). Reconciling conflicting results derived from experimental and survey studies of attitude change. *American Psychologist* 14, 8–17.
Hovland, C. I., and Weiss, W. (1951). The influence of source credibility on communication effectiveness. *Public Opinion Quarterly* 15, 635–650.
Hovland, C. I., Lumsdaine, A. A., and Sheffield, F. D. (1949). "Experiments on Mass Communication. Princeton University Press, Princeton, New Jersey. (Studies in Social Psychology in World War II, Vol. 3.)
Hovland, C. I., Janis, I. L., and Kelley, H. H. (1953). "Communication and Persuasion." Yale University Press, New Haven, Connecticut.
Howard, J., Liptzin, M. B., and Reifler, C. B. (1973). Is pornography a problem? *Journal of Social Issues* 29, No. 3, 133–145.
Hoyt, J. (1967). "Vengeance and Self-Defence as Justification for Film Aggression." Unpublished master's thesis, University of Wisconsin.
Hynes, J. C. (1972). Library work with brain damaged patients: a new mode of bibliotherapy. *Medical Library Association Bulletin* 60, 333–339.
Israel, H., Simmons, W. R., and Robinson, J. P. (1971). Demographic characteristics of viewers of television violence and news programs. *In* "Television and Social Behavior" (E. A. Rubinstein, G. A. Comstock, and J. P. Murray, eds.), Vol. 4, pp. 87–128. Government Printing Office, Washington, D. C.
Jackson, E. P. (1944). Effects of reading upon attitudes toward the Negro race. *Library Quarterly* 14, 47–54.
Jackson, E. P. (1962). Bibliotherapy and reading guidance: a tentative approach to theory. *Library Trends* 11, 118–126.
Jacoby, S. (1973). Altering sexism in the classroom. *Learning* 1, 63–67.
Janis, I. L., and Feshbach, S. (1953). Effects of fear-arousing communications. *Journal of Abnormal and Social Psychology* 48, 78–92.
Janis, I. L., and Field, P. B. (1959). A behavioral assessment of persuasibility:

consistency of individual differences. *In* "Personality and Persuasibility" (C. J. Hovland and I. L. Janis, eds.), pp. 29–54. Yale University Press, New Haven, Connecticut.
Janis, I. L., and Terwilliger, R. F. (1962). An experimental study of psychological resistance to fear-arousing communications. *Journal of Abnormal and Social Psychology* 65, 403–410.
Jones, E. E., and Gerard, H. B. (1967). "Foundations of Social Psychology." Wiley, New York.
Jordan, B. T., and Butler, J. R. (1967). GSR as a measure of the sexual component in hysteria. *Journal of Psychology* 67, 211–219.
Kaplan, A. (1964). "The Conduct of Inquiry." Chandler University Press, San Francisco, California.
Karp, E. E. (1954). "Crime Comic Book Role Preferences." Unpublished dissertation, New York University.
Katz, E. (1957). The two-step flow of communication: an up-to-date report of an hypothesis. *Public Opinion Quarterly* 21, 61–78.
Katz, E., and Lazarsfeld, P. F. (1955). "Personal Influence: The Part Played by People in the Flow of Mass Communications." The Free Press, Glencoe, Illinois.
Keating, C. H., Jr. (1970). Report of Commissioner Charles H. Keating, Jr. *In* Commission on Obscenity and Pornography. "Report," pp. 578–623. Bantam Books, New York.
Kerlinger, F. F. (1965). "Foundations of Behavioral Research." Holt, Rinehart and Winston, New York.
Kimmel, E. A. (1973). "Children's Reading and Attitude Change." Unpublished dissertation, University of Illinois at Urbana-Champaign.
Kinsey, A. C., Pomeroy, W. B., and Martin, C. E. (1948). "Sexual Behavior in the Human Male." Saunders, Philadelphia, Pennsylvania.
Kinsey, A. C., Pomeroy, W. B., Martin, W. B., and Gebhard, P. H. (1953). "Sexual Behavior in the Human Female." Saunders, Philadelphia, Pennsylvania.
Klapper, J. T. (1960). "Effects of Mass Communication." The Free Press, Glencoe, Illinois.
Kline, F. G. (1971). Media time budgeting as a function of demographics and life style. *Journalism Quarterly* 48, 211–221.
Kohlberg, L. (1969). Stage and sequence: the cognitive-developmental approach to socialization. *In* "Handbook of Socialization Theory and Research" (D. Goslin, ed.), pp. 347–380. Rand McNally, Chicago, Illinois.
Kozlowska, Sister M. V. (1973). "Study of the Effects on Racial Attitudes of Exercises in Values Clarification and Identification in Conjunction with the Poetry of a Black Poet and a White Poet." Unpublished dissertation, Temple University.
Kupperstein, L. (1971). The role of pornography in the etiology of juvenile delinquency: a review of the research literature. *In* Commission on Obscenity and Pornography. "Technical Report," Vol. 1, pp. 103–111. U. S. Government Printing Office, Washington, D. C.

Kutchinsky, B. (1973). The effect of easy availability of pornography on the incidence of sex crimes: the Danish experience. *Journal of Social Issues* **29**, No. 3, 163–181.

Lacy, D. (1965). The dissemination of print. In "The Public Library and the City" (R. W. Conant, ed.), pp. 114–128. MIT Press, Cambridge, Massachusetts.

Lancaster, J. W. (1971). "An Investigation of the Effect of Books With Black Characters on the Racial Preferences of White Children." Unpublished dissertation, Boston University, School of Education.

Larrick, N. (1965). The all-white world of children's books. *Saturday Review* **46** (Sept. 11), 63–65, 84–85.

Leedy, J. J. (1969). "Poetry Therapy." Lippincott, Philadelphia, Pennsylvania.

Leedy, J. J., ed. (1973). "Poetry the Healer." Lippincott, Philadelphia, Pennsylvania.

Levitt, E. E., and Hinesley, R. K. (1967). Some factors in the violences of erotic visual stimuli. *Journal of Sex Research* **3**, 63–68.

Lewis, I. R. (1967). "Some Effects of the Reading and Discussion of Stories on Certain Values of Sixth-Grade Pupils." Unpublished dissertation, University of California at Berkeley.

Livengood, D. K. (1961). "The Effect of Bibliotherapy Upon Peer Relations and Democratic Practices in a Sixth Grade Classroom." Unpublished dissertation, University of Florida.

Lockhart, W. B., and McClure, R. C. (1954). Literature, the law of obscenity, and the Constitution. *Minnesota Law Review* **38**, 295–395.

Loiselle, R. H., and Mollenauer, S. (1965). Galvanic skin responses to sexual stimuli in a female population. *Journal of Genetic Psychology* **73**, 273–275.

Lovass, O. J. (1961). Effect of exposure to symbolic aggression on aggressive behavior. *Child Development* **32**, 37–44.

Lovibond, S. H. (1967). The effect of media stressing crime and violence upon children's attitudes. *Social Problems* **15**, 91–100.

Lukenbill, W. B. (1972). "A Working Bibliography of American Doctoral Dissertations in Children's and Adolescent's Literature, 1930–1971." University of Illinois, Graduate School of Library Science, Urbana, Illinois. (Occasional Paper No. 103.)

McClaskey, H. C. (1970). "Bibliotherapy With Emotionally Disturbed Patients: An Experimental Study." Unpublished dissertation, University of Washington.

Maccoby, E. E. (1964). Effects of the mass media. In "Review of Child Development Research" (M. L. Hoffman and L. W. Hoffman, eds.), pp. 323–348. Russell Sage Foundation, New York.

Maccoby, E. E., Levin, H., and Selya, B. M. (1955). The effects of emotional arousal on the retention of aggressive and non-aggressive movie content. *American Psychologist* **10**, 359.

Maccoby, E. E., Levin, H., and Selya, B. M. (1956). The effects of emotional arousal on the retention of film content: a failure to replicate. *Journal of Abnormal and Social Psychology* **53**, 373–374.

McConaghy, N. (1967). Penile volume change to moving picture of male and female nudes in heterosexual and homosexual males. *Behaviour Research and Therapy* **5**, 43-48.
McDaniel, W. B., II (1956). Bibliotherapy: some historical and contemporary aspects. *ALA Bulletin* **50**, 584-589.
McGinnies, E. (1965). A Cross-cultural comparison of printed communication versus spoken communication in persuasion. *Journal of Psychology* **60**, 1-8.
McGuire, W. J. (1961a). The effectiveness of supportive and refutational defences in immunizing and restoring beliefs against persuasion. *Sociometry* **24**, 184-197.
McGuire, W. J. (1961b). Resistance to persuasion conferred by active and passive prior refutation of the same and alternate counter-arguments. *Journal of Abnormal and Social Psychology* **63**, 326-332.
McGuire, W. J. (1962). Persistence of the resistance to persuasion induced by various types of prior belief defenses. *Journal of Abnormal and Social Psychology* **64**, 241-248.
McGuire, W. J. (1964). Inducing resistance to persuasion. *In* "Advances in Experimental Social Psychology" (L. Berkowitz, ed.), Vol. 1, pp. 191-229. Academic Press, New York.
McGuire, W. J. (1969). The nature of attitudes and attitude change. *In* "The Handbook of Social Psychology" (G. Lindzey and E. Aronson, eds.), pp. 136-314. Addison-Wesley, Cambridge, Massachusetts.
McGuire, W. J. (1973). Persuasion, resistance, and attitude change. *In* "Handbook of Communication" (I. Pool, ed.), pp. 216-252. Rand McNally, Chicago, Illinois.
McGuire, W. J., and Papageorgis, D. (1961). The relative efficacy of various types of prior belief-defense in producing immunity against persuasion. *Journal of Abnormal and Social Psychology* **62**, 327-337.
Madden, L. E. (1970). "The Impact of Information About Negroes on Attitude Change." Unpublished dissertation, Ball State University.
Mann, J. (1971). Experimental induction of human sexual arousal. *In* Commission on Obscenity and Pornography. "Technical Report," Vol. 1, pp. 23-60. Government Printing Office, Washington, D. C.
Mann, J., Sidman, J., and Starr, S. (1973). Evaluating social consequences of erotic films: an experimental approach. *Journal of Social Issues* **29**, No. 3, 113-131.
Masters, W. H. (1967). Clinical significance of the study of human sexual response. *Medical Aspects of Human Sexuality* **1**, 14-20.
Masters, W. H., and Johnson, V. E. (1966). "Human Sexual Response." Little, Brown, Boston, Massachusetts.
Menninger, K. (1961). Reading as therapy. *ALA Bulletin* **55**, 316-319.
Meyerson, L. (1966). "The Effects of Filmed Aggression on the Aggressive Responses of High and Low Aggressive Subjects." Unpublished dissertation, University of Iowa.
Miller, D. R., and Swanson, G. E. (1960). "Inner Conflict and Defense." Holt, Rinehart and Winston, New York.

Monroe, M. E. (1971a). Reader services and bibliotherapy. *In* "Reading Guidance and Bibliotherapy in Public, Hospital, and Institutional Libraries," pp. 40–44. University of Wisconsin Press, Madison, Wisconsin.

Monroe, M. E. (1971b). Services in hospital and institution libraries. *In* "Libraries in the Therapeutic Society" (G. M. Casey, comp.), pp. 11–13. American Library Association, Chicago, Illinois.

Mortensen, C. D. (1972). "Communication: The Study of Interaction." McGraw-Hill, New York.

Moses, H. A., and Zaccaria, J. S. (1969). Bibliotherapy in the educational context: rationale and principles. *High School Journal* **52**, 401–411.

Mosher, D. L. (1971). Psychological reactions to pornographic films. *In* Commission on Obscenity and Pornography. "Technical Report," Vol. 8, pp. 255–312. Government Printing Office, Washington, D. C.

Mosher, D. L., and Greenberg, I. (1969). Females' affective responses to reading erotic literature. *Journal of Consulting and Clinical Psychology* **33**, 472–477.

Mussen, P. H., and Rutherford, E. (1961). Effects of aggressive cartoons in children's aggressive play. *Journal of Abnormal and Social Psychology* **62**, 461–464.

Mussen, P. H., and Scodel, A. (1955). The effects of sexual stimulation under varying conditions on TAT sexual responsiveness. *Journal of Consulting Psychology* **19**, 90.

Nawy, H. (1973). In the pursuit of happiness?: consumers of erotica in San Francisco. *Journal of Social Issues* **29**, No. 3, 147–161.

Obeler, E. M. (1974). "The Fear of the Word: Censorship and Sex." Scarecrow Press, Metuchen, New Jersey.

Osgood, C., and Tannenbaum, P. (1955). The principle of congruity in the prediction of attitude change. *Psychological Review* **62**, 42–55.

Otto, H. A. (1963). Sex and violence on the American newsstand. *Journalism Quarterly* **37**, 19–26.

Paul, J. C. N., and Schwartz, M. L. (1961). "Federal Censorship: Obscenity in the Mail." The Free Press, Glencoe, New York.

Peak, H., and Morrison, H. (1958). The acceptance of information into attitude structure. *Journal of Abnormal and Social Psychology* **57**, 127–135.

Peavler, W. S., and McLaughlin, J. P. (1967). The question of stimulus content and pupil size. *Psychonomic Science* **8**, 505–506.

Pelz, D. C., and Andrews, F. M. (1964). Detecting causal priorities in panel study data. *American Sociological Review* **29**, 836–848.

Pepitone, A., and Reichling, G. (1955). Group cohesiveness and the expression of hostility. *Human Relations* **3**, 327–337.

Peterson, R. C., and Thurston, L. L. (1933). "Motion Pictures and the Social Attitudes of Children." Macmillan, New York.

Phaedrus; A Newsletter of Children's Literature Research (1973+).

Pope, M. (1974). "Sex and the Undecided Librarian; A Study of Librarians' Opinions on Sexually Oriented Literature." Scarecrow Press, Metuchen, New Jersey.

Ramsey, G. (1943). The sexual development of boys. *American Journal of Psychology* **56**, 217–233.

Roach, W. J., and Kreisberg, L. (1971). Westchester College students' views on pornography. *In* Commission on Obscenity and Pornography. "Technical Report," Vol. 1, pp. 185–189. Government Printing Office, Washington, D. C.

Roberts, D., and Maccoby, N. (1973). Information processing and persuasion: counterarguing behavior. *In* "New Models for Mass Communication Research" (P. Clarke, ed.), pp. 269–307. Sage Publications, Beverley Hills, California.

Robinson, H. W., and Weintraub, S. (1973). Research related to children's interests and to developmental values of reading. *Library Trends* 21, 81–108.

Rokeach, M. (1960). "The Open and Closed Mind." Basic Books, New York.

Rokeach, M., and Mezei, L. (1966). Race and shared belief as factors in social choice. *Science* 151, 167–172.

Rongione, L. A. (1972). Bibliotherapy: its nature and uses. *Catholic Library World* 43, 495–500.

Rosenbaum, M. E., and de Charms, R. (1960). Direct and vicarious reduction of hostility. *Journal of Abnormal and Social Psychology* 60, 105–111.

Rosnow, R. L., and Robinson, E. J. (1967). "Experiments in Persuasion." Academic Press, New York.

Ryan, M. J. (1957). Bibliotherapy and psychiatry: changing concepts, 1937–1957. *Special Libraries* 48, 197–199.

Samuelson, M., Carter, R. F., and Ruggels, W. L. (1963). Education, available time, and use of mass media. *Journalism Quarterly* 40, 491–496.

Schiller, P. (1971). Effects of mass media on the sexual behavior of adolescent females. *In* Commission on Obscenity and Pornography. "Technical Report," Vol. 1, pp. 191–195. Government Printing Office, Washington, D. C.

Schmidt, G., and Sigusch, V. (1970). Sex differences in response to psychosexual stimulation by films and slides. *Journal of Sex Research* 6, 268–283.

Schmidt, G., Sigusch, V., and Meyberg, J. (1969). Psychosexual stimulation in men: emotional reactions, changes of sex behavior, and measures of conservative attitudes. *Journal of Sex Research* 5, 199–217.

Schramm, W., ed. (1963). "The Science of Human Communication." Basic Books, New York.

Schramm, W. (1971). The nature of communication between humans. *In* "The Process and Effects of Mass Communication" (W. Schramm and D. F. Roberts, eds.), pp. 3–53. University of Illinois Press, Urbana, Illinois.

Schramm, W., Lyle, J., and Parker, E. (1961). "Television in the Lives of Our Children." Stanford University Press, Stanford, California.

Schwoebel, B. (1973). Bibliotherapy: a guide to materials. *Catholic Library World* 44, 586–592.

Sears, D. O. (1969). Political behavior. *In* "The Handbook of Social Psychology" (G. Lindzey and E. Aronson, eds.), Vol. 5, pp. 315–458. Addison-Wesley, Reading, Massachusetts.

Sears, D. O., and Freedman, J. L. (1967). Selective exposure to information: a critical review. *Public Opinion Quarterly* 31, 194–213.

Sherif, C. W., Sherif, M., and Nebergall, R. E. (1965) "Attitude and Attitude Change." Saunders, Philadelphia, Pennsylvania.
Sherrill, L. L. (1972). "The Affective Response of Ethnic Minority Readers to Indigenous Ghetto Literature." Unpublished dissertation, University of Wisconsin.
Shrodes, C. (1960). Bibliotherapy: an application of psychoanalytic theory. *American Imago* 17, 311–319.
Shrodes, C. (1961). The dynamics of reading: implications for bibliotherapy. *ETC* 18, 21–33.
Siegel, A. (1956). Film-mediated fantasy aggression and strength of aggressive drive. *Child Development* 27, 365–378.
Siegel, A. (1958). The influence of violence in the mass media upon children's role expectations. *Child Development* 29, 35–56.
Sigusch, V., Schmidt, G., Reinfeld, A., and Wiedemann-Sutor, I. (1970). Psychological stimulation: sex differences. *Journal of Sex Research* 6, 10–24.
Steinberg, H. (1972). Books and readers as a subject of research in Europe and America. *International Social Sciences Journal* 24, 744–755.
Swanson, C. E. (1955). What they read in 130 daily newspapers. *Journalism Quarterly* 32, 411–421.
Taft, R. (1954). Selective recall and memory distortion of favorable and unfavorable material. *Journal of Abnormal and Social Psychology* 49, 23–29.
Tannenbaum, P. H. (1971). Emotional arousal as a mediator of communication effects. *In* Commission on Obscenity and Pornography. "Technical Report," Vol. 8, pp. 326–356. Government Printing Office, Washington, D. C.
Tauran, R. H. (1967). "The Influences of Reading on the Attitudes of Third Graders Toward Eskimos." Unpublished dissertation, University of Maryland.
Tews, R. M. (1969). Bibliotherapy. *In* "Encyclopedia of Library and Information Science" (A. Kent and H. Lancour, eds.), Vol. 2, pp. 448–457. Marcel Dekker, New York.
Tews, R. M. (1970). Progress in bibliotherapy. *In* "Advances in Librarianship" (M. J. Voigt, ed.), Vol. 1, pp. 171–188, Academic Press, New York.
Thibaut, J. W., and Coules, J. (1952). The role of communication in the reduction of interpersonal hostility. *Journal of Abnormal and Social Psychology* 47, 770–777.
Thornberry, T. P., and Silverman, R. A. (1971). Exposure to pornography and juvenile delinquency: the relationship as indicated by juvenile court records. *In* Commission on Obscenity and Pornography. "Technical Report," Vol. 1, pp. 175–179. Government Printing Office, Washington, D. C.
Toffler, A. (1970). "Future Shock." Random House, New York.
Troldahl, V. C., and Van Dam, R. (1965). Face-to-face communication about major topics in the news. *Public Opinion Quarterly* 29, 626–634.
Ulibarri, M. R. (1970). "The Socialization Process, Role Theory and a Teaching Taxonomy: An Application to Children's Literature." Unpublished dissertation, University of New Mexico.
Vidmar, N., and Rokeach, M. (1974). Archie Bunker's bigotry: a study in selective perception and exposure. *Journal of Communication* 24, 36–47.

Wallace, D. H. (1973). Obscenity and contemporary standards. *Journal of Social Issues* **29**, No. 3, 53–68.
Walters, R., and Thomas, E. (1963). Enhancement of punitiveness by visual and audio-visual displays. *Canadian Journal of Psychology* **17**, 244–255.
Walters, R., Thomas, E., and Acker, C. (1962). Enhancement of punitive behavior by audiovisual displays. *Science* **136**, 872–873.
Waples, D., Berelson, B., and Bradshaw, F. R. (1940). "What Reading Does to People." University of Chicago Press, Chicago, Illinois.
Weimerskirch, P. J. (1965). Benjamin Rush and John Minson Galt, II—pioneers of bibliotherapy in America. *Medical Library Association Bulletin* **53**, 510–526.
Weiss, W. (1969). Effects of the mass media of communication, *In* "The Handbook of Social Psychology" (G. Lindzey and E. Aronson, eds.), Vol. 5, pp. 77–195. Addison-Wesley, Reading, Massachusetts.
Weitzman, L. J., Eifler, D., Hokada, E., and Ross, C. (1972). Sex-role socialization in picture books for preschool children. *American Journal of Sociology* **77**, 1125–1148.
Wenger, M. A., Averill, J. A., and Smith, D. D. (1968). Autonomic activity during sexual arousal. *Psychophysiology* **4**, 468–478.
White, D. M., and Barnett, L. D. (1971). College students' attitudes on pornography' a pilot study. *In* Commission on Obsenity and Pornography. "Technical Report," Vol. 1, pp. 181–184. Government Printing Office, Washington, D. C.
Wilson, W. C. (1973). Law enforcement officer's perceptions of pornography as a social issue. *Journal of Social Issues* **29**, No. 3, 41–51.
Wilson, W. C., and Abelson, H. I. (1973). Experience with and attitudes toward explicit sexual materials. *Journal of Social Issues* **29**, No. 3, 19–39.
Wilson, W. C., and Goldstein, M. J., eds. (1973). Pornography: attitudes, use, and effects. *Journal of Social Issues* **29**, No. 3, 1–225.
Woodyard, M. A. (1970). "The Effects of Teaching Black Literature to a Ninth-Grade Class in a Negro High School in Picayune, Mississippi." Unpublished dissertation, University of Tennessee.
Worell, J. and Worell, L. (1974). Supporters and opposers of the women's liberation movement: some personality and parental correlates. *In* "Lecturas en Psicologia Social Contemporanea," Trillas, Mexico City.
Yungman, G. T. (1969). "An Experimental Comparison of Equivalent Pictoral-Auditory, Auditory and Written Modes of Disseminating Occupational Information among Inner City and Suburban Negro Adolescents." Unpublished dissertation, George Washington University.
Zaccaria, J. S., and Moses, H. A. (1968). "Facilitating Human Development Through Reading: The Use of Bibliotherapy in Teaching and Counciling." Stipes Publishing Co., Champaign, Illinois.
Zajonc, R. B. (1954). "Cognitive Structure and Cognitive Tuning," Unpublished dissertation, University of Michigan.
Zamansky, H. S. (1956). A technique for assessing homosexual tendencies. *Journal of Personality* **24**, 436–446.
Zimbardo, D. (1972). The tactics and ethics of persuasion. *In* "Attitudes.

Conflict, and Social Change" (B. King and E. McGinnies, eds.), pp. 84–99. Academic Press, New York.

Zucaro, B. J. (1972). "The Use of Bibliotherapy among Sixth Graders to Affect Attitude Change Toward American Negroes." Unpublished dissertation, Temple University.

Zuckerman, M. (1971). Physiological measures of sexual arousal in the human. *In* Commission on Obscenity and Pornography. "Technical Report," Vol. 1, pp. 61–101. Government Printing Office, Washington, D. C.

Trends in Library Education—Europe

DONALD DAVINSON

Leeds Polytechnic

I.	Introduction and Outline of Problems	218
II.	History and State of the Art in the United Kingdom	220
	A. Origins	220
	B. Postwar Development of Full-Time Education for Librarianship	223
III.	Library Education in Continental Europe	225
	A. Introduction	225
	B. Central Europe	228
	C. Eastern Europe	231
	D. Southern Europe	232
	E. Scandinavia	232
IV.	Issues in European Library Education	234
	A. Stratification of Professional Education	234
	B. Librarianship as an Academic Discipline	236
	C. Practice Work in Libraries	238
	D. Continuing Education	243
	E. Harmonization of Qualifications	245
V.	Intervention by Library Associations in Education for Librarianship	247
	A. United Kingdom	247
	B. Europe	248
	References	249

I. INTRODUCTION AND OUTLINE OF PROBLEMS

Attempting to draw out broad themes in library education over such a large area with such a diversity of cultural traditions as those represented in Europe is to run the risk of parading facile oversimplications or unhelpful generalizations from specific cases. Certainly to a British educator it is tempting to comment on the more apparent differences between Britain and the rest of Europe in the same terms as the proud mother watching her soldier son on parade. "Just look! Everybody is out of step except our Johnny," she said! There are such stark divergences of practice between Britain and the rest of Europe as to make the points of comparability difficult to organize into a coherent pattern. One is tempted to explore such interesting, but probably unprovable, theories as that which argues that in Europe senior librarians are often scholars first and professional librarians second. If provable, the contrast is with the British scene where, to a greater extent than anywhere else in Europe, librarianship itself has been exalted to the status of an academic study in its own right. Such statements are easy to make, but the elaboration of a rigorous theory based upon this is virtually impossible.

However, there are consistencies of theme in education for librarianship across Europe including Britain. The area with the most common ground is the recognition of the need for continuing education for senior staff and the need to develop improved programs for the education of school librarians. Also common in the literature, without achieving a similar unity of conclusion, is the discussion of the necessary integration of practical fieldwork with the theoretical study of librarianship. The considerable emphasis in Britain and eastern Europe upon considerations of the social role of the library—heavily overladen with outright political indoctrination in eastern Europe—is not common elsewhere in Europe. Generally speaking, the observer of the library education scene in Europe could expect to discern broad similarities, if not correspondence of fine detail, among nearly all countries. Having noted this, it must be said that the British scene would probably appear to be bafflingly unique, if not totally incomprehensible. When Piquard (1967) compiled his survey of patterns of library education throughout Europe, he found it necessary to place the United Kingdom in a separate (albeit very inadequate) section at the end, which quite appropriately stressed the role of the professional associations (the "Corporations," as he called them) as the principal sources of vocational education for librarianship.

A major difference between library education in Britain and most of the rest of Europe is the lack of an explicitly structured series of levels of education for different grades and types of libraries. This is seen, perhaps at its most extreme, in the development of formal courses for nonprofessional and even part-time staff in many European countries—an area virtually ignored in the United Kingdom. By contrast, the level of intervention of library associations in library education is hardly noticeable in many European countries but is all important in Britain and is fundamental to an understanding of the method and pattern of British library education.

The complex of levels, grades, and types of education for librarianship across Europe, as classified by Piquard, tends to support his suggestion that the British scene is unique and, perhaps, even wrongheaded, and underlines the fact that educational patterns tend to arise out of differing cultural traditions rather than out of rationality. The essential fact in Britian is that, historically, the prime influence on the pattern of development of education for librarianship has been that of the Library Association rather than of any individual academic institutions or group of such institutions.

While patterns are comprehensible in terms of structure, the approach to the formulation of policy for undertaking the task of teaching librarianship is less easy to elaborate. Theoretically, it might be possible to suggest that the poorer countries of Europe educate librarians, if at all, in a fashion very different from that in the richer countries. In particular, it would make sense to anticipate that only the richer, larger countries could boast established schools of librarianship with full-time teaching staff. An examination of the facts in the matter reveals such a thesis to be only partially supportable. Certainly, in southern Europe such education for librarianship as exists is restricted to the part-time, in terms of both teaching staff and students. Such a preference, however, exists in other countries (if not larger, then at least considerably richer ones), in northern Europe—Switzerland, Sweden, Holland, Belgium. Furthermore, in western Europe, if the United Kingdom, West Germany, and Denmark are eliminated from one's calculations, few programs that might be termed "full-time" can be detected.

More defensible, as a workable model for the analysis of library education in Europe, is one which divides countries into two groups: (1) those with a tradition of theoretical education for librarianship and (2) those that emphasize training in the routines and techniques associated with the work of one library or a group of similar libraries. In the former, the potential for research and the association of subject bibliography with academic subject study have created an obvious need for the development of widely acceptable general principles which transcend the more utilitarian and vocational approaches and which attempt to explain causes and effects in an "academic" as well as a "professional" way. Eastern Europe, West Germany, and the United Kingdom—especially the United Kingdom—fit this model. The impoverished state of development of librarianship in parts of southern Europe explains the rather prosaic concentration on training for practice in an individual library. Such a ready explanation eludes us when we observe a similar situation in such large and relatively rich countries as France, or such a technologically advanced and very rich country as Sweden, with its high level of educational excellence and library service. It implies that below a certain level of economic development a sophisticated system of education for librarianship is a luxury not to be afforded, while above a certain level of economic and social provision it is a system one can do without. It is certainly interesting to speculate why it is that the nature and extent of provision in neighboring countries of generally equivalent levels of political educational and economic development can be so different. Perhaps a more detailed analysis of these themes will clarify the situation somewhat.

II. HISTORY AND STATE OF THE ART IN THE UNITED KINGDOM

A. Origins

Formal programs of education for librarianship in the United Kingdom can be said to have begun in 1885, when the first examinations in librarianship were held at centers in London and Nottingham. This early direct intervention by the Library Association in the educational process represents the basic factor distinguishing the patterns of education for librarianship in the United Kingdom from those of the rest of Europe, if not the world. It is also the factor which makes the British system of education most difficult for the outsider to understand, and the one which makes a fairly detailed description of the British pattern necessary before any examination of trends and patterns in the rest of Europe can be attempted.

The early history of education for librarianship in the United Kingdom is centered principally around self-directed independent study under informal conditions. Correspondence courses administered by a Library Assistants Association (later to become the Association of Assistant Librarians and a constituent section of the Library Association) were available to students in rural areas. In London and some other major provincial cities, evening classes were sometimes available, and the various associations of librarians organized weekend and vacation courses. Only a very few enlightened employers gave any assistance to would-be students, either financially or by way of leaves of absence, for study purposes. Even the availability of programs of in-service training for the staffs in the larger libraries was a rare phenomenon.

The United Kingdom is characterized by a tradition, based in the nineteenth century, which tends to exalt self-help, puritanical self-denial, and suffering in order to obtain an education and fulfill one's calling. The remnants of such a tradition are still a factor to be reckoned with in the initiation of new educational programs. Harrison (1963) reviews this and other reasons why a strong tradition of part-time education has persisted in the United Kingdom.

Hogg (1969) expressed his astonishment at the fact that it was more than thirty years after the instigation of a pattern of examination and certification of librarians that the first program of full-time study was funded at University College, London, in 1919. Francis (1968), in dealing with the history of this, the first library school in the United Kingdom, dramatizes the controversial nature of this step. The worry was that the academic environment was likely to be altogether too rarefied and cerebral for what was thought of as a purely pragmatic and technical occupation. In fact, had it not been for a substantial financial contribution from the Carnegie United

Kingdom Trust to the University of London for the purpose of establishing a program in librarianship, Hogg's astonishment might well have grown, since the establishment of the first library school might have been delayed for many years. For, aside from the willingness of this single institution to accept charitable funds for the purpose of establishing a library school, there is no evidence of a ground swell of popular opinion in support of the concept of full-time education for librarianship in the post-World War I days.

This first halting step toward full-time education for librarianship had a limited impact, and University College, London, School of Librarianship and Archives, certainly did not have the same influence on the British scene as did the Graduate Library School at the University of Chicago in the United States. The slow progress made by the London school and the limited demand for places in its postgraduate course were not such as to inspire others to rush to emulate it.

Hogg (1969) identified two principal reasons why formal education for librarianship did not develop in British universities in the interwar years in spite of the great strides being made by libraries in the United Kingdom during that time. The first was that there was no tradition of professional education in the universities. Harrison (1963) had already pointed out that it was customary for virtually all vocational and quasi-professional education to be undertaken parttime in nonuniversity establishments. It was not until the mid-1960's, for example, that the first full-time business school was established in a British university. The second reason is that throughout the twentieth century the proportion of British secondary school graduates obtaining access to university education has been markedly lower than that of any other country boasting similar levels of cultural and economic development. They have, indeed, been less than those of countries of much lower levels of development. The reasons for this curious state of affairs are difficult to summarize. However, there is a definite strand in British educational philosophy which argues that entry to a university must be restricted to the gifted few. Those less gifted or, at least, less inclined to an academic, as opposed to a vocational or immediately relevant, education, were, and to some extent still are, obliged to seek their postschool education elsewhere. This is why the creation and continuation of a stronger and larger structure of postschool education outside of the university sector have been found to be more necessary in the United Kingdom as compared to virtually every other European country.

If the pre-World War II British universities thought at all about providing professional education their thoughts were confined almost entirely to postgraduate courses. Since the number of graduates of the relatively few universities in Britain was small and since the financial rewards of librarianship were generally poor, not many graduates went into librarianship. As a consequence there was little or no pressure on enrollment at the one existing graduate school of librarianship—certainly not enough to cause the development of more such schools in other universities.

The absence of any tradition of professional education for librarianship among university graduates with, or even without, any further graduate vocational training, coupled with an *established* tradition of association certification of the vast majority of the senior and middle ranks of the library profession, contributed to the state of affairs existing at the start of World War II. Librarianship at virtually every level was regarded as being based upon vocational skills rather than upon academic scholarship. Few, even among the most senior librarians outside of university libraries, were graduates; but many held the Library Association's professional certificate.

B. Postwar Development of Full-Time Education for Librarianship

In 1946 and 1947 a number of full-time programs of education for librarianship were established in various nonuniversity higher education centers in the United Kingdom, but they were not widely considered as anything but a purely temporary phenomenon. They were initiated to provide the means of swiftly enabling returning war veterans to catch up study time lost by five or so years of war service. Courses were of one academic year in duration and were designed to prepare students for the examinations of the Library Association. Both the examinations and the curricula were carefully stipulated by the Association. There was no question of individual educational institutions establishing their own programs. It was a considerable surprise to many observers when the purely "temporary" schools of librarianship proved to be attractive to young people who were not war veterans and who were not attracted by the thought of long periods spent in part-time study at the end of a full day's work as a means of obtaining professional certification.

Throughout the late 1940's and 1950's, the wisdom of providing opportunities for full-time education for librarianship was hotly debated. Although a wide measure of support existed for the availability of full-time education for some entrants, it was generally felt that part-time education was much to be preferred. The Library Association, however, never wavered from its view that full-time education must not only exist but in time become the norm. It is now, in the mid-1970's, perhaps, a matter for regret that the strength of the trend toward full-time education has been such that virtually all alternative methods of study for professional librarianship have been eliminated. Correspondence course tuition is no longer available, and very few opportunities for part-time study exist. In order to overcome opposition and succeed in the attempt to establish programs of full-time education it was necessary to denigrate the efficacy of alternative means, and these alternatives have now been virtually killed off. As a consequence, education for librarianship in Britain has none of the flexibility that is widely prevalent in, say, eastern Europe, where the existence of correspondence courses and part-time opportunities has apparently not affected the popularity of full-time courses.

By 1960 in the United Kingdom, full-time education for librarianship was firmly established. Further strengthening occurred at this time owing to two developments. The Library Association, for whose examinations every library school other than the University College, London, was still preparing students, doubled the length of its program from one to two years. The most immediate effect of this was to increase the size of the existing schools, not only in terms of students, but, more importantly, in terms of staff who were now able to specialize and to develop curricula, scholarly abilities, and facilities to a much greater extent. At the same time the undoubted success of vocational education in post-World War II Britain, in areas other than librarianship, caused the universities to begin to take an interest in the field. Several new university-based schools of librarianship were formed at this time.

In the mid-1960's further diversification and development became possible through the inauguration of the Council for National Academic Awards. This was an organization empowered by Government decree to offer facilities for nonuniversity higher education establishments to develop qualifications and other educational opportunities on equal terms with the university sector. In particular it was their aim to encourage the growth of programs in areas not hitherto considered to be traditional vehicles for academic study. The library schools were early contenders for such facilities, and the late 1960's saw the establishment of several programs of three to four years' duration, offering librarianship as an academic study in its own right, equal in status to that of traditionally academic fields such as history. Lewis (1973) has labeled this development in the United Kingdom as the most significant event in the history of library education. As a former library school lecturer and, more recently, a university librarian in one of Britain's largest universities, his further claim that British education for librarianship is the best in Europe might be considered by many to be a somewhat biased opinion. An important by-product of the evolution of these courses has been that the role of the Library Association, once preeminent in examination and syllabus design, is now much more limited in library education. Saunders (1969) has elaborated the complex structure of contemporary education for librarianship in Britain, drawing needed attention to the difficulties facing employers in assessing the relative merits of what New (1972) has called the diversity of qualifications which has arisen in the past ten years in British librarianship. The diversity retains, however, the unifying factor of fairly careful overall surveillance by the Library Association. All library schools have thought it worthwhile to seek dispensation from the Association so that their graduates may seek the designation "Associates of the Library Association" and describe themselves as "Chartered Librarians," subject only to completing a period of professional practice. Palmer (1970) surveys the impact of all of these developments.

III. LIBRARY EDUCATION IN CONTINENTAL EUROPE

A. Introduction

If, as was stated in the introduction, the patterns of continental Europe and the United Kingdom seem to diverge at almost every point, it must be quickly noted that there is one major point of similarity. Across much of Europe such library education as exists is of relatively recent origin compared to the history of her libraries. To be sure, traces of more or less formal education for librarianship can be found stretching back into the nineteenth or even the eighteenth century in most countries, but it is only recently that formal education for librarianship has gained noticeable influence and continuity in a few countries. Indeed, in most countries in Europe the conviction remains strong that only strictly on-the-job training, which is immediately relevant to a library's specific needs, is desirable as a method of education for professional librarianship.

A major difference between the British and continental European patterns has been the relative lack of commitment to the education of librarians by the various European library associations. The reasons for this and some of the results are discussed in Section IV.

A more puzzling dissimilarity, difficult to account for unless it be in terms of the effectiveness of the library associations, is that, generally speaking, the social status and levels of remuneration for librarians (relative to other professional groups) tend to be higher in Britain than elsewhere in Europe. This has occurred, moreover, against the background situation in the United Kingdom, perhaps the only country in Europe in which the necessity for senior librarians to be university graduates is seriously questioned, as the heated correspondence in the *Library Association Record* in 1974 and 1975 has shown.

Hjelmqvist (1968), in drawing out some of the points of difference between the pattern of activity in the Scandinavian countries as compared to West Germany, the Netherlands, and Czechoslovakia, rightly comments that many of the contrasts arise out of differences in the general educational and cultural traditions of the individual countries. He also points out something that is of fundamental significance in considering European patterns of education for librarianship and which, generally speaking, applies throughout the continent: that is, that the academic library tradition in Europe is both strong and long established. Libraries evolved patterns of training for their own individual staffs especially their senior staffs. Later, when libraries of this kind first thought of more formal structures of education for librarianship, it was the development of courses for assistants, rather than for senior staff, which occupied their attention. This tendency is probably explained by the fact that the senior staffs of European academic libraries have always been scholars and subject specialists first and, what one might term, general librarians, second. Such people would tend to have special techniques and knowledge relevant only to their own specific functions. On the other hand, their assistants, undertaking more of the housekeeping and routine functions of the library, would tend to have much more in common with assistants from other sections of the individual library and even with those of other academic libraries. The task of codifying some common body of technique and practice relevant to the needs of the junior staff and capable of being taught "off the job" was therefore both simpler and more pressing; hence a special structure of programs for such staff often evolved before any other type.

Furthermore, in many European countries the public library movement has not been so coherent, strongly rooted, and significant as in the United States and the United Kingdom. Therefore, when development of this sector began to occur, it did so, in contrast to the situation in the United States and the United Kingdom, at a different time from that of the academic libraries and, indeed, the special libraries. Consequently the patterns of education for academic libraries, already established, were often thought to be unfitted for the needs of other types of libraries and further special programs based on the needs of these other types tended to be the result. The consequent structuring, stratification, and fragmentation into small units, which is so much a feature of European education for librarianship, is described in detail in the International Federation of Library Associations (IFLA) special report (1966). This theme will be returned to later, but it is worth mentioning here that the virtually concurrent growth of academic and public libraries in the United States and the United Kingdom may well be a potent reason for the much greater coherence of education for librarianship in those countries. The indications are that in some parts of Europe the coherence, which has almost a natural growth in the two countries mentioned, is being painstakingly striven for against a background of entrenched vested interest and special pleading. On grounds of economy of operation of library education, such coherence is probably inevitable. On grounds of sheer efficiency of a nation's library network, it is probably also an essential requirement. Cooperation and creative joint development of library services are surely easier against a background in which the library staffs of the several participants began from the same starting points of professional education.

B. Central Europe

1. FRANCE

In France, one of the largest and certainly most traditionally library-conscious countries—at least in the academic world—the situation of professional education for librarianship is little short of incredible. De Grolier (1973) provides statistics which reveal that the total "stock" of professional librarians educated to the level that term might imply in the United States is only about 4,000 for a country of 52 million people. The consequences of such massive underprovision are in De Grolier's words, that: "Only a small elite is adequately served by good libraries, the great majority of the French population remaining with unsatisfactory services."

A major problem for the development of libraries and library education in France is that the traditional role of the librarian as a conservator of knowledge, rather than the means for its exploitation, is only very slowly being changed.

2. ITALY

Huckaby (1971) tends to contrast the unhappy state of provision in Italy with the relatively lavish provision in France in such a way as to underline the problems, bearing in mind De Grolier's strictures about France. In the early 1920's, properly constituted (if poor quality) formal programs of education for librarianship began to emerge. Roxas (1972) enumerates the large number of historical antecedents, none of which amount to very much more than in-service training exercises. More useful is her statistical appendix, indicating a persistent unwillingness of the library education programs established to grow in sustained fashion. There is a considerable shortage of professionally educated personnel and widespread dissatisfaction with the quality of those available. There are encouraging signs that the Italian Library Association is beginning to exert itself to tackle the problems of improving the quality of education available.

There are a number of major difficulties to face. Huckaby (1971) tells of one of them in drawing attention to a general lack of accepted principles of wide application between the different types of libraries and even between different libraries of the same type. For example, there is no code of cataloging practice that can be pointed to as being preeminent. Teaching programs at a level higher than that of the individual library are, therefore, hard to develop. As in France, the approach of senior library personnel in Italy to their tasks is often that of preservation rather than exploitation of stock, and it must be said that very high quality work in the field of book preservation is both undertaken and taught in Italy. The future in Italy is not easy to forecast. The country has emerged relatively recently from the economic underdevelopment typical of southern Europe, the region to which it belongs geographically, to relative affluence in the wake of the boom in northwestern Europe to which it is now politically linked. Italy now has the resources it once did not have to make rapid strides; but against the rising tide of affluence—especially in northern Italy—has to be balanced an apparently chronic disinclination to pay taxes to support public institutions and works of which education and libraries are so very much a part. Tentori (1972) reports the establishment of a "National List of Trained Librarians" and proposals for the establishment of degree courses in librarianship on the British model.

3. WEST GERMANY

The tradition of full-time education for librarianship in West Germany dates back to 1886, but, as in virtually all other parts of Europe, the significant development has been recent. In West Germany the European tradition of different types of library education being provided in separate programs is increasingly being challenged. The consequences of the separated patterns were elaborated by Frank (1967) as providing less potential for career mobility than British practice allows and as creating an unfortunate situation in which initial qualifications tend to predetermine career opportunities. Pflugk (1973) provides an account of the considerable progress made in recent years in the promotion of librarianship as an academic discipline in its own right. This development has enabled rapid progress to be made in widening the scope of courses to include a balanced mix of professional education, general education, and such desirable secondary skills as computing. Inevitably the newer developments do not meet every need or obtain total support. In West Germany there is a wide variety of programs of education for librarianship coexisting and under careful scrutiny to ascertain which is most likely to meet most adequately the current and future situation (Carroll, 1972). A major unresolved problem is that the ordered development of a widely acceptable revised scheme on a federal-wide basis is complicated by the wide range of powers for the control of libraries and the employment of librarians, which is held by the various provinces of the Federal Republic.

4. OTHER CENTRAL EUROPEAN COUNTRIES

Switzerland is a country sharing several common features with Sweden. These two are the richest countries in Europe in terms of gross national product per capita. They are also the only countries of any consequence which have had no enforced reappraisals and national reconstructions as a result of war damage in World War II. Cornaz (1967), in describing the state of the art of library education in Switzerland, pinpointed a further similarity between the two countries: the apparent lack of adequate facilities for advanced education of professional librarians. Facilities are very much geared to the library technician levels of staff.

In Belgium and Holland the basic difficulties of the stratification and specialization of library functions are complicated by a further series of problems. These arise in Belgium because of the existence of two language groups and in Holland by the fact that there are separate provisions for Protestants and Catholics. Attempts to coordinate and coalesce fragmentary programs in Belgium have been inhibited by, among other things, the large number of small and weak autonomous associations of librarians. In Holland a start has been made on the coordination of library education. Hjelmqvist (1968) makes particular reference to the establishment of the large multifunctional school of librarianship in Amsterdam but points out that one of the most serious problems is establishing effective programs quickly and on a large scale, where none previously existed. This problem is one which has been encountered in a number of other countries in Europe, such as Finland, Greece, and, most recently, Iceland. Particularly frustrating is the lack of sufficient teachers of librarianship possessing the necessary academic credentials and professional experience.

C. Eastern Europe

Eastern Europe represents the part of the continent where the broadest range of opportunities for the study of librarianship can be found. Basically the opportunities for full-time study are good throughout eastern Europe, and state financial support for students is very well developed. That such financial support is sometimes directly tied to examination results in a way which would be branded as elitist and unacceptable by student unions in nonsocialist countries is one of the minor mysteries of international politics. In addition to full-time courses, there are, typically in eastern Europe, extensive provisions for summer schools, part-time courses, and—an especially strong feature—correspondence courses organized by the library schools for students in rural areas. Library schools for the education of senior personnel are almost invariably housed in universities in eastern Europe, while the much more prevalent library schools for the middle range and junior professional staff are often housed in institutions for the education of school teachers. Indeed, joint qualifications as teachers and librarians is quite common.

The USSR boasts the most highly developed system of library education in eastern Europe, with close competition from East Germany. The Russian model is a strong influence on the rest of eastern Europe, especially in Hungary, Bulgaria, and Poland. For East Germany, Kunze (1970) reveals a pattern which is considerably more advanced than most. Like West Germany, however, East Germany has elevated librarianship to the rank of an independent academic study in its own right. While this is a trend likely to continue in eastern Europe, it is already much further developed in East Germany than anywhere else in Europe, other than the United Kingdom.

Abramov (1971) traces the origins of extensive programs for education for librarianship in the USSR in the 1930's, although there had been a program in St. Petersburg in prerevolutionary days. Rapid development, however, was delayed until the 1950's. Fonotov (1967) reports current annual production of more than 10,000 new professional librarians from 16 "high level" schools and 110 others.

Post-World War II development in eastern Europe is especially admirable, since there was little or no prewar basis of experience to draw upon in most countries. Strong and competent programs have developed, in spite of the rather stultifying effects of the conjoint development of ideological and professional education so prevalent in eastern Europe. A very real problem for the health of education for librarianship in eastern Europe is the restriction upon the freedom of movement of the people of the socialist countries. The inability of teaching staff to travel widely in the West and to study abroad has the unfortunate effect of reducing objectivity and breadth of vision. It is a feature of the educational system in most of eastern Europe that it is integrated with a national manpower plan, and librarianship is a part of such plans. In the context of such plans, and with associated measures for the direction of labor, the state is able to deploy qualified staff to areas of need regardless of personal inclination or specialization—at least in the early years of service.

D. Southern Europe

Development in southern Europe has been very slow relative to the rest of the continent. Hanz (1971) indicates that, since 1945, several major national education policy changes have severely disrupted the ordered development of education for librarianship in Yugoslavia. Greek and Turkish senior library personnel who have had professional education have usually obtained it abroad, generally in the United States. This circumstance creates considerable difficulty; it does little to create a pool of national experience in the development of locally relevant teaching for local library needs. The personnel educated overseas have the problem of acclimatization to a foreign tradition while studying and then a serious problem of reorienting their new knowledge when they return to their native land; some never do return.

E. Scandinavia

1. DENMARK

The baffling aspect of education for librarianship in Scandinavia is that, with the example of the remarkable Royal Danish Library School in their midst, the rest of the region has thus far an undistinguished record in education for librarianship. Denmark established a formal training program in 1918 that developed into the massive and monolithic Royal Danish School which has been frequently and comprehensively documented (e.g., Kirkegaard, 1971). The school provides programs at all levels, from advanced to those for part-time library assistants. This library school, perhaps unique in the world, has more than 1,000 students and nearly 100 staff, full-time and part-time. The Danish example proves that it is not only the larger countries which can provide a viable structure for education for librarianship.

2. SWEDEN

Sweden, Europe's richest country in terms of gross national product per capita, is, by contrast to Denmark, the scene of disarray and indecision. Ohlsson and Palmqvist (1970) note that students criticized the structure of professional education—they desired practical training *in* a specific library rather than what they claimed was outdated and irrelevant theoretical study in library schools. Such damaging admissions tend to indicate a deep-seated malaise and a lack of clear policy direction. Höglund and Jacobson (1973) provide a full account of the state of the art in Sweden. The most encouraging thing this report reveals is that since 1972 a College of Librarianship, patterned embryonically at least on the Danish model, has been established, providing common courses for all types of librarians with a core of full-time teaching staff providing a stability and consistency previously lacking.

3. OTHER SCANDINAVIAN COUNTRIES

It is a proud boast in Finland that the first chair in Library Science in Scandinavia was that established at the University of Tampere in 1971. Unfortunately the post has not been filled owing to a chronic shortage of adequately qualified teaching staff. Tammekann (1973) and Koskialla (1974) also draw attention to the one to one hundred staff-to-student ratio at the Tampere School. Further complications arise out of the need to provide facilities for the minority language group and the removal of the greater part of the education facilities from the capital city (Davinson, 1973).

Norway until recently had a very inadequate provision, but lately has apparently followed Denmark's example and established a special College of Library Studies (Rugaas, 1973). Iceland, the smallest

Scandinavian country, began to develop programs of library education on a full-time basis in 1973. An interesting overview of Scandinavian education for librarianship is that provided by Evans (1974), particularly valuable for its frequent comparison with the American situation.

IV. ISSUES IN EUROPEAN LIBRARY EDUCATION

A. Stratification of Professional Education

In many European countries the distribution of facilities for the education of librarians among educational institutions of different levels and qualities is usually accompanied by clear-cut distinctions in the nature of the education offered. These distinctions are to be seen, however, not simply in terms of the quality of education but also in terms of specialization as to the type of library the students are educated to enter. It is thus not uncommon in many European countries to find two or even three tiers of education for librarianship being offered in a number of educational institutions working in total isolation from each other. What might be termed a full professional education will be dealt with, in all probability, by university-level institutions. The training for subprofessional staff will be dealt with in a lesser grade of institution, probably that which is also responsible for primary and secondary school teacher training. The career opportunities of graduates of these programs will usually be severely limited. In some instances, a third tier of education or training will be provided for nonprofessional service assistants, either in still another category of educational establishment, or in individual libraries (Kovacs, 1966).

The practical effects of such stratification have often been to create a multiplicity of small schools of librarianship totally unconnected with each other and with each of them unable to provide the range of resources and staff necessary for a really effective system. An even more significant result of the dissipation of resources is that the several schools lack prestige and political strength within the institutions in which they are situated. Even greater confusion and still further opportunities for resource dissipation are provided by the practice of educating the subprofessional staff of academic and public libraries in isolation from each other. In some European countries the higher and lower echelons of the profession may be similarly separated. In many European countries the proposition that perhaps a greater degree of unification of the separate programs would result in improved quality is generally greeted with skepticism. Furthermore, a proposition that there is sufficient common ground between librarianship and that rather amorphous subject "information science" to justify unification would be greeted with outright derision. The nature of the complex stratification and specialization emerges from the study of such sources as the UNESCO/Bingley directory (1972) and from the situations in Russia, West Germany, and Italy (Carroll, 1973; Tentori, 1972; Zazersky, 1974). There is evidence of a shift of attitude in some European countries in favor of at least a certain amount of consolidation and integration into more effective and economical units. The country most interested in such a development is West Germany (Thauer, 1974).

It is certainly true that in Europe very often little attempt is made to isolate a body of general principles of librarianship. A great deal of the education offered in such circumstances becomes little more than the retailing of sets of predigested solutions to specific situations, rather than an attempt to provide opportunities for the development of programs intended to equip students for a more creative and innovative approach to the future problems of their profession. It is also possible to find evidence that education for librarianship is sometimes undertaken on the assumption that senior library staff are scholars interested more in academic than in professional pursuits. Education for such people often seems to be overly academic and research-oriented, aiming more at the creation of unassailable scholar credentials than at professional competence. A process which is intended to enhance the quality and status of the higher ranks of the profession can thus embody the inherent danger that it is also detrimental to the proper development of librarianship. It leads, in some countries, to the situation in which the level of academic qualification of an individual might be considered a higher imperative than professional competence in deciding on fitness for employment or promotion. There can be regulations governing the levels of academic, as distinct from professional, qualifications required to discharge the functions of a particular post. In circumstances such as these, the ambitious young librarian can be excused for devoting more attention to the pursuit of formal academic qualifications in a narrow subject area which may have no special relevance to librarianship, rather than to the development of professional competence. The consequences for the health and well-being of librarianship can rarely be happy.

There are few examples in the United Kingdom of closely defined qualifications appropriate to different levels of senior library personnel. Senior staff members in British university libraries are usually expected to be graduates in some traditional academic discipline, but, equally, they are also expected to be professionally qualified in librarianship. There is, indeed, a quite strong tradition of mobility between senior posts in different types of libraries. Some university librarians and most polytechnic librarians in the United Kingdom did, in fact, begin their careers in public libraries. Many industrial information specialists similarly began their careers in other branches of library work. Examples of individuals with senior experience in two, or even three, types of libraries are not hard to find. Such a situation would be unheard of in many European countries. Diversity of work experience among many senior British librarians has created a much stronger focus upon issues of general concern to the whole profession. In turn, this has assisted in the creation of large, multipurpose schools of librarianship committed to preparing students for all types of libraries. Even in Denmark, where there is one large school, it is, nevertheless, customary for different types of librarians to be taught largely in separated programs. Until some of the worst excesses of overspecialization and stratification are solved, education for librarianship in continental Europe will fall short of its obvious potential.

B. Librarianship as an Academic Discipline

As Lewis (1973) has said, the great achievement in the 1960's in the United Kingdom was the development of an appreciation of librarianship as an academic discipline, fit, in its own right, to stand alongside other and more traditional academic disciplines. Thus far this concept has not attracted much support elsewhere in Europe, despite the establishment of university chairs of librarianship in some countries. Indeed, as will be demonstrated elsewhere, the countries in which librarianship is regarded as a skill or technique outnumber those with any pretensions, at any level, for introduction of a more rigorous theoretical approach. Where chairs in librarianship, or indeed information science, exist in continental Europe, it is often in recognition of postgraduate research activities, rather than recognition of rigorous and demanding teaching at a more basic level. To be fair, the same might be said for many of the "chairs" in the United Kingdom, since it has been the polytechnic and college-based library schools which have pioneered much of the development of first-degree courses with librarianship as the core academic discipline.

In West Germany the question of how far librarianship can be regarded as a distinctive discipline is currently, if rather tentatively, being examined. The traditional concept of librarianship as a skill to be acquired by graduates of "established" academic disciplines appears to be dying hard in West Germany, but, as Pflugk (1973) indicates, a new dimension is being added in some library schools. Integrated programs, composed of courses in librarianship, an academic discipline, and its associated bibliography, have been introduced in some centers. The intention in West Germany seems to be to provide for a range of different programs of education for librarianship and to evaluate them comparatively as they evolve.

Anthony C. Foskett (1972), in describing an approach to integrating the two areas of education, examines the question of whether librarianship can stand on its own right or needs to be, as it were, supported by studies in more established academic disciplines. Much emotion can be generated by a discussion of the academic respectability, or lack thereof, of librarianship. It is perhaps right that it should be so, but those who would vehemently deny the likelihood of the subject's ever attaining an established status would do well to reflect upon the history of educational development. If one goes back far enough it is possible to discern a pattern of similar arguments just as vehement. Huckaby (1971), reporting on Italy, finds that approaches to library education in Italy, other than those which have, as a prerequisite, the classical education, are only slowly emerging. This situation is not confined to Italy, and, indeed, in many European countries the tradition that the study of the Latin and Greek civilizations absolves its recipients of the need for anything further in the way of vocational education is still a standpoint seriously held and tenaciously argued by some.

The question of the purity and respectability of librarianship as an academic discipline has surely to do with attitudes toward the teaching and learning process. Greek or Latin, history or theology, badly taught to poor students will not necessarily provide the same level of intellectual challenge as librarianship or, say, hotel management well taught, with clear educational objectives, to lively students well motivated and convinced of the worthiness of their task.

C. Practice Work in Libraries

Too much education seems to proceed from the wrong starting point. This is as true of librarianship as of any other area. Too many curricula are devised without regard to whether they will achieve desired goals or, indeed, without much attention being paid to the consideration of what those goals are. D. J. Foskett (1972) is in no doubt about the matter: "For a profession, the identification of objectives must precede the description of the technology required; the reverse approach in which the technology is allowed to dictate the objectives has led to a trail of disasters without parallel in the history of library and information science. . . ."

Many librarians in many countries find themselves in a real quandary when they attempt to teach librarianship. Are they to provide an education *for* librarianship or a training *in* librarianship? Education *for* librarianship implies the recognition of widely applicable principles and the design of teaching to be not simply a preparation for a specific first job, but a basis for the development of a full professional career. Educators and the more thoughtful students want "education for." Many employers, however, with their different perspective and, perhaps pressing short-term needs, would often settle for library schools which offered "training in." The apprentice and "learning on the job" traditions, mentioned by Harrison (1963), tend to reinforce this different perspective. D. J. Foskett (1972) again provides *les mots juste*:

> It is clear that the employer would be very pleased to receive from the library schools young would-be professionals who are mentally alert and vigorous, full of knowledge about the very latest techniques and at the same time malleable and amenable to the practical instruction of those who have been in the system for some time and are already in positions of authority. But the employer wants more than this: he wants to recruit from the schools new employees who can immediately be posted to a particular job already having the ability to do that job, requiring very little practical instruction from the employer and thus causing the minimum of "wasted time."

For the library school, it is easy to adopt the view that the objectives are to teach people to pass their examinations and leave the task of fitting them into particular library situations to the employers.

It is a matter for concern that what New (1969) calls the "educational escalator" pulls or pushes library schools into a pattern of conformity with general educational objectives. This effect can well serve to create a conflict between library schools and libraries. Library schools in the United Kingdom see their commitments as being, first, to their parent institutions and their students; second, to the profession; and only third, to the needs of the individual library. The library, as represented by its chief librarian, tends quite naturally to think of its own needs first and, only after that, of the needs of the profession generally. Rarely, if ever, will the appreciation of the overall objectives of education enter his or her calculations. The pressures operating upon each party create what New terms "a credibility gap." Each party understands too little of the other's problems. The divergence of their primary objectives is perhaps unavoidable, but it does not help to cement good relationships. The consequences for curriculum design in library schools are that syllabuses are often an uneasy compromise between the education-for approach and the training-in approach. Compromises are rarely pleasing.

The difficulties regarding the objectives of library education and the heritage left by the apprentice training background is perhaps the principal reason why many library schools feel it necessary to introduce periods of practice work into their full-time courses. For students with no previous experience in library work it forms the opportunity to "taste" the profession they are aspiring to join. Students with previous library experience are afforded the opportunity to work for a while in a contrasting type of library. Practice periods in libraries are regarded as an essential part of a program of studies in many European countries, with 6 to 12 weeks appearing to be the most favored duration. Sinkevicius (1971), Rugaas (1973), and Höglund and Jacobson (1973) comment on the situation from Russian, Norwegian, and Swedish points of view.

Whether such practice is in fact worthwhile is very much an open question. There is a need to resolve just what it is that such periods are designed to achieve. Is it a test of motivation? Is it to provide an opportunity for testing concepts learned in the classroom in practice? Is it an attempt to provide, or increase, an amount of practical experience such as will enable students completing the courses to find a post more easily and to settle into it quickly? The probable answer is that all three of these things are hoped-for outcomes, although in the United Kingdom the principal reason for including practical fieldwork is to provide a sop to that professional opinion which has never quite reconciled itself to full-time education for librarianship.

In assessing whether or not such programs are valuable, so much depends upon the quality of the receiving libraries—and even the best can have their off times when staff shortages, illnesses, or work pressures make dealing with short-stay, visiting students a nuisance. Some students find it difficult to adjust quickly to unfamiliar surroundings and may give an unduly poor account of themselves in the short term, or otherwise fail to reap benefits from the period. It can even happen that practical work periods in libraries of less than top quality are counterproductive in causing students to decide against seeking subsequent employment in a library of similar type or, even worse, to leave librarianship altogether.

Too little really clear and rational thinking has gone into the question of the value of practical fieldwork periods. The costs incurred by the libraries, the cost to the library school in providing supervision, and the costs to the student are considerable. Are the benefits derived equal to the costs? Students themselves seem to feel the need for some elements of practical work in their courses. The desire they feel for a period of practical work seems to arise out of the need to have a period of doing some concrete work during a course that is largely concerned with more or less abstract concepts. The desire for practical work can be satisfied in ways other than the usual posting to one particular library for a period of generalized work experience. A useful method is to attempt to focus upon a specific task that can be undertaken in a particular library. Most chief librarians have a mental list of desirable projects to be initiated when opportunity and staff resources allow. Such projects might be the reorganization of a music library or the development of a current awareness service for some category or other of library user. If a librarian can be persuaded to allow a group of students to plan and develop such projects in association with library staff and their teachers, not only is a valuable learning situation created, but a piece of concrete and useful work is completed. The feeling of many students about a period of generalized attachment to a library is that they were manifestly supernumerary and that their presence, if not actually inhibiting the work of the library, did nothing of consequence to further it. To have the feeling at the end of a practical work attachment that something has actually been achieved is good for student morale.

It is, perhaps, the emphasis on the development of programs for nonprofessional staffs, concentrating on the purely technical routines and skills, which has tended to blur the focus in many European countries as to the objectives of professional education for librarianship. Perhaps, also, the insistence on high levels of preentry academic qualifications for persons wishing to aspire to the more senior posts in librarianship in many European countries reduces the need to think of library education as anything other than a parade of immediately relevant skills.

The advocates of library-based training in librarianship (Heaney, 1973) and the proponents of the policy of short-stay library school lecturers quickly returning to the practice of the profession (Cowley, 1971) have an unflattering view of the achievements of library schools. The standpoint of the former group appears to be that there has been total failure on the part of the library schools, and the latter seem to believe that no special expertise or experience is needed for education for librarianship—that any librarian can drop in on a library school, deliver the perfect lecture on clear and consistent objectives, and expect it to fit a coherent program perfectly.

The practice of education is so complex, with the constant need to introduce new methods and new technology, that to expect part-time and short-stay lecturers to have the energy to develop new approaches is unrealistic. A mix of both full-time career lecturers in librarianship with part-time and visiting lecturers is probably the ideal to be aimed at (Lewis, 1973).

Quite understandably, the demand of potential employers of librarians is usually for students who have been thoroughly grounded in the techniques presently in use in their own particular libraries (Wilson, 1971). The perspective of an employer is necessarily much shorter than that of the individual employee. Employers are not always concerned—even if they should be—with the needs of their potential employees for an education offering the prospects of a coherent and satisfying career development. It is a clear responsibility of the library school to provide an education with more than only the immediate consumer in mind. The almost exclusively part-time staffing of the many European library schools carries with it the inevitable result that much of the program administered is concerned with short-term training needs rather than any larger perspective.

Only in circumstances in which library schools are considered to be at least equal partners in the task of setting the objectives of library education can there be any assurance that the right balance between immediate and longer term educational needs is met. Only in such circumstances is it possible for library schools to aspire to the kind of leadership and innovative thinking in the development of the profession generally, which seems so necessary (Wasserman, 1970). There are a number of European countries where the lack of a policy and sound status for library education could be argued as one of the principal inhibitors of progress of librarianship as a whole.

Naturally the immediate needs of the profession in regard to education for librarianship must not be ignored in favor of the evolution of more grandiose long-term aims. In fact, it could be argued that it is only when the process of library education has been thoroughly grounded in the fulfillment of immediate needs that the way is clear for more imaginative curriculum development. What is often alarming in European librarianship, however, is the way concentration on the immediate needs becomes not only an end in itself, but a positive contributor to a progressively lower standard of attainment. Practical work, visits to libraries, and study tours of groups of libraries might begin as attempts to illuminate aspects of the theoretical teaching but all too soon devolve into simple demonstrations of how a job is done in a given situation, with no attempt to infer broader lessons.

The constant interaction between theory and practice is an essential element of vocational education. Whether the practice must always be in a real life situation or whether simulation techniques will be at least as effective and perhaps cheaper and less intrusive upon the continuity of a course is a question often debated (Baylis, 1973; Burkett, 1970; Köttelwesch and Halbe, 1973; Needham, 1970). There are some strong arguments for the replacement of much of what is traditionally regarded as necessary "out of library school" practice work, by simulation techniques such as role playing, case studies, and the creative use of the library school's own specially developed practice collection (Prytherch, 1973).

In any event librarians can not continue to demand and receive students from library schools fully polished and immediately suited to their specific needs. Across Europe the necessity for the development of clear lines of policy relative to what is best taught in a library school, and what is best learned on the job, is obvious. A three-tier process seems to be indicated in which a basic program concentrates upon the "why" and the "what," and is followed by practical in-service training in the "how" of a specific library's operations. The third stage is the very important one of continuing whole-life refreshment and reorientation (Bungay, 1970).

D. Continuing Education

The term "continuing education" is educational jargon which restates in brief the old adage that education ought to be a lifelong process. For librarianship the swift development of such applications of modern technology as the computer and audiovisual materials provides obvious areas in which the more senior library staffs will need to refresh, reorient, or amplify their knowledge. With libraries and their finances tending to grow at a considerable rate, increasing specialization of knowledge in more traditional librarianship studies also calls for further education, as does the need for senior staff to develop more sophisticated management techniques and expertise.

Activities in the continuing education of librarians are perhaps one of the areas of dynamic growth throughout Europe. The need for senior librarians to extend their education beyond the basic level is not a new phenomenon. The formation of the various library associations is one evidence of this need, especially through their organization of conferences and meetings.

As organizations already suitably equipped and staffed with experts, library schools have an important part to play in the presentation of programs of continuing education. Norway, for example, has such a pattern (Rugaas, 1973). It must be remembered, however, that at least some of the continuing education needs of librarians will be in subjects other than librarianship. An important reason why programs of continuing education should be provided as part of a total educational effort is that it makes certain decisions about the structures of basic library education easier. The availability of resources for the further education of librarians at various points in their careers makes the temptation to overfill basic courses easier to resist.

Continuing education can be provided in various forms, including full-time courses of the type available in the United States as "sixth year specialist programs" (Danton, 1970) and part-time courses of a duration long enough to add up to the equivalent of a full-time year. The problem with full-time courses of any length is that the senior staff members for whom such courses are intended are often difficult for an employer to spare for any length of time. It is also true that family obligations or the need to maintain a second home create financial difficulties for potential students of full-time continuing education programs. The Danish pattern of making financial grants, both to course participants to cover their expenses and to employing libraries to help cover the costs of temporary staff to replace those away, is obviously a valuable provision (Bredsdorff, 1973). With part-time courses of considerable duration, advantages can be that participants can probably rearrange their timetables to create the minimum disturbance to their library work while attending the course, and, of course, they do not need to live away from home. Disadvantages are that part-time courses tend to be viable only in areas of large population, and the rates of dropout of students from part-time courses are usually very high.

For most purposes the most popular and convenient forms of continuing education are short full-time residential courses of one day to one month's duration. Courses of this nature are the norm across Europe and provide economical and swift means of responding to new developments as well as opportunities for participants to carry their newly acquired knowledge immediately into practice. There is evidence to suggest that while the effects are not necessarily long lasting without further reinforcement, they are considerable in the short term (Revill, 1973).

The ideal pattern of continuing education for librarians is one which combines the benefits of formal "off the job" courses with a continuous process of in-service training and refreshment of skills. The All-Union Institute of Scientific and Technical Information, Institute for the Further Training of Information Specialists in the

USSR has, since 1963, organized courses of various lengths, from 1 hour to 5 month's duration, in a variety of forms. Apart from full-time "off the job" courses, many of the shorter sessions are organized to take place in individual factories or groups of factories with similar interests (Arutjunov, 1974).

A good deal of interest is being shown in the development of international programs of education for librarianship. Obviously these will be most effective if they are provided at the senior level and designed to promote international understanding and cooperation. Proposals have been made for the establishment of an International School of Librarianship (Marco, 1970). Attention is also being paid to including material on international librarianship at the basic education level. Such courses, while basic to the nationals of a particular country, can form useful means of continuing education for foreign nations (Carroll, 1972).

E. Harmonization of Qualifications

Desultory and inconclusive efforts to arrive at working agreements on the mutual recognition of the qualifications of several different country's librarians have been made for more than twenty years involving Australia, Canada, the United States, and the United Kingdom (Stokes, 1970). A further complicating dimension to the problem of reciprocity of qualifications has recently been added for the United Kingdom, at least, when she joined the European Economic Community (EEC). The Community's measures, designed to ensure the mobility of employment throughout the whole area for the nationals of each member country, require that moves should be made to devise principles for the reciprocal recognition of professional qualifications between member countries.

Initial proposals by the Community for the assessment and comparison of the levels and quality of programs of librarianship across Europe were based principally upon a simple equation of the numbers of years, months, and even hours spent in postschool education generally. With the tradition in the United Kingdom for relatively short, intensive university courses (typically three years), followed by one year of full-time study for a masters degree, there was danger of severe undervaluation of British qualifications relative to those available in other EEC countries, where, in some cases, a first-degree program is of five years' duration. The apparently logical system of counting the duration of postschool study breaks down in the face of the different cultural traditions noted earlier.

The problem is a very difficult one for the United Kingdom and is made more so by the persistent unwillingness of British librarianship to accept the requirement that the top echelons of the profession always be university graduates. Such unwillingness immediately marks off a distinction between the United Kingdom and the rest of Europe. Despite the high standards of purely professional education in the United Kingdom, it poses an immediate difficulty in the harmonization (as the offical EEC terminology has it) of qualifications. Antiacademic, antigraduate urges have deep roots in British culture. Although attitudes are slowly changing, and most professions are making graduate entry the norm for their higher echelons, whether librarianship will join them in the near future is still a somewhat open question (Library Association, 1973). Fears concerning the recognition of graduate entry as the norm in British librarianship have been based upon the feeling that any influx of graduates at the bottom of the senior ranks of the profession would pose a threat to the job security and further promotion prospects of the nongraduate, professionally qualified librarians already in posts. The fears of the nongraduate professional librarian in the United Kingdom appear to indicate almost the reverse of the situation in the United States, where opposition to the growth of a nongraduate library technician level is based on the fear that the technicians will take over jobs previously held by full professionals (Asheim, 1975). In the United Kingdom the strong emotional reaction is fear that the entry of large numbers of graduates, to the future total exclusion of nongraduates, will somehow force the remaining nongraduates into a technician type role regardless of their experience.

In the United Kingdom, as in the United States, the lack of a clear focus on what is, and what is not, professional activity is part of the problem. The more explicit definition of levels of work in many European countries renders the task of assessing the relative merits of different types of qualification easier. The development in West Germany and the United Kingdom of programs of library education which feature librarianship as a formal academic, as well as professional, discipline adds a further dimension of confusion to the task of the comparative assessment of European qualifications. There is the risk that the qualifications in the countries with the highest content and quality of professional librarianship could be undervalued relative to the rest of the European community. This could happen if the nonlibrarianship, traditional academic study was inferior to that in programs of European countries where professional education is less well developed, for example, France, Italy, and the Low Countries. The Library Association is currently keeping a very close watch on a situation which could be the most serious threat to its role as arbiter of professional standards that it has ever faced. It is not too dramatic to suggest that it is possible that, for at least certain categories of libraries, it could break their traditionally strong position in the sense that even if traditional academic qualifications have been specified as essential in some libraries, so, too, have professional library qualifications. The Library Association (1973) created a fairly open system of transitional arrangements for the harmonization process in order to secure as long advance notice as possible of changes which might radically affect their members' careers.

V. INTERVENTION BY LIBRARY ASSOCIATIONS IN EDUCATION FOR LIBRARIANSHIP

A. United Kingdom

The central role of the Library Association in the development of education for librarianship mirrors a generally high level of concern for the direction and quality of professional education by learned and professional societies of all types in the United Kingdom. It is a concern that leads to the situation in a number of professions in which persons are legally debarred from the practice of that profession unless they are subscribing members of the appropriate society. Although the powers of the Library Association are not as wide as those of some professional bodies, they are, nevertheless, of sufficient consequence to be described as "awesome" (Lancour, 1968). No other professional association of librarians in Europe, and perhaps in the world, has had such a strong influence over such a prolonged period. The directions which the patterns of influence have taken have been both internal, in the sense of formulating and formalizing the scope and intellectual content of the subject field and its several parts, and external, in the sense of strong advocacy of the need for strong programs of education for librarians in the country. In the internal sense, since 1885, the Library Association has controlled a program of examination and certification of librarians and has awarded the distinctive titles "Fellow of the Library Association" or "Associate of the Library Association." In recent years, with the development of alternative forms of qualification for librarianship through examinations established by individual universities and colleges, the high standing of the two designations mentioned has been underlined by the fact that each of such education institutions has felt it worthwhile to negotiate for recognition by the Library Association of their degrees as providing exemption from the Association's qualifications for purposes of securing the designation "Associate of the Library Association." Such recognition has, in fact, been accorded to all established programs in the United Kingdom. Recognition has, however, not been automatic and has sometimes been conditional upon the strengthening in specified ways of the academic content of the courses offered. Lancour's reference to the awesomeness of the intervention by the Library Association doubtless includes a comprehension of the unhesitating manner in which the Association is prepared to offer comments on educational quality to the universities and colleges despite the traditional dignity and feelings of independence of such establishments (Palmer, 1970).

B. Europe

Conceivably, the very strong traditions of independence of the European universities have limited the opportunities of library associations in Europe to make any significant impact upon the patterns of education for librarianship. Direct comparisons of Europe and the United Kingdom in regard to professional and vocational education may be unfair because of the very different cultural and educational traditions. It is, however, often a matter of considerable surprise to British librarians observing the European situation to find how ineffectual librarianship associations often are. In some cases they appear to be totally disinterested. Schur (1972, pp. 108–109) states: "One of the principal aims of a professional organization is to promote the maintenance of high professional standards. In this, organizations in a few countries have been eminently successful, whilst in most countries the organizations have so far, largely failed."

The situation Schur was observing was one in which, in many European countries, the multiplicity of associations of librarians for various specialist groups or different levels of staff within a particular group makes difficult the development of clear, influential statements of policy. The situation is difficult enough in the larger countries such as West Germany, where elaborate systems of coordinating joint committees have been developed to try to provide a common forum on major issues (Frank, 1967). In countries, such as Belgium and Finland, with only a relatively small number of librarians, the fragmentation of associations of librarians further reduces the prospects of developing a coherent power base for the creation of interest in matters affecting the well-being of librarians and library service in such countries.

The indications are that the library associations of Europe are developing their interest in, and influence on, education for librarianship. In Italy, the Italian Library Association has developed plans for the creation of a national register of librarians along the lines of the British Library Association. It has also put on record its ideas as to the proper content and form of programs for all levels and categories of librarian (Vianello, 1972). The Swiss Library Association has sought representation on the governing body of the Library School of the School of Social Studies in Geneva. In return it has granted recognition to the School's diploma (Cornaz, 1967).

The Finnish Library Association has begun to give very active consideration to matters of library education. Perhaps wisely, in circumstances in which too vehement a stand on matters of professional library education might offend other interests, their most advanced work is concerned with the provision of formal education for library assistants—the area least likely to cause controversy (Tammekann, 1973). In Denmark, a happy feature of the annual conference of the Library Association is that the Director of the Royal Danish School of Librarianship presents a report to the delegates on the work of the school (Kirkegaard, 1971).

REFERENCES

Abramov, K. I. (1971). Library education in the USSR. *Indian Librarian* **25**, 199–200.
Arutjunov, N. B. (1974). Training and refresher courses for information specialists in the U.S.S.R. *UNESCO Bulletin for Libraries* **28**, 29–33.
Asheim, L. (1975). Trends in library education—United States. *In* "Advances in

Librarianship" (M. J. Voigt, ed.), Vol. 5, pp. 147–201. Academic Press, New York.

Baylis, C. T. (1973). The teaching of reference work. *An Leabharlann* 2, 174–179.

Bredsdorff, V. (1973). Courses and seminars at the Danish School of Librarianship. *Scandinavian Public Library Quarterly* 6, 81–87.

Bungay, F. (1970). The future librarian—what do we need? *In* "Looking at Ourselves" (T. D. F. Barnard, ed.), pp. 12–19. The Library Association, London and Home Countries Branch, London.

Burkett, J. (1970). The practical element of library school teaching. *Library Association Record* 72, 232–233.

Carroll, F. L. (1972). Internationalism in education for librarianship. *International Library Review* 4, 103–126.

Carroll, F. L. (1973). West German library schools, 1968–1972. *International Library Review* 5, 329–333.

Cornaz, M. L. (1967). The Swiss School for Librarians. *UNESCO Bulletin for Libraries* 21, 261–262.

Cowley, J. (1971). Education, training and utilisation of library staff. *Assistant Librarian* 64, 98–102.

Danton, J. P. (1970). "Between M.L.S. and Ph.D; A Study of Sixth Year Specialist Programs in Accredited Library Schools." American Library Association, Chicago, Illinois.

Davinson, D. E. (1970). The education of librarians in an age of mechanisation. *In* "Men and Machines" (P. W. H. Pickup, ed.), pp. 28–42. The Library Association, County Libraries Group, London.

Davinson, D. E. (1973). Finland the good. *New Library World* 74, 35–36, 39.

DeGrolier, E. (1973). Education for librarianship in France. *In* "Encyclopeadia of Library and Information Science," Vol. 9, pp. 67–79. Marcel Dekker, New York.

Evans, E. (1974). An American's view of Nordic education programs for library personnel. *Scandinavian Public Libraries Quarterly* 6, 2–15.

Fonotov, G. (1967). The libraries of the USSR during the last fifty years. *UNESCO Bulletin for Libraries* 21, 240–248.

Foskett, A. C. (1972). An integrated approach to subject and professional education. *In* "Proceedings of the International Conference on Training for Information Work" (G. Lubbock, ed.), pp. 169–171. International Federation for Documentation, The Hague. (FID Publication 486.)

Foskett, D. J. (1972). The education of librarians. *In* "The Metropolitan Library" (R. W. Conant and K. Molz eds.), pp. 233–247. MIT Press, Cambridge, Massachusetts.

Francis, Sir F. C. (1968). Education for librarianship in Great Britain. *In* "Library Education: An International Survey" (L. E. Bone ed.), pp. 55–71. The Illini Union Bookstore, Champaign, Illinois.

Frank, J. (1967). The German library pattern: a British view. *Library Association Record* 69, 120–123.

Hanz, B. (1971). Library school histories: (7) Yugoslavia: library education in Yugoslavia. *International Library Review* 31, 113–120.

Harrison, J. C. (1963). Education for librarianship abroad: the United Kingdom. *Library Trends* 12, 123–142.
Heaney, H. J. (1973). The relevance of library education. *An Leabharlann* 2, 145–154.
Hjelmqvist, B. (1968). Library education in continental Europe. In "Library Education: An International Survey" (L. E. Bone, ed.), pp. 29–53. The Illini Union Bookstore, Champaign, Illinois.
Höglund, A. L., and Jacobson, T. P. (1973). The Swedish College of Librarianship. *Scandinavian Public Library Quarterly* 6, 106–115.
Hogg, F. N. (1969). Library education and research in librarianship in Great Britain. *Libri* 19, 191–203.
Huckaby, S. (1971). Education for librarianship in Italy: an historical view. *Journal of Library History* 6, 5–20.
International Federation of Library Associations (1966). La formation professionnelle des Bibliothécaires en Europe. *Libri* 16, 282–311.
Kirkegaard, P. (1971). Library schol histories: (1) Denmark: The Royal School of Librarianship, Copenhagen. *International Library Review* 3, 77–81.
Koskialla, S. (1974). Our friends from last year. *Kirjastolehti* 67, 322–323.
Köttelwesch, C., and Halbe, H. G. (1973). Noch einmal: die praktische Ausbildung. In "Bibliotheksarbeit Heute" (G. Lohse and G. Pflugk, eds.), pp. 59–67. Klostermann, Frankfurt am Main. (Zeitschrift für Bibliothekswesen und Bibliographie. Sonderheft No. 16.)
Kovacs, M. (1966). The education and training of librarians in Hungary. *Libri* 16, 18–48.
Kunze, H. (1970). The training of librarians and documentalists in the German Democratic Republic. *Journal of Librarianship* 2, 42–55.
Lancour, H. (1968). Library associations and library education. In "Library Education: An International Survey" (L. E. Bone, ed.), pp. 373–384. The Illini Union Bookstore, Champaign, Illinois.
Lewis, P. R. (1973). Policy interactions in the development of library education in Great Britain. *Libri* 23, 241–250.
Library Association (1973). Library qualifications in the European Communities: statement by the Library Association Council. *Library Association Record* 75, 53, 56.
Marco, G. A. (1970). The idea of an international library school. *Library World* 72, 191, 193.
Needham, C. D. (1970). Particulars and principles: case studies in librarianship. *Journal of Librarianship* 2, 56–71.
New, P. G. (1969). Educational escalation. *Library Association Record* 71, 202–204.
New, P. G., ed. (1972). "British Qualifications in Librarianship." The Library Association, Library Education Group, London.
Ohlsson, J., and Palmqvist, B. (1970). Biblioteksskolan. *Biblioteksbladet* 55, 45–51.
Palmer, B. I. (1970). Professional education in Britain. *Herald of Library Science* 9, 1–5.
Pflugk, U. (1973). Der Hamburger Ausbildungsplan von 1970. In "Bibliotheks-

arbeit Heute" (G. Lohsc and G. Pflug, eds.), pp. 92–99. Klostermann, Frankfurt am Main. (Zeitschrift für Bibliothekswesen und Bibliographie, Sonderheft 16.)

Piquard, M. (1967). The training of librarians in Europe. *UNESCO Bulletin for Libraries* 21, 311–317.

Prytherch, R. J. (1973). Library based teaching. *New Library World* 74, 170–172.

Revill, D. H. (1973). Course effect. *New Library World* 74, 102–103, 107.

Roxas, S. A. (1972). "Library Education in Italy: An Historical Survey, 1870–1969." Scarecrow Press, Metuchen, New Jersey.

Rugaas, B. (1973). Education for librarianship in Norway. *Scandinavian Public Libraries Quarterly* 6, 116–121.

Saunders, W. L. (1969). Education for librarianship in Great Britain. *Australian Library Journal* 18, 386–392.

Schur, H. (1972). "Education and Training for Information Specialists for the 1970's," Organization for Economic Cooperation and Development, Paris, Sheffield Post-Graduate School of Librarianship and Information Science, Sheffield University, Sheffield, England. (DAS/STINFO/72.9.)

Sinkevicius, K. (1971). Library school histories: (6) U.S.S.R. Lithuania: higher education of librarians in Soviet Lithuania. *International Library Review* 3, 109–111.

Stokes, R. B. (1970). Equation of qualifications. *Library Association Record* 72, 234–235.

Tammekann, E. M. (1973). The training of librarians in Finland. *Scandinavian Public Libraries Quarterly* 6, 78–80.

Tentori, M. C. (1972). Italian Libraries Association's contribution for the professional training of librarians. *In* "International Conference on Training for Information Work" (G. Lubbock, ed.), pp. 138–141. International Federation for Documentation, The Hague.

Thauer, W. (1974). Stand und Gegenswarts probleme der bibliothekarischen Ausbildung im Bereich der öffentlichen Bibliotheken. *In* "Bibliothekarische Kooperation: Aspekte und Möglichkeiten" (P. Kägbeing, ed.), pp. 89–99. Klostermann, Frankfurt am Main.

UNESCO (1972). "World Guide to Library Schools and Training Courses in Documentation." Clive Bingley, UNESCO, London, Paris.

Vianello, N. (1972). "Proposals for Professional Training." Associazone Italiana Bibliotheche, Rome.

Wasserman, P. (1970). Professional adaptation: library education mandate. *Library Journal* 95, 1281–1288.

Wilson, B. J. (1971). Library theory and practical vocational training: a forum. *ASLIB Proceedings* 23, 225–236.

Zazersky, E. J. (1974). System of librarians training in the USSR. *International Library Review* 6, 219–229.

The Role of Middle Managers in Libraries

BEVERLY P. LYNCH

Association of College and Research Libraries,
American Library Association

I.	The Manager's Work	255
II.	Factors That Influence the Role of the Middle Manager	259
	A. Environment	260
	B. Technology	263
	C. Professionalism	265
III.	Leadership in the Context of the Organization	266
	A. Trait Theory	267
	B. Ohio State University Studies in Leadership	268
	C. Survey Research Center, University of Michigan	269
	D. Current Perspectives	269
IV.	Summary and Discussion	272
	References	274
	General References	276

The traditional model of the middle manager, used frequently to describe the library middle manager, emphasizes the manager's downward authority over the people who report to him or her. The middle manager is described in terms of a functional department head, a librarian responsible for the work of others. Little attention is paid to the new managers in the library, the budget analysts, systems analysts, research and development officers—the middle managers without command authority who are responsible for providing information to top management and other middle management. Like other complex organizations, libraries generally have been structured hierarchically, managers being responsible to a superior for the actions and decisions of subordinates as well as for their own. The superior's scope of authority over the subordinate is clearly prescribed. The hierarchical (or bureaucratic) authority provides the means for coordinating organizational goals, but it is in contrast to professional authority, which is based upon the recognition of the personal competence of the position holder. Reflecting a concern for authority, the library literature emphasizes the influence of formal hierarchies upon the individuals involved. Since authority relationships within organizations are necessary to achieve organizational goals, formal hierarchies of authority form the most common pattern of organizational relationships we know.

Librarians working in large libraries, where hierarchies are firmly established, recently have begun to investigate other modes of organization. Modeling themselves on the autonomous professional, they have demanded greater participation in the library's decision-making in order to make changes in the organizational characteristics which affect them. Although there is as yet little evidence to indicate that libraries of the future will be organized in ways other than hierarchical, there is great interest in the role of the middle manager and the part the manager would play should different patterns of organization emerge. Advocates of participation predict the decline of middle management jobs, while other observers predict an expansion of middle management jobs, staffed by nonlibrarian specialists.

The recent literature has emphasized the beliefs and feelings librarians have about job satisfaction, supervisory relationships, and the constraints the library's bureaucratic structure places upon the professional. Little attention has been given to how the librarian's professional beliefs might influence the way he does his job. No consideration of the extent of the librarian's professionalism has yet appeared.

This chapter, while identifying some of the characteristics, attitudes, and problems of middle managers, considers the organizational environment in which library managers work. It suggests that the nature of library work and the environment in which that work is performed are important factors that influence the type of organizational structure applied by the library. It also suggests that the degree of professionalism held by the librarian will have an effect upon the role of the librarian in the library. Distinctions are made between the concepts of leadership, power, and authority, since these concepts loom large in the discussion of managers in organizations.

I. THE MANAGER'S WORK

Authorities on management generally assume that management is a distinct type of work and that managers perform the same functions regardless of what or whom they manage (Dale, 1973; Drucker, 1974). The management functions identified by Gulick (1937), continue to be used to describe the work of the manager. Planning, organizing, directing, staffing, and controlling are the most frequently mentioned, although Drucker (1974) provides a somewhat different analysis. To the functions of planning and organizing, he adds integrating and measuring. Integrating refers to the task of relating the manager's work to others inside and outside the unit. Measuring refers to the analysis, appraisal, and interpretation of performance. In most of the literature describing the management functions, a hierarchical form of organization is assumed, each supervisor being responsible for the actions of the workers in the unit and, in turn, reporting to a supervisor above him. By assigning to the manager the classic management functions, it is assumed that the worker has little interest or expertise in the activities necessary for the successful performance of the unit.

Many library managers plan, organize, direct, control, and staff. Some manage by consulting with the people in the unit, while others manage without much consultation. In some libraries the expectations of the library managers have conflicted with the expectations of the librarians within the unit. As the role of the autonomous professional is advocated and implemented (Standards for faculty status for college and university libraries, 1972), librarians expect direct participation in all affairs of the unit that relate to the performance of the unit. They want to participate in the decisions that affect their own professional goals and objectives. Instead of the library manager dominating the unit and its activities, the expectation of the librarian is that the supervisory style of the library manager will be one of collaboration, in which the manager and the librarians will influence the decision-making. These expectations of librarians have brought about a change in the role of some library middle managers, resulting in greater collaboration and consultation with unit members. The expectations have brought conflict and disharmony in other situations where the role of the manager has not changed, or has changed in a direction not anticipated by the librarians.

Although assumptions are made about the work of the library manager as well as the work of the librarian, very little is known about what the middle manager in libraries really does. The importance attached to the various classic management functions varies from unit to unit and from library to library. In some units the middle manager acts more as a technical supervisor than a general manager. The knowledge the supervisor has about the unit's work requirements and the work itself bears directly upon the managerial style of the supervisor and upon the attitudes the librarians in the unit will have toward the manager.

Although a large body of literature exists that confronts the issues of professionals in organizations (Hall, 1968; Hall and Lawler, 1970; Kornhauser, 1962), the role of librarians within the organization has not been adequately explored. The literature on other types of organizations suggests that the attitudes of professionals toward the work they do differ significantly from the attitudes of other executives and managers in the organization. According to the profiles found in the literature, professionals tend to identify themselves primarily with their disciplines. In judging themselves and their work, professionals tend to compare themselves with fellow professionals in the same discipline. Professionals are inclined to acknowledge authority based on excellence in their disciplines or on collective colleague opinion. They place particular value on opportunities to pursue intellectual excellence, carry self-selected tasks to their logical conclusions, and work with guidance rather than supervision. They prefer an open mode of operation that avoids secrecy and places special emphasis on the receipt of aesthetic and technical satisfactions from their work.

This profile summarizes the opinions of many librarians now working in libraries about their role in the library. Their attitudes toward middle management and top management are influenced heavily by this perspective.

By contrast, the profile of the executive portrays the executive as one who identifies primarily with the employing institutions. Executives use peers and seniors within the same organization as their basis of judgment. They acknowledge the authority as derived from the administrative hierarchy of the employing institutions. They prefer confidentiality within the organization to sharing information outside that might result in a loss in competitive advantage. They place great emphasis on achieving practical results in their work (Sofer, 1970).

This profile summarizes the opinions of other librarians, the perspective influencing the way some library managers view the work of the unit as well as their own work.

The few existing studies of librarians as managers emphasize the characteristics of the individuals in these jobs and reflect one or the other profile. Plate (1970) is influenced by the profile of the executive. Using data gathered from seventy-eight middle managers in sixteen major research libraries, Plate found little professional orientation among the middle managers in his sample. Most managers derived their greatest satisfaction from having their work recognized by people within the library instead of by the profession at large. Although membership in regional and national library associations was held by more than 80 percent of the sample, only one-third of the middle managers were in favor of providing time and resources for any librarians to engage in writing or research. In response to a question about qualities required for a middle management position, the middle managers cited experience most often, followed by administrative ability and the ability to get along with people. Professional competence and commitment were cited less than ten times.

Plate emphasizes the influence a supervisor has on the behavior and attitudes of subordinates. He assumes that librarians identify themselves with their employing library, that librarians acknowledge the hicrarchical authority of the library, and that professional librarians in a subordinate role reflect the attitudes and behaviors of supervisors in order to enhance their own advancement. If one accepts

Plate's assumption that librarians who are supervised by these middle managers are heavily influenced by them, it would follow that librarians working in large research libraries generally are not professionally oriented, and the classic bureaucratic assumption would apply: librarians expect to learn their jobs and gain their greatest satisfactions from within the library. Plate's data neither support not deny the assumption. His work is heavily influenced by his perspective derived from the literature describing the executive.

Morrison's study (1969) reflects the profile of the professional in the organization. Morrison found that academic librarians are very active in professional and scholarly organizations, more so than the public librarians studied by Bryan (1952). The source of job satisfaction cited most frequently by the library executives in Morrison's study was "service to the people." The service motive is considered to be one of the distinguishing marks of the professional (Goode, 1961). "Work with books" was the second most frequently cited source of job satisfaction. "Stimulating environment and interesting colleagues" ranked third.

Only one-fourth of the executives in the Morrison study cited administration and planning as a source of satisfaction.

> ... the major executive complains that, although he likes this phase of library work, it tends to separate him from bibliographic activity which remains his first love. Nor do middle managers seem to care much for the administrative responsibilities that result from separating the various levels of work in well-managed libraries. They seem to feel that the administrative and "intellectual" aspects of the profession are antagonistic rather than parts of a coordinated whole (Morrison, 1969, p. 68).

Several additional studies of the librarian as professional have tried to identify the professional characteristics of librarians (Douglass, 1957; Farley, 1967; Guttsman, 1965; Nash, 1964). Not one of the studies attempts to assess the effect of librarians' professionalism upon the way they do their work. In order to understand the role of the managers who are professional librarians managing other professional librarians, data are needed on the "professionalism effect." Although the librarians are interested in the beliefs and feelings about job satisfaction and superior/subordinate relationships, we have yet to learn whether library managers who have a high degree of professionalism do their jobs differently than do library managers who are less professionally oriented, or whether the degree of professionalism among the librarians in the unit influences their perspectives and attitudes toward the manager as well as the way they do their work. Librarians generally assume that the professionalism of the librarian is increasing and that the role of the middle manager in libraries is changing from that of a supervisor in the classic authoritarian sense to that of a supervisor in the more consultative sense. There are no data to confirm or deny the assumption.

Although it is likely that the degree of professionalism of the managers will influence the way they do their jobs, other factors also may bear upon the issue. The nature of the organization's tasks and the environment within which the organization operates will influence the supervisory styles useful in achieving the organization's goals. Studies of other organizations show that the supervisory styles of middle managers vary from unit to unit and from organization to organization. The characteristics of the management styles have been related to the nature of the work done in the organization (Blauner, 1964; Burns and Stalker, 1961; Fullan, 1970; Sofer, 1970). There is no one pattern of supervisory behavior, nor is there one role for the middle manager that is optimum or ideal. Different situations call for different responses. To be successful, middle managers are called upon to develop sensitivities to problems and situations, not just to the problems of human relations, but to technical and organizational problems as well.

II. FACTORS THAT INFLUENCE THE ROLE OF THE MIDDLE MANAGER

A universal description of the effective middle manager does not exist. Nor is there a single set of traits which can be used to define the ideal middle manager. The role of the middle manager varies according to the characteristics of the organization such as external environment, the technology or the nature of the work, the characteristics of the individual members of the organization, the "fit" between the environmental and technological characteristics, and the organizational structure designed to carry out the organization's goals and objectives.

This section considers the middle manager in the context of the milieu of the library and its organizational structure. The prevailing view of the manager's job, stressing as it does the human relations problems and problems of leadership encountered on the job, is not emphasized. The relationships of library units to one another, the degree of centralization of decision-making, the values, expectations, and goals of the organization's members are considered, with attention to the influence of the environment on the organization and the importance of technology in relation to the organization's structure and its goals.

A. Environment

The literature of librarianship reflects the profession's search for the one best way to organize the library, while practice has supported numerous managerial styles and structures. External environments of libraries do vary. Differences in staffing patterns and organizational structures reflect these variations.

The impact of the environment upon the organization is featured prominently in much of the current organizational literature (Crozier, 1964; Duncan, 1972; Lawrence and Lorsch, 1967; Lorsch and Morse, 1974; Thompson, 1967) and has begun to influence the library literature (Lynch, 1974a; Sloan, 1973) but the dimensions of the environment have yet to be clearly defined.

Lawrence and Lorsch describe the external environment of an organization along three dimensions: the certainty or uncertainty of information available to organizational members, the length of time it takes the members to get feedback about their actions, and the variations in the "dominant strategic issue" that confront each unit in the organization. Basing their analysis upon industrial organizations, Lawrence and Lorsch propose that since an organization must deal with more information than a single manager or group of managers can handle, organizations are divided into functional groups, each group dealing with a different aspect of the environment. Thus a marketing unit deals with the marketing sectors of the environment as it forecasts product demand, the production unit deals with the economic and technical sectors of the environment, and a research unit deals with the scientific segments of the environment.

Although the particular functional units will vary, depending upon the type of organization, the same environmental analysis can be applied to libraries. No one library manager can handle the information required to deal with all aspects of the library's environment. Functional units of selection, acquisition, cataloging, circulation, and reference each deal with a different aspect of the library's environment. The selection unit deals with the requirements of the clientele and various aspects of the book trade; the acquisitions unit deals with the economic sectors of the environment; the cataloging unit deals with the technical sectors of the environment, the circulation and reference units deal with the needs of diverse users. Variations within each of these functional units can be predicted on the environmental properties identified by Lawrence and Lorsch (1967). The information coming into the unit varies on a continuum of certainty to uncertainty. The "time-span of feedback" varies. For example, a cataloger may never know if his or her product, the description and classification of a book, is useful to the user, while an acquisition librarian knows fairly promptly whether or not a desired book is purchased. The dominant strategic issue also will vary across departments. The reference department may see its major issue as meeting the needs of individual users of the library regardless of the variations in cost and in time and effort, while the catalog department is forced to emphasize issues of cost and efficiency, even though delays in processing some items result in wanted items not being immediately available for some users.

Like other organizations, libraries have environments composed of suppliers, competitors, clients, and regulatory agencies. They exist in the complex milieu of the communities. Since environmental influences impinge directly upon the library, most libraries will respond by attempting to stabilize and control the influences. Thus, within the library, techniques such as the use of book jobbers, reliance upon a particular library school for staff, or detailed rules governing the conduct of borrowers, are used to stabilize and control the environment.

Environmental changes result in a fluctuation in the demand for library materials. New areas of interest come to the attention of the public; information is available in new formats. New courses are established; the contents of old courses change. In order to deal with the environment routinely and in a predictable way, the library establishes rules and procedures within the various units. For example, complex rules are made to routinize purchasing decisions.

Selection specialists are hired and selection committees established in order to reduce the unpredictability in the supply of library materials. Responding to such rules, the branch librarian or the librarian in the circulation department might complain about the cumbersome selection and order policies. The librarian in a public service unit thinks he or she knows best what the client wants, yet a technical service staff member charged with selection responsibilities may make a different choice. The acquisitions librarian may order a book from a jobber instead of buying it at the local bookstore where the client has seen it and expects the library to buy it. Such decisions add to the problems of the public service librarian, and the librarian, whose major goal is service regardless of cost, may complain about the lack of a service goal in the selection and acquisitions units and the inefficiency of those units. The librarian in acquisitions, however, may have decided that a large order to a single jobber would save money, or that one supplier is more reliable than another, although supplying the materials may take longer.

Although the division of the organization's work into functional departments enables the organization to deal with its environment more effectively, the segmenting of units requires techniques of collaboration and coordination in order to avoid intraunit conflicts that do occur. Traditionally, organizational disputes have been resolved by referring the dispute up the line to the first shared supervisor. Within the context of the classical theory of organizations all conflicts are resolved in this way. This method of conflict resolution is successful only if the units in conflict have similar environments and are structured in the same way to meet these environments. If the units involved in the dispute are different, that is, if one unit has more formal rules and procedures than the other; if the units' goals are very different, that is, if one is concerned with costs and efficiency and the other is concerned with satisfying client needs; if the time orientation regarding the units' goals is different, the use of coordination through the management hierarchy may not be successful.

The differentiation of an organization into functional units will result in continuing basic and legitimate conflict. The manager, understanding the required and actual patterns of differentiation in the library, will work to clarify the reasons for conflict, to understand the differences in judgment that will occur among the librarians, and to find the knowledge necessary to resolve the conflict. Depending upon the environment and the unit structures, other methods besides sending the conflict up the line will be found to resolve it.

B. Technology

Librarians have proposed changes in the internal structure of libraries in attempts to resolve the inevitable conflicts that occur among functional units (Bundy, 1966; Guttsman, 1973). Most of the proposals emphasize the work done in libraries and do not stress the environmental perspectives of the organization (Booz et al., 1973; Ricking and Booth, 1974).

Recent studies of other organizations suggest that the internal structure of organizations is influenced greatly by the nature of the work done in the organizations (Blau and Schoenherr, 1971; Hage and Aiken, 1969; Van de Ven and Delbecq, 1974; Woodward, 1965). These organizational analyses suggest that organizations vary in terms of their technologies and that those technologies influence various aspects of organizational structure. Woodward pioneered in the study of the effect of technology upon organizational structure. Her work was designed to understand the effectiveness of approximately one hundred businesses on the basis of the classic principles of management, particularly the degree of functional specialization, the number of hierarchical levels, and the optimum span of control. Only after she had grouped the firms according to the technical complexity of their overall production systems, did patterns emerge. Three types of production systems were identified: unit and small batch which included manufacturers of machine tools and custom furniture, large batch, assembly, and mass production which included companies that mass-produced clothing, automobiles, and industrial equipment; and process production, including oils and chemicals. Despite the variety of products produced, those firms with similar technologies showed similarities in terms of organizational structure. The number of levels in the managerial hierarchy increased according to the technical complexity of the production system. The span of control of the chief executive was larger in the process firms than in the other types of firms. More delegation and decentralization were observed in the process firms than in the large batch and mass firms.

In addition to the relationships between technology and structure, Woodward identified two organizational mechanisms for resolving conflicts and problems, a technical function which coordinates the work and a social function which enables people to work together. She related these functions to the variability of the organization's technology. In the processing firms the technical function of coordination was designed into the plant itself, enabling management in these firms to spend more time on the social function. This was less true in mass firms. The small batch firms required both methods of coordination.

Woodward's study also provides insight into the problem of which functional group is most important within the organization: it depends upon the technology of the production system.

Woodward's important contribution in bringing a new variable into the study of organizations was limited in its conception to industrial producers. Perrow (1967) freed the perspective by defining organizational technology in terms of the frequency of exceptional cases encountered in the work, which refers to the perceived nature of the raw materials, and the search behaviors undertaken by individuals when exceptional cases appear, which refers to the actions of workers in response to the perceived nature of the materials. Perrow's perspective enables a comparison of library work across functional units (Lynch, 1974b,c) and provides a means of understanding the work and structure of various library units.

Perrow theorizes that the technology, or nature of the work as he defines it, will influence the discretion and power of the workers in the organizational unit, the methods of coordination used by the unit, and the interdependence of the units within the organization. For units whose work is routine, that is, when few exceptional cases occur and the search strategies to deal with them are easily analyzed, little discretion will be allowed the supervisor or the worker, the work will be governed by rules and standard procedures, coordinated through advance planning. Little interdependence will occur among work groups. For units whose work is nonroutine, where there are many exceptional cases and unanalyzable search strategies, there will be a great deal of discretion and much interdependence, and coordination will be through mutual feedback.

Hage and Aiken (1969), drawing upon Perrow's model for their theoretical perspective in a study of social welfare agencies, found that in the more routine agencies, the decision-making regarding organizational policies was more centralized, the use of rules and procedures more prevalent, and the jobs more structured. In the routine agencies, staff members were more likely to emphasize the organizational goals of efficiency and numbers of clients served than they were to emphasize quality of service, staff morale, or innovativeness.

A library manager who analyzes the unit's environment and the nature of the work done in the unit will be able to identify suitable strategies for conflict resolution and develop patterns of work coordination and integration that will assist the unit in its effectiveness and efficiency. This perspective suggests that a successful manager in an effective unit will be able to fit the unit's organizational characteristics to its environmental and technological setting. It suggests that managerial techniques will vary and that a manager who successfully applies one set of strategies in one situation may find the same set of strategies inappropriate to another situation. It suggests that librarians working in a unit where the environment is certain and where the work is routine may be more effective if formal rules and procedures are established and advance planning is done. It suggests that for some units a bureaucratic structure rather than a participatory one will lead to greater unit effectiveness.

C. Professionalism

Although organizational environment, technology, and structure are described quite simply, the concepts are complex, as are the relationships among them and other organizational variables. The complexity of the relationships is compounded by the variation in the characteristics of the organization's members and the relationships between the members and the organization.

Beginning librarians, steeped in the ethics and values of librarianship, often fail to recognize that librarianship is practiced within an organizational setting. They expect to work as autonomous professionals in an environment in which the work of others does not impinge upon their own. They do not expect to be concerned about the overall effectiveness of the unit in which they work or of the library itself.

Librarians coming to their jobs with tendencies to act in certain already established ways learn the expectations of the library from signals given by peers, subordinates, and managers. They observe the formal patterns of organization and the methods of control, measurement, and evaluation of performance. The librarians learn to what extent they are expected to follow rules and orders, the extent to which supervisors are expected to show a personal interest in the subordinates, the extent to which organizational relationships are conducted according to general rather than specific standards, the extent to which supervision is detailed, and the extent to which they are to strive for achievement and advancement (Katz and Kahn, 1966).

Having been socialized to accept the role of the autonomous professional, librarians may be shocked to find that their expectations regarding the work they do cannot be fully realized. The change in expectations forced upon the librarians by the library may generate considerable conflict. Professional standards must be reconciled with the reality of the job. The librarian must learn to deal with administrators and managers, a group with whom the beginning librarian has not been prepared to deal (Abrahamson, 1967).

Not all librarians necessarily accept the role of the autonomous professional. By assuming that the model has been adopted generally throughout the profession, that it is shared by all professionals working in the library, or that it can be applied in all units or types of libraries, librarians may limit their perspective and their understanding of the role they have in the organization and the management of libraries.

III. LEADERSHIP IN THE CONTEXT OF THE ORGANIZATION

The term "management" has several meanings. It can refer to the broad activities that make up the control of the organization. It can be used to describe the levels of authority in the organization. It can describe the functions of managers, those mental and physical processes by which organizational objectives are carried out by members. In terms of each usage managers are expected to be responsible for organizational performance, and the manager's relationship to the subordinates usually is conceived as one-way. Management is defined as the process by which resources are organized and employed to accomplish specific purposes or objectives.

Leadership, by contrast, implies a two-way relationship. "Leadership constitutes an influence relationship between two, or usually more, persons who depend upon one another for the attainment of certain mutual goals within a group structure" (Hollander and Julian, 1969). The typical view of leadership as one person directing another is misleading. The leader does provide a valuable resource to the group, but the group's resources are not the leader's alone to manipulate or deploy. In attempting to understand the process of leadership and particularly the role of the appointed leader, i.e., manager, leadership must be viewed as a process of influence involving an exchange relationship over time.

Leadership is one of the most researched topics in the management field. Recent developments indicate that the evaluation of leadership is a highly complex problem to which simple solutions cannot be applied. Some research instruments have been widely used and have been applied to studies of library management, but few conclusions can be drawn so far from these studies. The knowledge of the theories of leadership supporting the investigations can help the practicing manager and subordinates begin to understand their own behavior and the responses of others to it.

A. Trait Theory

Surveys conducted before World War II tried to identify the characteristics of traits of leaders. Although these studies at first seemed to indicate that leaders differed from followers in one or more specific traits, Bird's review (1940) of the studies and Stogdill's review (1948) concluded that only a few traits were common to more than one study, and the extent to which the leader's traits differed from situation to situation seemed to depend upon the situation in which the leader was found. These conclusions led to a shift in the definition of leadership from the characteristics held by the leader to that of a relationship between persons. A leader with certain traits could be effective in one situation and ineffective in another.

B. Ohio State University Studies in Leadership

In 1947 the Personnel Research Board of Ohio State University developed a series of leadership studies under the direction of Carroll Shartle, which concentrated on issues of organizational effectiveness and on descriptions of leader behavior and its impact in formal organizations. Leadership behavior was studied in relation to criteria of group satisfaction and group performance. From these studies the categories of consideration and structure emerged (Halpin and Winer, 1957). Reflecting upon the early stages of the research, Fleishman (1973) defined the two factors:

> ...*consideration* seemed to involve behavior indicating friendship, mutual trust, respect, a certain warmth and rapport between the supervisor and his group. As we continued to do research with these, the emphasis on friendship seemed to drop and the tolerance for two-way communications seemed to become a key feature of this dimension.... *Initiating structure* seemed to involve acts which imply that the leader organizes and defines the relationships in the group, tends to establish well defined patterns and channels of communication and ways of getting the job done.

Fleishman's "Supervisory Behavior Description Questionnaire" (1970), which identifies the expectations of subordinates toward the supervisor, has been applied in a variety of organizational settings and is the best known and most widely used outcome of this work. Evidence from the many studies conducted by the researchers at Ohio State shows that subordinates regard more favorably those leaders who show consideration, but that superordinates do not share these expectations. Further, there is little correlation between productivity and the reports by subordinates of their leaders' behavior regarding consideration and structure. Stogdill's model (1969), developed from the Ohio State studies, suggests that successful leaders must be concerned with both the satisfaction of the group's members and the productivity of the work group.

The effective supervisor alternates behavior as the situation demands, emphasizing structure when necessary, showing consideration when desirable. What the studies do not yet indicate is what decision rule the supervisor uses to alter his or her behavior. The basic question remains: What is in the situation that leads to what kind of response on the part of the leader in order to produce effective group behavior (Jacobs, 1970)?

C. Survey Research Center, University of Michigan

The studies in human relations that were begun at the Survey Research Center at the University of Michigan about the same time as the leadership studies got underway at Ohio State concentrated on small work groups, particularly emphasizing the behavior of foremen in relation to levels of productivity and group satisfaction. The Michigan group expected high satisfaction to be associated with high productivity. This position differed from the Ohio State emphasis which was that satisfaction and productivity would be influenced by the leadership process.

The Michigan studies focused on productivity and group morale, trying to identify that leadership behavior which would facilitate production, morale, and satisfaction. The results of the Michigan studies suggest that the supervisor, to be effective, must differentiate his or her role from that of the persons supervised, doing those things which he or she alone can do well and refraining from those which the subordinates can do as well or better.

D. Current Perspectives

Authority, power, and leadership are different concepts, yet difficult to define and separate. All are used to describe organizational relationships in which one person exerts influence over another.

1. AUTHORITY

It is recognized that authority as a relationship between positions in an organization relies upon the acceptance or consent of individuals. Essentially there are two perspectives. One views authority as being legitimized by the acceptance or consent of subordinates. The other sees authority as being legitimized by the consensus of the superordinates (Peabody, 1964). The discussion of authority in libraries generally emphasizes one or the other of these perspectives. It has not contrasted these perspectives or recognized the further reality that there are several types of authority which may exist simultaneously.

Bureaucratic authority is based upon position. It derives legitimacy largely from the organization's regulations and the consensus of superordinates. The position given responsibilities for goal definition and goal attainment is inevitably supervisory. The manager's attempts to exercise bureaucratic authority will fail if the subordinates do not recognize the position of authority and see the attempts to influence as illegitimate.

Professional authority is the type based upon the position holder's personal competence as to knowledge or techniques. Its legitimacy is derived largely from the perceptions of others as to the person's competence in his or her area of expertise (Meyer, 1968a,b).

Despite efforts to increase participation and to exercise decision-making through consensus, libraries find it necessary to place people in positions of authority in order to accomplish the library's goals. It is difficult for a library to find a way to achieve its goals by group consensus. Outcomes of group decision-making are found to be unreliable. Libraries find it necessary to give managerial positions bureaucratic authority. The success of the middle manager in a library will depend largely on whether subordinates accept his or her authority. If the middle manager is a librarian, the perceptions of subordinates regarding his or her professional authority as well as bureaucratic authority will affect the middle manager's performance and the performance of the unit. If subordinates perceive the manager's authority as being weak or illegitimate, they will resist attempts by the manager to exercise authority. Many or even all attempts to influence the behavior of the subordinates in terms of the work they do will be ignored, and organizational conflict will occur.

2. POWER

The exercise of power also can lead to organizational conflict, resistance, and resentment among the organization's members. Power is the ability of one person to influence another to do something that person would not otherwise do. It is a coercive form of influence, since the person who is able to influence the behavior of another despite that person's opposition is able to do so because he has the capacity to withhold benefits or inflict punishment. In organizational studies, power is viewed as a relationship between people, not as a personal characteristic or attribute (Jacobs, 1970).

Within organizations, persons who are the target of the power will attempt to find ways to reduce the differential between themselves and the more powerful. Through means such as collective bargaining or legislation, members will attempt to restrict the range of legitimate power or define the areas in which power can be exercised. Weaker members of the organization will form coalitions or cliques in a collective attempt to reduce the power of the stronger. Social behavior, such as "apple-polishing," may be used by weaker members to influence the stronger member's use of power (Cartwright, 1965). A response to the power differential that can adversely affect the effectiveness of the organization is the tendency on the part of subordinates to restrict the amount and accuracy of the information they can provide. Managers in organizations complain frequently that they do not know what is going on and that they are displeased with the communication they have from subordinates. When a situation of power differential is present, it is unlikely that the less powerful will increase the amount and accuracy of information or initiate more interactions with the powerful (Lawler *et al.*, 1968).

Library managers and others with power should recognize that the very presence of the power differential poses a threat to the weaker members. Since managers have the potential power to cause subordinates harm or distress, subordinates are sensitive to the behavior of managers and will strive to contain it.

3. LEADERSHIP

A great deal of confusion exists concerning the concepts of authority, power, and leadership. A librarian complaining that the department head is not a leader fails to distinguish between leader and leadership.

Leadership is a process of influence involving an exchange relationship over time. In the process one person, the leader, provides some kind of information so that the other person modifies his or her behavior, having been convinced that the change in behavior will lead to a more desirable outcome. The leader in such a situation recognizes the need for persuasive interaction, particularly if the other person holds different ideas about the subject in question.

"Leadership depends on the competence of the leader at the task at hand, on his ability to understand the motives of his followers in order to provide convincing evidence of the desirability of an act that he desires, and on his tolerance for counter-influence attempts" (Jacobs, 1970, p. 233).

Two-way communication is the behavior that distinguishes the process of leadership from authority and power. Two-way communication may occur in an influence attempt based on authority, but it is not necessary since the influence is directed mainly from the top down. Two-way communication rarely occurs in an influence attempt based on power.

Each of the three processes of influence occurs in libraries. Leadership, being a set of behaviors used by superordinates as the situation demands, is not required in many of the organizational activities supervised by the middle managers in libraries.

IV. SUMMARY AND DISCUSSION

The library manager responsible for certain aspects of the library's performance must analyze, appraise, and interpret the performance of others, relating that performance to the unit's effectiveness and the library's goals. Planning, organizing, directing, staffing, and controlling are essential parts of the manager's job. The precise techniques used by the manager will vary from library to library and unit to unit depending upon the characteristics of the library's environment, the particular work situation and the nature of the work, and the personal skills of the manager.

In order for the library to carry out its mission effectively, the manager works to reduce the conflicting goals and forces that exist in the library. To ensure that conflict is reduced so that organizational goals can be attained, control mechanisms are employed, centered on the processes of authority, power, and leadership.

Bureaucratic authority assumes that the subordinate has little interest or expertise in the activities necessary for successful performance of the unit. The assumption is correct for some libraries and there is evidence to suggest that bureaucratic authority is the type of influence most generally accepted by librarians in the field. The model of the autonomous professional also assumes that the librarian has little interest in the overall effectiveness of the unit or the library. According to this model, the work of the individual librarian is the most important function. Yet the effectiveness of the unit and of all other units in the library is essential to the success of the library. Taking all things into consideration, the library will employ the management model that will best ensure organizational effectiveness.

The attempt by librarians to change the role of the library's middle manager, by introducing methods of group decision-making and decision-making by consensus, are attempts to bring about a change in the library's (or the unit's) goals, to reduce the manager's authority and power, or to shift the focus of control so that the differential in power that exists between the manager and the subordinates is reduced. Some management models based upon consensus have been tried in libraries, but the results have usually been less than satisfactory. As noted earlier, library administrators generally have found the results of group decision-making to be inconsistent and unreliable. Decision-making through the consensus of individuals will be employed only to the extent that it is evident that the consensus model leads to greater organizational effectiveness than the authority model.

It is not enough that library managers know the elements comprising the functions of management or the techniques of supervision. They must know the nature of the work being done in the unit, the differences in the underlying characteristics of the work of library units, and the internal and external environments in which the work is conducted. The organizational complexity brought about by professionals working in libraries is such that the successful manager must analyze the extent of the professionalism in the library and attempt to assess its impact on the various units and the library itself. A high degree of professionalism is likely to bring about some change in the role and function of the manager of a given library unit, but there is little evidence to show that the present level of professionalism generally is great enough to reduce the role of the library's middle manager or eliminate the manager altogether. The norms and values of the librarians in the unit and the library will influence the manager and the forms of influence used by the manager, but the functions of management are essential to the library and will continue for some time to be assigned to the manager, not to the group.

REFERENCES

Abrahamson, M. (1967). "The Professional in the Organization." Rand McNally, Chicago, Illinois.
Bird, C. (1940). Leadership. *In* "Social Psychology" (R. M. Elliot, ed.), pp. 369–395. Appleton-Century-Crofts, New York.
Blau, P. M., and Schoenherr, R. A. (1971). "The Structure of Organizations." Basic Books, New York.
Blauner, R. (1964). "Alienation and Freedom." University of Chicago Press, Chicago, Illinois.
Booz, Allen & Hamilton, Inc. (1973). "Organization and Staffing of the Libraries of Columbia University." Redgrave Information Resources Corp., Westport, Connecticut.
Bryan, A. I. (1952). "The Public Librarian." Columbia University Press, New York.
Bundy, M. L. (1966). Conflict in libraries. *College & Research Libraries* **27**, 253–262.
Burns, T., and Stalker, G. M. (1961). "The Management of Innovation." Tavistock Publications, London.
Cartwright, D. (1965). Influence, leadership, control. *In* "Handbook of Organizations" (J. G. March, ed.), pp. 1–47. Rand McNally, Chicago, Illinois.
Crozier, M. (1964). "The Bureaucratic Phenomenon." University of Chicago Press, Chicago, Illinois.
Dale, E. (1973). "Management: Theory and Practice," 3rd ed. McGraw-Hill, New York.
Douglass, R. R. (1957). "The Personality of the Librarian." Unpublished dissertation, University of Chicago.
Drucker, P. F. (1974). "Management: Tasks, Responsibilities, Practices." Harper & Row, New York.
Duncan, R. (1972). Characteristics of organizational environment and perceived environmental uncertainty. *Administrative Science Quarterly* **17**, 313–327.
Farley, R. A. (1967). "The American Library Executive." Unpublished dissertation, University of Illinois.
Fleishman, E. A. (1970). "Supervisory Behavior Description Questionnaire." Science Research Associates, Chicago, Illinois.
Fleishman, E. A. (1973). Twenty years of consideration and structure. *In* "Current Developments in the Study of Leadership" (E. A. Fleishman and J. G. Hunt, eds.), pp. 1–40. Southern Illinois University Press, Carbondale, Illinois.

Fullan, M. (1970). Industrial technology and worker integration in the organization. *American Sociological Review* **35**, 1028–1039.
Goode, W. J. (1961). The librarian: from occupation to profession? *Library Quarterly* **31**, 306–320.
Gulick, L. (1937). Notes on the theory of organization. *In* "Papers on the Science of Administration" (L. Gulick and L. F. Urwick, eds.), pp. 1–45. Institute of Public Administration, Columbia University, New York.
Guttsman, W. L. (1965). "Learned" librarians and the structure of academic libraries. *Libri* **15**, 159–167.
Guttsman, W. L. (1973). Subject specialization in academic libraries: some preliminary observations on role conflict and organizational stress. *Journal of Librarianship* **5**, 1–8.
Hage, J., and Aiken, M. (1969). Routine technology, social structure, and organizational goals. *Administrative Science Quarterly* **14**, 366–376.
Hall, D. T., and Lawler, E. (1970). Job characteristics and pressures and the organizational integration of professionals. *Administrative Science Quarterly* **15**, 271–281.
Hall, R. J. (1968). Professionalization and bureaucratization. *American Sociological Review* **33**, 92–104.
Halpin, A. W., and Winer, B. J. (1957). A factorial study of the leader behavior descriptions. *In* "Leader Behavior: Its Description and Measurement" (R. M. Stogdill and A. E. Coons, eds.), pp. 39–51. Bureau of Business Research, Ohio State University, Columbus, Ohio. (Research Monograph No. 88.)
Hollander, E. P., and Julian, J. W. (1969). Contemporary trends in the analysis of leadership processes. *Psychological Bulletin* **71**, 387–397.
Jacobs, T. O. (1970). "Leadership and Exchange in Formal Organizations." Human Resources Research Organization, Alexandria, Virginia.
Katz, D., and Kahn, R. L. (1966). "The Social Psychology of Organizations." Wiley, New York.
Kornhauser, W. (1962). "Scientists in Industry." University of California Press, Berkeley, California.
Lawler, E. E., Porter, L. W., and Tennenbaum, A. (1968). Managers' attitudes toward interaction episodes. *Journal of Applied Psychology* **52**, 432–439.
Lawrence, P. R., and Lorsch, J. W. (1967). "Organization and Environment." Graduate School of Business Administration, Harvard University, Boston, Massachusetts.
Lorsch, J. W., and Morse, J. J. (1974). "Organizations and Their Members." Harper & Row, New York.
Lynch, B. P. (1974a). The academic library and its environment. *College & Research Libraries* **35**, 126–132.
Lynch, B. P. (1974b). An empirical assessment of Perrow's technology construct. *Administrative Science Quarterly* **19**, 338–356.
Lynch, B. P. (1974c). A framework for the comparative analysis of library work. *College & Research Libraries* **35**, 432–443.
Meyer, M. W. (1968a). Expertness and the span of control. *American Sociological Review* **33**, 944–951.

Meyer, M. W. (1968b). The two authority structures of bureaucratic organization. *Administrative Science Quarterly* **13**, 211–228.

Morrison, P. D. (1969). "The Career of the Academic Librarian." American Library Association, Chicago, Illinois.

Nash, W. V. (1964). "Characteristics of Administrative Heads of Public Libraries in Various Communications Categories." Unpublished dissertation, University of Illinois.

Peabody, R. L. (1964). "Organizational Authority: Superior-Subordinate Relationships in Three Public Service Organizations." Atherton Press, New York.

Perrow, C. (1967). A framework for the comparative analysis of organizations. *American Sociological Review* **32**, 194–208.

Plate, K. (1970). "Management Personnel in Libraries." American Faculty Press, Rockaway, New Jersey.

Ricking, M., and Booth, R. W. (1974). "Personnel Utilization in Libraries." American Library Association, Chicago, Illinois.

Sloan, E. (1973). "The Organization of Collection Development in Large University Libraries." Unpublished dissertation, University of Maryland.

Sofer, C. (1970). "Men in Mid-Career: A Study of British Managers and Technical Specialists." University Press, Cambridge, England.

Standards for faculty status for college and university librarians (1972). *College & Research Libraries News* **33**, 210–212.

Stogdill, R. M. (1948). Personal factors associated with leadership: a survey of the literature. *Journal of Psychology* **25**, 35–72.

Stogdill, R. M. (1969). "Individual Behavior and Group Achievement: A Behavioral Model of Organization." Paper presented at the Annual Meeting of the American Psychological Association, Washington, D. C.

Thompson, J. D. (1967). "Organizations in Action." McGraw-Hill, New York.

Van de Ven, A. H., and Delbecq, A. L. (1974). A task contingent model of work-unit structure. *Administrative Science Quarterly* **19**, 183–197.

Woodward, J. (1965). "Industrial Organization: Theory and Practice." Oxford University Press, London and New York.

GENERAL REFERENCES

Axford, H. W. (1975). The interrelations of structure, governance and effective resource allocation. *Library Trends* **23**, 551–557.

Buckland, M. K. (1974). The management of libraries and information centers. *Annual Review of Information Science and Technology* **9**, 335–379.

Dix, W. S. (1960). Leadership in academic libraries. *College & Research Libraries* **21**, 373–380.

Gibb, C. A. (1969). Leadership, *In* "Handbook of Social Psychology" (G. Lindzey and E. Aronson, eds.), Vol. 4, pp. 205–282. Addison-Wesley, Reading, Massachusetts.

Haga, W. J., Graen, G., and Dansereau, F. (1974). Professionalism and role making in a service organization. *American Sociological Review* **39**, 122–133.

Hall, R. J. (1967). Some organizational considerations in the professional-organizational relationship. *Administrative Science Quarterly* **12**, 461–478.

Kay, E. (1974). "The Crisis in Middle Management." American Management Association, New York.

Smith, E. (1969). Do libraries need managers? *Library Journal* **94**, 502–506.

Smith, G. C. K., and Schofield, J. L. (1973). A general survey of senior and intermediate staff deployment in university libraries. *Journal of Librarianship* **5**, 79–96.

Stewart, R. (1967). "Managers and Their Jobs." Macmillan, New York.

Wickert, F. C., and McFarland, D. E. (1967). "Measuring Executive Effectiveness." Appleton-Century-Crofts, New York.

Author Index

Numbers in italics refer to the pages on which the complete references are listed.

A

Abelson, H. I., 156, 157, *202*, *215*
Abelson, R. P., 181, *202*
Abrahamson, M., 266, *274*
Abramov, K. I., 231, *249*
Acker, C., 170, *215*
Adorno, T., 183, *202*
Aiken, M., 263, 265, *275*
Allen, A. P., 263, *274*
Allport, C. W., 187, 188, 192, *202*
Altman, E., 31, 33, 38, 42, *46*, *47*
Anderson, A. R., 83, *135*
Anderson, W. H. L., 63, *75*
Andrews, F. M., 147, *212*
Appleberry, M. H., 197, *202*
Aring, C. D., 193, *202*
Aronson, E., 181, 184, *202*
Arutjunov, N. B., 245, *249*
Asheim, L., 246, *249*
Atkin, C. K., 149, 183, *202*, *205*
Atkinson, A. B., 63, *75*
Averill, J. A., 162, *215*
Axford, H. W., *276*

B

Baker, N. R., 26, *46*
Baker, R. K., 166, 169, *202*
Ball, S. J., 166, 169, *202*
Bandura, A., 150, 174, 175, 176, *202*, *203*

Barcus, F. E., 168, *203*
Barhydt, G. C., 133, *135*
Barnett, L. D., 157, *215*
Baughman, J. C., 14, *46*
Baumanis, G. J., 99, 130, 131, 132, 133, *136*, *137*
Baumol, W. J., 54, 58, 59, *75*
Baylis, C. T., 242, *250*
Bazelak, L. P. 196, *203*
Beasley, K. E., 12, 31, 33, *46*, *47*
Beatty, W. K., 193, 194, *203*
Becker, J., 190, *203*
Bekkedal, T. R., 198, *203*
Belenky, M., 159, *207*
Bell, D., 81, 92, *135*
Belnap, N. D., Jr., 83, *135*
Ben-Veniste, R., 163, *203*
Berelson, B., 145, 148, *203*, *215*
Berkowitz, L., 167, 170, 171, 172, 173, *203*, *204*, *206*
Berlyne, D. E., 149, *204*
Bernotavicz, F. D., 22, *46*
Berry, M., 98, *136*
Besen, S. M., 64, *75*
Bird, C., 267, *274*
Blackman, A., 13, *46*
Blau, P. M., 263, *274*
Blauner, R., 259, *274*
Blum, B., 173, *204*
Blum, E., 168, *204*
Bogart, L., 143, *204*
Bonn, G. L., 32, *46*
Bonner, M. R. W., 27, *48*

279

Bookstein, A., 25, *46, 50*
Booth, R. W., 263, *276*
Booz, 263, *274*
Borko, H., 56, *76*
Bowers, J. W., 145, *204*
Bradford, D. A., 59, *76*
Bradford, S. C., 89, 103, *135*
Bradshaw, F. R., 141, *215*
Bramel, D., 173, *204*
Braucht, G. N., 164, *205*
Bredsdorff, V., 244, *250*
Breuer, J., 172, *204*
Brimmer, M. R. W., 27, *48*
Brock, T. C., 164, *204*
Brookes, B. C., 103, *135*
Brooks, W. D., 145, *206*
Brown, J. D., 189, 190, 192, *204*
Bryan, A. I., 258, *274*
Bryson, R. J., 196, *204*
Buckland, M. K., 26, *46, 47, 276*
Bundy, M. L., 263, *274*
Bungay, F., 243, *250*
Burgoon, M., 184, *204*
Burkett, J., 242, *250*
Burns, T., 259, *274*
Burt, L. N., 198, *204*
Bush, V., 95, *135*
Busha, C. A., 165, *204*
Buss, A. H., 167, 172, *204*
Butler, J. R., 162, *209*
Butterworth, R. F., 169, *204*

C

Cairns, R. B., 162, *204*
Capon, N., 179, *205*
Carey, J. W., 150, *205*
Carnap, R., 83, *135*
Carroll, F. L., 230, 235, 245, *250*
Carter, R. F., 150, *213*
Cartwright, D., 271, *274*
Case, R. N., 20, 21, *47*
Certain, C. C., 14, *47*
Chaffee, S. H., 149, 182, *205*
Chein, I., 182, *207*
Childers, T. A., 18, 31, *47*
Christenson, C. V., 164, *206*
Cianciolo, P. J., 196, *205*
Clark, K., 192, *205*
Clark, R. A., 161, *205*

Clelland, R. C., 27, *48*
Cleverdon, C. W., 98, *135*
Cohen, R., 157, *202*
Coleman, J. S., 7, *47*
Comstock, O. O., 169, *205*
Conklin, M., 187, *208*
Cooper, E., 150, 184, *205*
Cooper, W. S., 85, 107, 108, 114, 115, 122, *135*
Cornaz, M. L., 230, 249, *250*
Corwin, R., 170, *204*
Coules, J., 172, *214*
Cowley, J., 241, *250*
Craig, C. E., 57, 60, 61, 62, 64, 65, *76*
Crowley, T., 31, *47*
Crozier, M., 260, *274*
Cuadra, C. A., 99, 100, 102, 129, 130, 131, 132, 133, *135*

D

Dale, E., 255, *274*
Dansereau, F., *277*
Danton, J. P., 244, *250*
Darling, R. L., 17, *47*
Davinson, D. E., 233, *250*
Davis, K. E., 164, *205*
Deason, H. J., 43, *47*
de Charms, R., 173, *213*
De Gennaro, R., 54, *76*
DeGrolier, E., 228, *250*
DeHart, F. E., 30, *50*
Delbecq, A. L., 263, *276*
Denison, E. F., 60, 64, *76*
Dennis, J., 190, *205*
DeProspo, E. R., 33, 38, 42, *47*
De Rath, G. W., 176, *205*
Dervin, B., 191, *205*
Diamond, P. A., 64, *76*
Diwan, R. K., 64, *76*
Dix, W. S., *276*
Dollard, J. 167, 172, *205*
Domar, E. D., 64, *76*
Donohew, L., 183, *205*
Doob, L., 167, 172, *205*
Dougherty, R. M., 30, *47*
Douglass, R. R., 258, *274*
Doyle, L. B., 98, *135*
Drucker, P. F., 255, *274*
Dudick, T. S., 66, *76*

Author Index

Dudley, L., 64, 76
Duncan, R., 260, 274

E

Egan, M. E., 88, 137
Ehrlich, H. J., 176, 186, 187, 205
Eifler, D., 189, 191, 215
Emmerich, W., 205
Emmert, P., 145, 206
Evans, E., 56, 76, 234, 250

F

Fabricant, S., 55, 56, 58, 60, 63, 64, 65, 76
Fairthorne, R. A., 102, 103, 104, 135
Farley, R. A., 258, 274
Farrell, W., 190, 206
Favazza, A. R., 194, 206
Ferguson, P., 56, 76
Feshbach, S., 173, 179, 206, 208
Festinger, L., 181, 206
Field, P. B., 150, 208
Fisher, F. L., 197, 206
Fisher, G. H., 63, 76
Fiske, M., 165, 206
Flanders, J. P., 150, 206
Fleishman, E. A., 268, 274
Fleming, M. C., 63, 76
Floyd, H. H., 190, 206
Fonotov, G., 231, 250
Foskett, A. C., 237, 250
Foskett, D. J., 85, 109, 135, 238, 250
Francis, Sir F. C., 221, 250
Frank, J., 229, 249, 250
Frankel, H. H., 196, 197, 206
Freedman, J. L., 149, 213
Frankel-Brunswick, E., 183, 202
Freud, S., 172, 204
Freund, K., 162, 206
Fuchs, V. R., 60, 66, 76
Fullan, M., 259, 275
Fulton, W. R., 19, 47

G

Gagnon, J. H., 164, 206
Galbraith, C. G., 161, 206

Gaver, M. V., 23, 42, 47, 48
Gebhard, P. H., 158, 160, 164, 206, 209
Geen, R., 170, 172, 204, 206
Gerard, H. B., 178, 184, 185, 209
Gerber, A., 151, 207
Gerbner, G., 168, 207
Gersoni-Stavin, D., 189, 207
Geyer, J. J., 198, 207
Gibb, C. A., 276
Gifford, C., 131, 136
Gillespie, J. T., 42, 48
Gillig, P. M., 179, 207
Gilligan, C., 159, 207
Gintis, H., 64, 76
Goffman, W., 88, 91, 97, 108, 111, 120, 121, 136, 138
Goldberg, P. A., 159, 207
Golden, B. W., 184, 202
Goldman, K. S., 205
Goldstein, M. J., 155, 160, 161, 164, 207, 215
Goode, W. J., 258, 275
Gooler, D. D., 11, 50
Gordon, D. R., 142, 207
Gore, D., 32, 33, 48
Graen, G., 277
Granberg, D., 184, 207
Greenberg, B., 186, 191, 205, 207
Greenberg, I., 159, 161, 212
Greenberg, L., 56, 58, 64, 65, 76
Greene, E., 42, 48
Greenwald, A. G., 179, 207
Griliches, Z., 64, 76
Guerrero, J., 182, 205
Gulick, L., 255, 275
Gupta, S., 64, 76
Guttsman, W. L., 258, 263, 275

H

Haga, W. J., 277
Hage, J., 263, 265, 275
Halbe, H. G., 242, 251
Hall, D. T., 256, 275
Hall, R. J., 256, 275, 277
Halpin, A. W., 268, 275
Hamburg, M., 27, 48
Hamilton, 263, 274
Hamreus, D., 23, 48
Haney, R., 173, 207

Hanneman, G., 186, 207
Hannigan, J., 44, 48
Hannigan, M. C., 195, 207
Hansen, H. S., 149, 207
Hanz, B., 232, 250
Harding, J., 182, 207
Harmon, G., 111, 136
Harris, M. H., 141, 207
Harris, R. C., 57, 60, 61, 62, 64, 65, 76
Harrison, J. C., 221, 222, 238, 251
Hartmann, D. P., 173, 176, 186, 187, 188, 207
Haskins, J. B., 168, 207
Hayes, M. T., 187, 196, 208
Heaney, H. J., 241, 251
Heaton, E., 157, 202
Heironimous, M., 170, 204
Henne, F., 14, 48
Herminghaus, E. G., 197, 208
Hess, E. H., 162, 208
Hicks, D., 175, 176, 208
Hillman, D. J., 85, 97, 122, 136
Hines, T. C., 30, 43, 48
Hinesley, R. K., 160, 210
Hjelmqvist, B., 226, 230, 251
Hodges, E. D., 42, 48
Höglund, A. L., 233, 239, 251
Hoffman, J. M., 133, 136
Hogg, F. N., 221, 222, 251
Hokada, E., 189, 191, 215
Hollander, E. P., 267, 275
Holmes, D. S., 172, 204
Horne, E. M., 194, 195, 208
Hoult, T. F., 169, 208
House, E. R., 9, 48
Hovland, C. I., 146, 147, 178, 179, 180, 184, 208
Howard, J., 163, 208
Hoyt, J., 171, 208
Huckaby, S., 228, 229, 237, 251
Hulbert, J., 179, 205
Husband, C., 176, 186, 187, 188, 207
Huston, A. D., 175, 203
Hynes, J. C., 193, 198, 208

I

Israel, H., 169, 208

J

Jackson, E. P., 195, 196, 208
Jacobs, T. O., 269, 271, 272, 275
Jacobson, T. P., 233, 239, 251
Jacoby, S., 189, 208
Jahoda, M., 150, 184, 205
Janis, I. L., 146, 150, 178, 179, 208, 209
Jencks, C., 7, 48
Johnson, V. E., 162, 211
Jones, E. E., 178, 184, 185, 209
Jordan, B. T., 162, 209
Jorgenson, D. W., 64, 76
Julian, J. W., 267, 275

K

Kahn, R. L., 266, 275
Kant, H. S., 155, 160, 161, 164, 207
Kaplan, A., 145, 209
Karp, E. E., 169, 209
Katter, R. V., 99, 100, 102, 129, 130, 131, 132, 133, 135, 136
Katz, D., 266, 275
Katz, D. A., 59, 77
Katz, E., 150, 209
Kay, E., 277
Keating, C. H., Jr., 144, 209
Kelley, H. H., 146, 178, 208
Kemp, D. A., 85, 109, 110, 136
Kent, A., 98, 136
Kerlinger, F. F., 145, 209
Kilgour, F. G., 56, 59, 74, 77
Kimmel, E. A., 197, 209
Kinsey, A. C., 158, 160, 209
Kirkegaard, P., 233, 249, 251
Klapper, J. T., 149, 150, 209
Kline, F. G., 150, 209
Kochen, M., 92, 116, 136
Köttelwesch, C., 242, 251
Kohlberg, L., 159, 207, 209
Kolers, P. A., 198, 207
Kornhauser, W., 256, 275
Koskialla, S., 233, 251
Kovacs, M., 234, 251
Kozachkov, L. S., 105, 136
Kozlowska, Sister M. V., 196, 197, 209
Kreisberg, L., 158, 213

Author Index

Kuhns, J. L., 119, *136*
Kunze, H., 231, *251*
Kupperstein, L., 163, *209*
Kurfeerst, M., 130, *138*
Kutchinsky, B., 163, *210*
Kutner, B., 182, *207*

L

Lacy, D., 149, *210*
Lampman, R. J., 57, 59, 77
Lancaster, J. W., 196, *210*
Lancour, H., 247, *251*
Larrick, N., 189, *210*
Lawler, E. E., 256, 271, *275*
Lawrence, P. R., 260, 261, *275*
Lazarsfeld, P. F., 148, 149, *203, 209*
Leedy, J. J., 193, *210*
Leimkuhler, F. F., 26, *48*
Leonard, L. E., 30, *47*
Lerner, J., 159, *207*
Lesk, M. E., 133, *136*
Leuhrs, F. U., 98, *136*
Levenson, I. F., 63, 77
Levin, H., 175, *210*
Levison, D., 183, *202*
Levitan, K. M., 23, *49*
Levitt, E. E., 160, *210*
Lewis, I. R., 197, *210*
Lewis, P. R., 225, 236, 241, *251*
Liesener, J. W., 23, 24, 25, 41, *48, 49*
Line, M. B., 103, *136*
Lipsman, C. K., 29, *49*
Liptzin, M. B., 163, *208*
Livengood, D. K., 196, 198, *210*
Lockhart, W. B., 152, *210*
Loiselle, R. H., 158, 162, *210*
Lorsch, J. W., 260, 261, *275*
Lotka, A. J., 104, *136*
Lovass, O. J., 175, *210*
Lovibond, S. H., 175, *210*
Lowrey, A. M., 21, *47*
Lucey, P. J., 57, 77
Lukenbill, W. B., 198, *210*
Lumsdaine, A. A., 178, *208*
Lundberg, E., 63, 77
Lyle, J., 166, 175, *213*
Lynch, B. P., 260, 264, *275*

M

McClaskey, H. C., 198, *210*
McClure, R. C., 152, *210*
Maccoby, E. E., 175, 198, *210*
Maccoby, N., 180, *213*
McConaghy, N., 162, *211*
McDaniel, R., 42, *49*
McDaniel, W. B., II, 193, *211*
McFarland, D. E., *277*
McGinnies, E., 142, *211*
McGuire, W. J., 150, 180, 181, 202, *211*
McLaughlin, J. P., 162, *212*
McLeod, J. M., 149, *205*
McPhee, W. N., 148, *203*
Madden, L. E., 196, 198, *211*
Malt, R. A., 59, 76
Mann, J., 162, 163, *211*
Marco, G. A., 245, *251*
Marcus, M., 54, 58, 59, 75
Marcus, S., 99, 130, 131, 132, 133, *137*
Marimont, M. L., 65, 77
Maron, M. E., 119, *136*
Martin, C. E., 158, 160, *209*
Martin, W. B., 158, 160, *209*
Mason, E., 56, 77
Masters, W. H., 162, *211*
Meier, R. L., 28, *49*
Menlove, F. L., 174, *203*
Menninger, K., 193, *211*
Mesarović, M., 81, *136*
Meyberg, J., 162, *213*
Meyer, M. W., 270, *275, 276*
Meyerson, L., 175, *211*
Mezei, L., 184, *213*
Miller, D. R., 158, *211*
Miller, G., 184, *204*
Miller, G. A., 102, *136*
Miller, N., 167, 172, *205*
Milstein, J. T., 159, *207*
Mollenauer, S., 158, 162, *210*
Monroe, M. E., 29, 49, 194, *212*
Mooers, C. S., 96, *136*
Morrison, H., 185, *212*
Morrison, P. D., 258, *276*
Morse, J. J., 260, *275*
Morse, P. M., 26, 27, *49*
Mortensen, C. D., 178, 180, *212*
Moses, H. A., 195, 196, 197, *212, 215*

Mosher, D. L., 158, 159, 161, *206, 212*
Mowrer, O., 167, 172, *205*
Murdick, R. G., 63, 77
Mussen, P. H., 161, 175, *212*

N

Nash, W. V., 258, *276*
Nawy, H., 158, *212*
Nebergall, R. E., 184, *214*
Needham, C. D., 242, *251*
New, P. G., 225, 239, *251*
Newburn, R. M., 60, 65, 77
Newcomb, T. M., 181, *202*
Newill, V. A., 108, 121, *136*
Nordhaus, W. D., 63, 77

O

Oates, W. E., 59, *76*
Obeler, E. M., 151, *212*
O'Connor, J., 100, 107, 131, *137*
Oglesby, W., 23, *49*
Ohlsson, J., 233, *251*
Olson, E. E., 24, *49*
Orr, R. H., 24, *49*
Osgood, C., 181, 184, *212*
Ottersen, S., 17, *49*
Otto, H. A., 168, *212*

P

Palmer, B. I., 225, 248, *251*
Palmer, D. C., 17, *49*
Palmgreen, P., 183, *205*
Palmqvist, B., 233, *251*
Papageorgis, D., 180, *211*
Parker, E., 166, 175, *213*
Paul, J. C. N., 152, 162, *204, 212*
Peabody, R. L., 269, *276*
Peak, H., 185, *212*
Peavler, W. S., 162, *212*
Pelz, D. C., 147, *212*
Pepitone, A., 172, *212*
Perrow, C., 264, *276*
Perry, J. W., 96, 98, *136, 137*
Pestel, E., 81, *136*
Peterson, R. C., 150, *212*
Pflugk, U., 229, 237, *251*

Pings, V. M., 24, *49*
Piquard, M., 218, *252*
Pizer, I. H., 24, *49*
Plate, K., 257, *276*
Polt, J. M., 162, *208*
Pomeroy, W. B., 158, 160, 164, *206, 209*
Pope, M., 165, *212*
Porter, L. W., 271, *275*
Porter, R. C., 63, 77
Prentiss, S. G., 18, *49*
Price, D. J., de S., 87, 88, 104, 111, *137*
Proshansky, H., 182, *207*
Prytherch, R. J., 243, *252*

R

Raffel, J. A., 75, 77
Ramist, L. E., 27, *48*
Ramsey, G., 160, *212*
Rath, G. J., 101, 130, *137*
Rawlings, E., 170, 173, *204*
Reder, M. W., 65, 77
Rees, A. M., 99, 100, 108, 130, 131, 132, 133, *137*
Reichling, G., 172, *212*
Reifler, C. B., 163, *208*
Reinfeld, A., 162, *214*
Resnick, A., 101, 130, 133, *137*
Revill, D. H., 244, *252*
Ricking, M., 263, *276*
Roach, W. J., 158, *213*
Roberts, D., 180, *213*
Robinson, E. J., 179, *213*
Robinson, H. W., 196, *213*
Robinson, J. P., 169, *208*
Rockart, J. F., 60, 65, 77
Rokeach, M., 12, *50,* 183, 184, *213, 215*
Rongione, I. A., 197, *213*
Rosenbaum, M. E., 173, *213*
Rosenberg, M. J., 181, *202*
Rosnow, R. L., 179, *213*
Ross, C., 189, 191, *215*
Ross, D., 150, 175, *203*
Ross, J. E., 63, 77
Ross, S. A., 151, 175, *203*
Rothenburg, L., 99, 130, 131, 132, 133, *137*
Rothstein, S., 10, 31, *50*
Roxas, S. A., 228, *252*
Rubinstein, O. O., 169, *205*

Rugaas, B., 233, 239, 243, *252*
Ruggels, W. L., 150, *213*
Rutherford, E., 175, *212*
Ryan, M. J., 193, *213*

S

Sales, S. M., 64, 77
Salton, G., 133, *136*
Samuelson, M., 150, *213*
Sandison, A., 103, *136*
Sanford, R., 183, *202*
Saracevic, T., 99, 100, 101, 104, 105, 108, 130, 131, 132, 133, *137*
Saunders, W. L., 225, *252*
Savage, T. R., 101, 130, 133, *137*
Schiller, P., 160, *213*
Schmidt, G., 162, *213*, *214*
Schoenfield, M., 42, *48*
Schoenherr, R. A., 263, *274*
Schofield, J. L., *277*
Schramm, W., 142, 148, 166, 175, 178, *213*
Schultz, D. G., 99, 130, 131, 132, 133, *137*
Schur, H., 248, *252*
Schutz, A., 82, 84, 110, 111, 130, 131, 132, 134, *137*
Schwartz, M. L., 152, *212*
Schwoebel, B., 194, 195, *213*
Scodel, A., 161, *212*
Scriven, M., 10, *50*
Sears, D. O., 149, 178, 184, *213*
Sears, R., 167, 172, *205*
Selya, B. M., 175, *210*
Shannon, C. E., 91, *137*
Sheffield, F. D., 178, *208*
Shera, J. H., 88, *137*
Sherif, C. W., 184, *214*
Sherif, M., 184, *214*
Sherrill, L. L., 198, *214*
Shirey, D. L., 130, *138*
Shoffner, R. M., 59, 77
Shore, R. E., *205*
Shrodes, C., 195, *214*
Sidman, J., 163, *211*
Siegel, A., 150, 175, *214*
Sigusch, V., 162, *213*
Silber, K., 22, *50*
Silverman, R. A., 159, 163, *214*

Simmons, P., 30, *50*
Simmons, W. R., 169, *208*
Singer, R. D., 173, *206*
Sinkevicius, K., 239, *252*
Slamecka, V., 26, *50*
Sloan, E., 260, *276*
Smith, D. D., 162, *215*
Smith, E., *277*
Smith, G. C. K., *277*
Smith, I. G., 56, 61, 77
Sofer, C., 257, 259, *276*
South, D. R., 190, *206*
Spirt, D. L., 42, *48*
Stake, R. E., 11, *50*
Stalker, G. M., 259, *274*
Stamm, K., 182, *205*
Starr, S., 163, *211*
Steedman, I. A., 64, *76*
Steele, L., 184, *207*
Steinberg, H., 141, *214*
Steiner, G. A., 145, *203*
Stern, M., 99, 130, 131, 132, 133, *137*
Stewart, R., *277*
Stiglitz, J. E., 63, *75*
Stogdill, R. M., 267, 268, *276*
Stokes, R. B., 245, *252*
Suder, C., 157, *202*
Sutherland, Z., 42, *50*
Swanson, C. E., 168, *214*
Swanson, D. R., 25, *46*, *50*
Swanson, G. E., 158, *211*

T

Taft, R., 185, *214*
Tammekann, E. M., 233, 249, *252*
Tannenbaum, P. H., 171, 181, 184, *202*, *212*, *214*
Taub, B., 173, *204*
Taube, M., 96, *138*
Tauran, R. H., 197, *214*
Tennenbaum, A., 271, *275*
Tentori, M. C., 229, 235, *252*
Terwilliger, R. F., 179., *209*
Tesovnik, M. L., 30, *50*
Tews, R. M., 194, 195, *214*
Thauer, W., 235, *252*
Thibaut, J. W., 172, *214*
Thomas, E., 170, *215*
Thompson, G. D., 169, *204*

Thompson, J. D., 260, *276*
Thornberry, T. P., 159, 163, *214*
Thurston, L. L., 150, *212*
Toffler, A., 149, *214*
Treadway, A. B., 65, *78*
Troldahl, V. C., 149, *214*
Trueswell, R. W., 33, *50*

U

Ulibarri, M. R., 197, *214*
Urquhart, D. J., 104, *138*

V

Van Dam, R., 149, *214*
Van de Ven, A. H., 263, *276*
Van Orden, P., 42, *48*
Vianello, N., 249, *252*
Vidmar, N., 184, *215*

W

Wallace, D. H., 157, *215*
Wallington, J., 22, *46, 50*
Walters, R. H., 170, 176, *203, 215*
Waples, D., 141, *215*
Warheit, I. A., 55, 59, *78*
Warren, K. S., 88, *138*
Wasserman, P., 242, *252*
Weaver, W., 91, *137*
Webster, D. E., 27, *50*
Weech, T. L., 31, *51*
Weiler, G., 125, *138*
Weimerskirch, P. J., 193, *215*
Weintraub, S., 196, *213*
Weiss, W., 178, 186, *208, 215*

Weitzman, L. J., 189, 191, *215*
Welch, F., 64, *78*
Wenger, M. A., 162, *215*
Wessel, C. J., 27, *51*
White, D. M., 157, *215*
Whitfield, R. M., 27, *48*
Wickert, F. C., *277*
Wiedemann-Sutor, I., 162, *214*
Wiener, N., 91, *138*
Wilson, B. J., 241, *252*
Wilson, P., 85, 115, 123, 134, *138*
Wilson, W. C., 155, 156, 157, *215*
Winer, B. J., 268, *275*
Wishnet, J., 162, *204*
Woodward, J., 263, *276*
Woodyard, M. A., 196, 197, *215*
Worell, J., 190. *215*
Worell, L., 190, *215*
Wynar, C. L., 42, *51*

Y

Yungman, G. T., 142, *215*

Z

Zaccaria, J. S., 195, 196, 197, *212, 215*
Zajonc, R. B., 150, *215*
Zamansky, H. S., 158, *216*
Zazersky, E. J., 235, *252*
Ziman, J. M., 87, 88, 92, 111, *138*
Zimbardo, D., 180, 183, *216*
Zipf, G., 104, *138*
Zucaro, B. J., 196, *216*
Zuckerman, M., 162, *216*
Zull, C., 99, 130, 131, 132, 133, *137*

Subject Index

A

Academic libraries, *see* College and university libraries
Administration, *see also* Management
  library, 253–274
Aggression, 167–172
American Association of School Libraries, 14–15
  School Library Manpower Project, 20–22
  Standards for School Media Programs, 13–14, 23
American Library Association
  Joint Committee on Elementary School Standards, 14
Association of Assistant Librarians, 221
Association of Educational Communications and Technology, 15
Association of Research Libraries
  Management Review and Analysis Program (MRAP), 27
Attitude
  effect of reading, 176–193

B

Bibliometrics, 102–106
Bibliotherapy, 193–199
  definition, 193
  history, 193–194
  research, 194–197
Bradford Law, 103–104

C

California
  Bureau of Audio-Visual and School Library Education, 16

Carnegie United Kingdom Trust, 221–222
Case studies (in research), 147–148
Cataloging
  productivity measurement, 66–74
Chicago, University of
  Graduate Library School, 222
Circulation
  measurement, 29–30, 43
College and university libraries
  Europe, 227
  growth, 54–55
  operations research, 25–27
  productivity measurement, 54–75
College of Librarianship (Sweden), 233
College of Library Studies (Norway), 233
Communication, 91–93
  cognitive consistency theories, 181–182
  ecology, 88–89
  effectiveness, 82
  message variables, 179–180
  research, 139–202
    implications for information professionals, 199–202
  scientific, 87–88
  source variables, 178–179
  systems, 93–94
Content analysis, 148, 189–190
Continuing education, *see* Education, continuing
Cranfield Project, 98
Council for National Academic Awards, 224
Cybernetics, 113–114

D

Danish Library Association, 249
Decision-making, 273–278

E

Education
  aims, 11
  continuing, 243–245
  library, see Librarians, education
  professional, see Professional education
Erotic stimuli, 159–165
ESEA, see U. S. Elementary and Secondary Education Act (ESEA)
European Economic Community, 245–247
Evaluation, see Performance measurement, evaluation

F

Finnish Library Association, 249

I

Inferential statistics, 38–39
Information
  processing
    effect of prejudice, 183–185
    relevance, 80–135
  retrieval
    false drops, 96
    logic, 95
    relevance, 80–135
    utility measurement, 114–119
  science, 85–89
  systems, 93–94
International School of Librarianship (proposed), 245
Iowa
  Department of Public Instruction, 16
Italian Library Association, 228, 249

J

JIMS, see Jobs in Instructional Media Study (JIMS)
Jobs in Instructional Media Study (JIMS), 22–23

L

Lancaster, University of
  Library Research Unit, 26

Leadership, 266–272
  characteristics, 267–268
LIBGIS, see Library General Information Survey Project (LIBGIS)
Librarians
  education
    Belgium, 219, 230, 249
    Bulgaria, 231
    Central Europe, 228–231
    continuing, 243–245
    Czechoslovakia, 226
    Denmark, 219, 232–233, 236, 244
    Eastern Europe, 218, 220, 231–232
    Europe, 217–249
      levels of training, 234–236
    Finland, 230, 233, 249
    France, 220, 228, 247
    Germany (Democratic Republic), 231
    Germany (Federal Republic), 219–220, 226, 229–230, 235, 237, 246, 249
    Greece, 230, 232
    Hungary, 231
    Iceland, 231, 233–234
    Italy, 228–229, 235, 237, 247, 249
    Netherlands, 219, 226, 230
    Norway, 233, 239, 243
    Poland, 231
    policy, 238–242
    practical training, 238–242
    reciprocity, 245–247
    role of library associations, 247–249
    Russia, 231, 235, 239, 244–245
    Scandinavia, 226, 232–234
    Sweden, 219–220, 233, 239
    Switzerland, 219, 230
    Turkey, 232
    United Kingdom, 217–249
      history, 220–225
    Yugoslavia, 232
  professionalism, 265–266
  qualifications, 245–247
Librarianship
  as an academic discipline, 236–238
Libraries, see also, College and university libraries; Public libraries; School libraries.
  administration, 253–274
  collections
    evaluation, 32–33
  cost effectiveness, 27–28
  economics, 54–55

Subject Index

environment, 260–263
management, 253–274
    effect of technology, 263–265
    organization, 260–263
    performance measurement, 1–46
    statistics, 17–18
Library Assistant Association, *see*
    Association of Assistant Librarians
Library Association, 219, 221, 223–225, 247–248
Library collections
    evaluation, 42–43
Library education, *see* Librarians, education
Library General Information Survey Project (LIBGIS), 17–18
Library schools
    education policy, 238–242
Library technical assistants, 246
    education, 234–235

M

Management
    authority, 269–270
    functions, 255–259
    leadership role, 266–272
    library, 253–274
    use of power, 270–271
Maryland
    State Department of Education, 15–16
Mass media, 141–142
Media centers, *see* School libraries, media centers
Media services, *see* School libraries, media services
Michigan, University of
    Survey Research Center, 269
Middle management, 253–274
Missouri
    State Department of Education, 16
MRAP, *see* Association of Research Libraries, Management Review and Analysis Program (MRAP)

N

National Center for Educational Statistics, *see* U. S. Office of Education, National Center for Educational Statistics (NCES)
National Council of Teachers of English, 14

National Education Association
    Department of Audiovisual Instructions, 15
National Science Foundation, *see* U. S. National Science Foundation
NCES, *see* U. S. Office of Education, National Center for Educational Statistics (NCES)

O

Obscenity, 151–165
    Miller case, 154
    Roth-Alberts case, 153–154
Ohio
    Association of School Libraries, 16
    State University
        Personnel Research Board, 268–269
Operations research, 25–27
Oregon
    State System of Higher Education
        Teaching Research Division, 23

P

Pennsylvania
    Department of Education, 16
Performance measurement, 1–46
    checklists, 19–25
    definition, 10–11
    evaluation, 10–11, 23–25, 44–45
    inventories, 19–25
    systems analysis, 37–38
Persuasion
    innoculation theory, 180–181
Pertinence (concept), 108
Pornography, 151–165
    community standards, 156–158
    demographics, 158–160
    effects, 155–165
        on sex offenders, 163–164
    Hicklin rule, 151–152
Prejudice
    as portrayed in the media, 186–188
    effect of reading, 176–193
    effect on information processing, 183–185
    in children's literature, 187–188
    racial
        effect of reading, 182–188
    reinforcement through reading, 185–188

Productivity
  meaning, 55–57
  measurement, 54–75
    capital, 60
    in cataloging, 66–74
    input, 64–65, 68–71
    labor, 58–60, 72–73
    levels, 62–63
    output, 65–68
Philadelphia, Pennsylvania
  Free Library, 28
Professional education
  United Kingdom, 222–223
Public libraries
  performance measurement, 27–29
Public Library Measurement Study, 33–36
Purdue University
  Industrial Engineering School, 26

R

Racial prejudice, see Prejudice, racial
Reading
  effect on attitude, 176–193
  effect on behavior, 139–202
    sexual, 151–165
    violent, 165–176
  selective perception, 184
  selective retention, 185
Reference services
  measurement, 31–32
Relevance, 80–135
  definition, 99–100
  "destination's view", 98–102
  logic, 83–84, 122–124
  measurement, 120–122
  "pertinence view", 107–112
  philosophy of, 84–85
  pragmatic view, 112–119
  situational, 115–116
  "subject knowledge view", 107–112
  "subject literature view", 102–106
  "system's view", 95–98
  theories, 119–124
Research
  case studies, 147–148
  design, 145–148
  experimental, 145–146
  scientific method, 142–145
  survey technique, 146–147
Royal Danish Library School, 232–233, 249

S

Sampling (statistics), 38
School libraries
  goals and objectives, 11–13
  media centers, 23
    standards, 13–17
  media services, 12–13, 22–25
  performance measurement, 1–47
  standards, 13–17
  statistics, 17–18
School Library Manpower Project, see
  American Association of School
  Libraries, School Library Manpower
  Project
School of Social Studies, Geneva
  Library School, 249
Scientific method, see Research, scientific
  method
Sexual behavior
  effect of reading, 151–165
Sexism
  as portrayed in the media, 189–190
  effect of reading, 188–192
  male attitudes, 190–191
Standards for School Media Programs, see
  American Association of School
  Libraries, Standards for School Media
  Programs
Statistics
  inferential, 38–39
Supervision, 255–259
Surveys (in research), 146–147
Swiss Library Association, 249

T

Tampere, University of, 233
Technical services
  measurement, 30–31

U

University College, London,
  School of Librarianship and Archives,
  221–224
U. S. Commission on Obscenity and
  Pornography, 155–156
U. S. Comstock Act, 152
U. S. Elementary and Secondary Education
  Act (ESEA), 17

U. S. National Commission on the Causes
    and Prevention of Violence, 166–172
U. S. National Science Foundation, 99
U. S. Office of Education, National Center
    for Educational Statistics (NCES), 17

V

Violence
    catharsis, 172–174
    definition, 166–168
    effect on children, 174–176
    effect of reading, 165–176

W

Wisconsin
    Department of Public Instruction, 16